WINES

OF ARGENTINA

Texts: Michel Rolland and Enrique Chrabolowsky
Photography: Carlos Calise
Editor-in-Chief: Enrique Chrabolowsky
Writing Supervision: Carmen Pérez
Production: Viviana Fernández y Verónica Gordillo
Copy Editing: Osvaldo Gac

Design and Art Managing: Alejandra Rodón and Mirta Leucrini

Photography
Editors: Carlos Calise
Image Database: Photo Estudio Calise
Image Processing: Mirta Leucrini y Carlos Calise
Photographs: Arturo Ballester Molina, Federico García, participating Wineries and Mendoza
and Neuquén Tourism Undersecretariats. Salta Tourism Secretariat.

Graphics Information: Claudia Saavedra

Translators (Spanish/English): Kim Mandel

Photochrome: Color Center
Printing: Aprinta S.A.

Cover Photo: Carlos Calise.
Dancers: Enzo Fabián De Lucca and Andrea Vázquez.

Chrabolowsky, Enrique
Wines of Argentina / Enrique Chrabolowsky y Michel Rolland; con prólogo de:
Robert Parker - 2a ed. - Buenos Aires: Mirrol, 2005.
228 p.; 31x23 cm.

Traducido por: Kim Mandel

ISBN 987-20926-3-X

1. Vinos-Argentina. I. Rolland, Michel II. Parker, Robert, prolog. III. Mandel, Kim trad.
IV. Título
   CDD 663.209 82

Printed in Argentina, 2005
© Mirrol S.A.
echrabolowsky@speedy.com.ar

WINES

OF ARGENTINA

MICHEL ROLLAND
ENRIQUE CHRABOLOWSKY

"ARGENTINE LEADERSHIP"

BY ROBERT PARKER

I have known Michel Rolland since the spring of 1983, when I first met him while tasting the young 1982 vintage. In the 25 years that I have been a wine writer and critic, no one has had the impact on the high quality of wines we drink today as has Michel Rolland.

In 1983, he was a respected, but provincial oenologist working out of his cramped office in Libourne, mainly advising his clients in Pomerol and St. Emilion. Twenty years later, he has clients at the best addresses in every top viticultural region of the world, including Spain, California's Napa and Somona Valleys, Tuscan, and one of the world's most exciting new wine regions, Argentina. His strong convictions that vineyards produce the finest wines, and that the winemaker's role is to translate the essence of a vineyard's spirit and terroir into wines of undeniable flavor and complexity led him to take a serious interest in Argentina's great potential.

Michel Rolland, more than any other world famous oenologist, has understood better than anyone that low yields, ripe fruit, and careful meticulous, non-interventional handling of grapes results in wine with great sensual and intellectual pleasure. His belief in the high quality of Argentine wines, particularly those made from a varietal long ignored in, but which has flourished in Argentina –Malbec– has literally transformed the world's impression of this grape. Thanks to Michel Rolland, as well as to some of his most serious colleagues, Malbec and Argentine wines have achieved a long overdue place on the world's stage. The potential and challenge for world class quality from Argentina's finest vineyards continues to be more and more evident with each new vintage, not only with Malbec, but also with Cabernet Sauvignon, Merlot and Chardonnay, all noble varietals. No one is more capable of exploiting this challenge than Michel Rolland.

It is an honor and privilege to have Michel Rolland put down in a book his thoughts about wine quality, which have so revolutionized the world of wine we all love. Certainly my life, not only as a wine critic, but as a wine taster and wine lover, has been rewarded time and time again by the brilliant quality of his work.

With the publication of this new edition, all of those who love this exceptional beverage will be enlightened by the genius of Michel Rolland, who has been at the epicentre of the revolution which has so dramatically improved the quality of the world's wines.

My deepest thanks to Arnaldo Etchart and his family for allowing
me to travel to Argentina and discover such a great country.
I also would like to thank all those who supported us in our first great
adventure as authors, and those who have encouraged us to write
this new edition of Wines of Argentina.

Argentina's potential for winemaking is amazing and the diversity of its future prospects is dramatic. This fact is far better understood by all those who have attempted to turn away from preconceived production systems bogged down in conservative attitudes, contrary to any possibility of change. If there is anywhere a place that encompasses the perfect match of climate, soil, costs, human resources, and, above all, freedom for creativity and minimal bureaucracy to hinder the genuine development of a new and exceptional viticulture, that place is undoubtedly Argentina

Michel Rolland

In 1988, during his first visit to the country, when the Etchart wineries had hired him, Michel Rolland wanted to find out about Argentine wines. He tasted the best 38 wines on the market. His disappointment was enormous: "Only two or three were rather acceptable, and the rest were very bad quality", recall the great oenologist from Bordeaux. From then on, as has occurred in the rest of the world, his innovative vision of viticulture has been accepted by all those local producers aspiring to make top quality wines.

Fifteen years later at the Mendoza Park Hyatt Hotel, Rolland tasted 191 wines produced by the major Argentine wineries. The results were more than promising and his comments were included in our first book. "I didn't find any bad wine; there are some better than others", he told journalists after finishing his review. "However, in accord with international quality standards, they are all totally acceptable to meet consumer's demands worldwide. They are increasingly more balanced and have excellent fruity flavors, whether or not they aged in oak barrels. Great effort and intense though back up each of these wines. I can vouch that Argentina has fully understood international tastes."

The excellent acceptation of our first book in 2003 −two reprinting− has encouraged us to write this new 2005 edition. We have added more pages, including an update of information and tourist areas that accompany the Argentine wine route. The wineries whose 191 wines that Michel Rolland tasted and commented on have now increased to 252 from 105 wineries. The majority of the photos have been renewed as well.

The idea of writing a book on Argentine wines arose from a fact that concerned many pro-ducers, winemakers, consumers, wine traders and exporters. All of those for whom wine means passion and pride. Until now, despite the fact that Argentina is the fifth largest producer in the world and has top quality wines, the space devoted to the country in all the international specialized publications was minimal, almost non-existent. Rolland, whose heart is close to Argentina, accepted the challenge and a book that would serve as an introduction to Argentina in the fascinating world of wine was born.

Each chapter is preceded by comments from Michel Rolland. In the final chapter on the prin-cipal wineries, Rolland makes an objective evaluation and comments on the 252 main Argentine wines available on international mar-kets.

Enrique Chrabolowsky

CHAPTER 1

ARGENTINA
IN THE WORLD

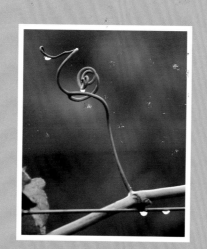

"A CHANGE OF MIND"

BY MICHEL ROLLAND

Even though the shift from quantity to quality implied a decline in production, Argentina is among the top five world wine producers (the USA pushed the country back to fifth place). However for a long time, it did not export any wines because the domestic market was so huge. International markets were neither known nor necessary. When local consumption started to fall off, some companies considered the alternative of foreign markets and realized that both time and buyers had been lost. Apart from France and Italy, traditional wine exporting countries, Chile, Australia and South Africa —with good products and prices— were far ahead. The negative image of Argentina had to be overcome in order to gain lost ground: anyone who has made a bad deal does not forget about it overnight. It was necessary to clarify that quali-

ty and competitive prices were possible. This task has required great effort, and has only just started. However, future prospects can be very promising if things are done properly.

At present, Argentina has a significant proportion of good wines since many winemakers understood the philosophical principles underlying export activities. Prices have dropped due to the fact that the peso is no longer pegged to the dollar, and the good price-quality equation enables competitive entry into international markets. In any case, it must be understood that entry into an international market cannot be gained overnight. On the contrary, it is a slow and gradual process that calls for responsibility and good products. A lucky coup that works just once is worthless.

We have been delighted to see many Argentine

wines being awarded prizes at wine shows, which in itself is good proof of the existing potential. However, winning a medal is meaningless if the award is an isolated prize or the wine is not improved from year to year. Wines need to be produced consistently so as to make Argentina a reliable and trustworthy partner for its customers around the world.

Although there are still practices that can be improved, the changes made to date are remarkable. There are many wine growers who are painstakingly working to improve stocks and more vines per hectare, while managing irrigation systems rationally. Nevertheless, much remains to be done: there are too many vineyards that are still being managed without any changes whatsoever.

When Argentine wines are talked about in the world, some of them are praised, but some are not due to their poor quality. The latter do not contribute to the country's image. It is precisely those products where the most effort must be made.

For instance, everyone knows yields must be lowered in order to improve quality and that excessive irrigation at a certain time of the vine development endangers it. However, many vineyard owners, in spite of being aware of this, continue to irrigate excessively. This has to change, and it will take time. It is not possible to change overnight and there will always be someone left behind, watching as progress passes by. It is important for Argentina that the change be as swift as possible.

Change entails a different attitude, hard work, and, lastly, investment. It does not require much money. However, change demands people's commitment, which perhaps is much harder to achieve.

ARGENTINA
IN THE WORLD

THE GREAT VITICULTURE OF SOUTH AMERICA

"Argentum" is a Latin word meaning "silver", the silver of the New Continent that dazzled from the far South. Argentina is the homeland of Jorge Luis Borges, Julio Cortázar, Juan Manuel Fangio, Diego Maradona, and Tango. It is the country of getting together with friends, of barbecues ("asados"), Carlos Gardel, nature, passion, and where soccer dominates daily conversations. It is a country of diversity and contrasts, with a large national area covering 2,791,810 square kilometers of continental lands and 973,331 square kilometers corresponding to the Antarctica and the South Atlantic Islands. Argentina has a population of over 38 million inhabitants.

The country's ethnic and cultural origins have been greatly influenced by European immigration –mainly Italian and Spanish, who came to

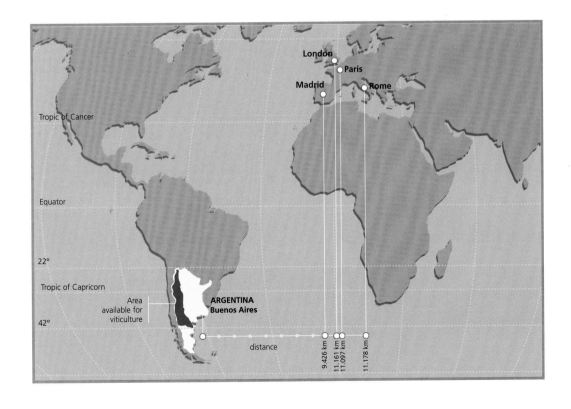

Comparative advantages

Within a geographical context featuring a wide range of landscapes, the principal wine-growing areas are located between the 22° and 42° South latitude, on the Andean mountain range.

Vineyards are located between 300 and 2,300 meters above sea level. This altitude combines perfectly with Argentine viticulture's main asset: the comparative advantages of the richness of its agricultural and climatic factors, such as:

- continental, semi-arid desert climate with scarce rainfall allowing the normal growth of the stock without excessive use of fertilizers;
- wide range in temperatures, that is, the difference in temperature between day and night that sometimes is over 20 °C;
- the perfect exposure of the plants to sunlight helps develop color and aromas in the clusters while preventing disease;
- clear skies over the whole viticulture landscape.

These privileged natural conditions allow the development of an environmentally friendly and sustainable viticulture, with outstanding wines, that bear witness to the uniqueness of Argentine terroirs.

Sunlight. *Fully ripened grapes give birth to aromatic, concentrated and balanced wines.*

the country during the end of the 19th century and the beginning of the 20th century. Along with this legacy, cultural expressions from copper-colored native people, siblings of the four elements –earth, air, water, fire– still survive.

The country is politically organized as a Federal State with 24 provinces and the Autonomous City of Buenos Aires-the Federal Capital District.

Due to its vast expanse and its particular geographical location, Argentina boasts a great variety of landscapes. For example, the vast eastern plains contrast with the Andes to the west, an impressive mountain range which forms the natural geographical boundary with Chile. Across the whole country, from north to south, the Andes frame such diverse landscapes as the northwestern plateaus or the

The majestic Andes. *The magnificent mountain range frames one of the highest vineyards in the world.*

lakes, and the woodland and glacier districts in Patagonia. The greatest winegrowing region in Argentina and South America can be found in the west of Argentina.

RENOVATION IN VITICULTURE

Viticulture is one of the most productive activities in the central western and northwestern provinces of the country, hence its importance in the development of regional economies. Along with winegrowing and fine winemaking, it has given rise to important interrelated industries with tourism standing out for its promising potential.

Indeed, from the 90's onwards, the sector has undergone a profound transformation propelled by new concepts in the art of winemaking.

Vineyards of the world

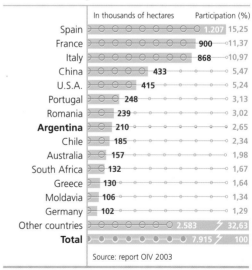

	In thousands of hectares	Participation (%)
Spain	1.207	15,25
France	900	11,37
Italy	868	10,97
China	433	5,47
U.S.A.	415	5,24
Portugal	248	3,13
Romania	239	3,02
Argentina	210	2,65
Chile	185	2,34
Australia	157	1,98
South Africa	132	1,67
Greece	130	1,64
Moldavia	106	1,34
Germany	102	1,29
Other countries	2.583	32,63
Total	7.915	100

Source: report OIV 2003

World yield of grapes

	In thousands of quintals	Participation (%)
Italy	73.939	11,97
France	68.535	11,09
U.S.A.	66.577	10,78
Spain	58.797	9,52
China	44.795	7,25
Turkey	35.000	5,67
Iran	27.040	4,38
Argentina	22.444	3,63
Chile	18.723	3,03
Australia	17.539	2,84
South Africa	15.001	2,43
Germany	13.180	2,13
Brazil	11.206	1,81
India	11.100	1,80
Egypt	11.038	1,79
Portugal	10.986	1,78
Romania	10.700	1,73
Greece	10.000	1,62
Other countries	91.219	14,76
Total	617.819	100

Source: report OIV 2003

Nobility. *Paradoxically generous, stone is the perfect cradle for the vines watered by state-of-the-art irrigation systems.*

This process includes all levels of production. Vineyards have achieved qualitative improvement, systematically incorporating technology to optimize the production line. The professionalism of human resources has improved communication, distribution, and trading. All these indicate the constant renovation that the sector has undergone. The close interrelationships of such processes have enabled Argentine wines to excel and to strengthen their position in international markets as a result of a generous character and a winemaking tradition capable of surprise and innovation.

DIVERSIFIED PRODUCTION

Argentina has a winegrowing area of over 210,000 hectares distributed in 25,180 vineyards. Grapes are grown in 13 of the 24 provinces of the country; however, only in 7 of them is viticulture economically meaningful: Salta, Catamarca, La Rioja, San Juan, Mendoza, Neuquén and Rio Negro.

Some 94% of the area with grapes (about 188,000 hectares) is dedicated to winemaking and grape juice concentrate. The rest are varieties either used as table grapes (4.5%) or for making raisins (1.8%). Reverse seasonal trading favors exports to countries in the European Community.

Argentina is the major world concentrated grape juice exporter and this commodity is basically traded in the United States, Japan and Canada, and increasingly in developing markets, such as Russia and South Africa.

QUALITY STARTS
IN THE VINEYARD

Argentina's interest in fulfilling consumer demands and being competitive in the global wine business hastened the technological revolution that was started in the vineyards, and

Protection. *Grape quality is protected against hail by mesh netting.*

subsequently improved its raw material. The main changes recorded in primary production are as follows:

- **Drip irrigation systems:** allow rational water management, as well as incorporating new areas apt for viticulture.

- **Hail protection mesh:** its use has been widespread to prevent the damaging effect of hail.

- **Improvement of vineyard techniques:** agricultural professionals emphasize controls in the grapes yield and protect the virtues that the terroir expresses in the fruit.

- **International Consultants:** many winery owners sought the advice of international experts to asses the technological level of their procedures, recommend cuttings, follow up the maturing process, and broaden their knowledge on international wine consumption trends.

This advice allows, in turn, the transfer of expertise from the wineries to their grape suppliers, which is very important since many wineries work on a joint venture basis with the suppliers whom they advise and control. In some cases the wineries receive up to 70% of the raw material from their suppliers.

WINERIES:
INNOVATION AND STYLE

The process also introduced dramatic changes regarding technical and production procedures for winemaking, bottling and packaging. This technological revolution implied,

above all, new machinery, modern equipment and cooling systems for wine cooling during the harvest, pneumatic presses, automated temperature controls. stainless steel tanks, more versatile and efficient bottling procedures, and oak casks, among other additions. As regards wines to be cellared, the wineries have understood the importance of an adequate ageing-in-wood process.

Important progress regarding technical and commercial management, and trading techniques has also been remarkable.

At the same time, packaging designs follow definite world tendencies featuring the characteristics that make an Argentine wine a unique experience, beginning with its packaging.

Many investors have renovated and refurbished old existing facilities to produce wines in limited amounts, with a "boutique" style. Thus, small wineries have mushroomed and where the wine's quality in enveloped in the warmth of architecture that emphasizes the region's cultural features. Wineries of different scales and profiles are a wine tourism attraction offering tastings, guided visits, culinary and cultural options.

FROM THE INVESTORS' VIEWPOINT

From 1990 onwards, the dramatic changes undergone by the sector resulted in important foreign investment. The main flow came from the United States, Chile, France, Spain and the United Kingdom, and to a lesser extent, from the Netherlands and Portugal.

These new players settled mainly in Mendoza, in rich and historically important areas such as Luján de Cuyo, Maipú, Tupungato, Tunuyán, San Rafael and San Martín. Recently, San Juan, Neuquén and Salta have also attracted interest and very good land for special viticulture has been "rediscovered".

THE GREAT DOMESTIC MARKET

Argentina ranks sixth among the world's wine consuming countries, an important fact not be overlooked.

Annual consumption per capita in Argentina follows the world tendency, which is between 40 and 90 liters in traditional wine drinking countries. In Argentina, this figure is between

World yield of wine

	In thousands of hectolitres	Participation (%)
France	45.818	17,44
Italy	44.086	16,78
Spain	40.758	15,52
U.S.A.	20.770	7,91
Argentina	13.225	5,03
Australia	10.194	3,88
South Africa	8.853	3,37
Germany	8.191	3,12
Portugal	7.340	2,79
Chile	6.682	2,54
Romania	5.555	2,11
Hungary	3.887	1,48
Greece	3.799	1,45
Brazil	2.620	1,00
Austria	2.526	0,96
Other Countries	38.396	14,62
Total	262.700	100

Source: OIV 2003

Wine Consumption per inhabitant

	In litres per year	Participation (%)
Luxembourg	63	8,7
France	57	7,8
Italy	55	7,5
Portugal	50	6,8
Switzerland	41	5,6
Argentina	39	5,4
Spain	36	4,9
Uruguay	32	4,5
Austria	32	4,3
Hungary	30	4,1
Denmark	29	4,0
Greece	25	3,4
Germany	24	3,2
Romania	22	3,1
Australia	20	2,8
Other Countries	175	23,9
Total	732,63	100

Source: OIV 2003

Vineyards in Argentina

	In hectares
Mendoza	146.081,73
San Juan	47.842,50
La Rioja	8.046,18
Río Negro	2.803,80
Catamarca	2.338,58
Salta	1910,97
Neuquén	956,00
Córdoba	333,19
La Pampa	122,16
Tucumán	43,30
Chubut	20,00
San Luis	16,80
Santiago del Estero	8,80
Buenos Aires	3,52
Misiones	2,25
Total	210.530,00

Source: INV 2003

Efficiency. *State-of-the-art procedures maximize each stage in the winemaking process.*

40 liters per person, per year. Currently, the great domestic market is leading companies to optimize even more, the price-quality ratio in all price ranges. Table wines continue being very important in the industry's development, although there is an important presence of different varietals in the market, that the consumer appreciates for their excellent price-quality ratio.

Currently, Argentine consumers are more curious, require more information, are attracted by new and better opportunities to enjoy the marvelous union between tourism and viticulture. They are attentive to the growth of wineries and the varied range of products they offer. In a country where wine is part of a specially rich culture, there are numerous possibilities to enjoy food, tour wineries and live moments that contribute to a better quality of life.

OPEN TO THE WORLD

In recent years, Argentina has made an even more focused effort to export, exploring emerging markets and consolidating its position in those that have known about Argentine wine for some time. The ten principal destinations for Argentine wines are the United Kingdom, the United States, Germany, the Netherlands, Canada, Brazil, Denmark, France, Japan and Switzerland. These markets are the most profitable since mainly high and medium price wines are bought by these countries. Other important markets are the Scandinavian countries, where wine consumption has increased surprisingly in recent years.

Latin America is also a nearby market of great importance, especially for table wines. In the Southern Cone Market, Brazil is very interesting and undoubtedly one of the export challenges most important to Argentina.

The sale of sparkling wines is also growing, with exports mainly to the United States. New possibilities are arising in Russia, China and Korea where there is a growing interest in Argentine wines, especially red, closely followed by whites. The experts consider these markets have huge potential.

CHAPTER **2**

IN THE BEGINNING
WAS THE SUNLIGHT

IN THE BEGINNING
WAS THE SUNLIGHT

GRAPEVINES AND THE CONQUEST

Five centuries have passed since the first records of grapevines in America and the current launching and consolidation of Argentina's hold on the wine industry. No doubt, this time period is but a moment if that 500-year-span is compared to the ancient chronology of vinegrowing and winemaking, dating back to the Greek Dyonisian celebrations or the Roman bacchanalians before the Christian era.

When adventurous seamen started to expand the boundaries of the known world, the conquerors from the Old World found great riches in this promising land. In the early 16th

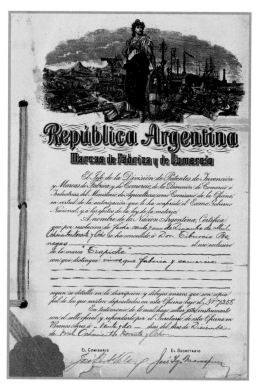

The Beginning. *Record of Trademark from the late 1800's.*

century, priests from missionary orders began settling in America. They brought along elements needed for their religious celebrations: wine, bread and holy oil. One historical account mentions that Spanish friars and conquerors introduced grapevines in the New Continent. Garcilaso de la Vega, in his "Comentarios Reales" (Royal Comments), reports that the Spanish conqueror Francisco de Caravantes was responsible for bringing grapevine cuttings from Mexico to Peru. Between 1550 and 1560, the plants grew in most Chilean and Peruvian houses and monasteries. However, it was not until the early 17th century that vines started being used for making a wonderful beverage.

The Jesuits played a leading role in encouraging vinegrowing: they took grapevines with them wherever they settled. However, vinegrowing only developed in the northern Argentine provinces, and at the Andean foothills, where they found the perfect soil and conditions to grow.

At that time, the chronicles record an anecdote about the origins of vinegrowing in

Processes. *By 1910, winemaking added technology and started to reach industrial status.*

Harvest scene. *Work by men and women established a cultural root that becomes richer with every harvest.*

Argentina. Towards the end of 1557, the inhabitants of the Argentine province of Santiago del Estero, in the central northern part of the country, needed the religious services of a priest. Thus, Father Juan Cidrón of the Order of Mercy, bringing along the first cuttings that were eventually grown in Argentina.

THE FIRST
CREOLE WINES

The first grapes, called Creole of Spanish origin, were not the most suitable for winemaking. However, in the last decades of the 16th century, vinegrowing had reached the provinces of Mendoza and San Juan.
By mid- 17th century, vineyards had become increasingly important in the Argentine region of Cuyo, and wine trading started to have a dramatic impact on the country's economy. The Jesuits appreciated the local regional

wines since they considered those wines "very generous and strong, able to tolerate long journeys without spoiling".

THE EUROPEAN
VINE STOCKS

The first Malbec vine stocks were introduced to Mendoza around 1860. This produced a great change in the winemaking activity since only Creole vines had been cultivated in the country until then. Nevertheless, due to the poor technology used, it was not until the 19th century that significant changes in the quality of the product were made.
Towards 1850, the French agronomist Michel Aimé Pouget arrived in Mendoza. His arrival had a significant impact since he introduced French varieties of higher oenological quality. The first stocks came from Chile and later, Pouget brought stocks directly from France, which he planted in the area dedicated to the

Evangelizing Orders. The first grapevines were brought by the missionaries.

Royal anecdote

In 1595, in an effort to maintain the Spanish wine market monopoly, King Philip II of Spain prohibited wine growing and wine making in all the New Continent colonies. Despite the regulations, settlers continued growing vines, so the authorities allowed some "exemptions, provided a 20% tax on the annual yield was paid to the Spanish crown.

Agrarian Plots and the Model Winery built in 1902. The latter was the first specialized institution for teaching agrarian techniques, while focusing on winemaking. The first Argentine oenologists graduated from there, and the building is now part of the country's historic and cultural heritage.

Mendoza already stood out as a winemaking area and the opening of the railway in 1885 greatly contributed to improve its status. The 1,100 kilometer railroads connected the province to the port in Buenos Aires and greatly reduced transportation problems while increasing the flow of trade. Production rose and the wines made in Mendoza became popular in the main cities.

THE IMMIGRANTS' CONTRIBUTION

In the 1880's, the Mendoza government hired an Italian engineer César Cipolletti to standardize the irrigation network in the province. Cipolletti played an essential role in the development of all the irrigation works, and the building of canals and dams, not only in Mendoza but also in San Juan. The struggle against the desert was won and the planting of trees, a landmark in the region, was encouraged.

Immigrants. The first winemakers brought the practices learned in their homelands.

Roots. *Argentine viticulture incorporates the legacy of European traditions with the New World's innovative spirit.*

At that time, Argentina became the Promised Land for thousands of European immigrants who were fleeing war and poverty. Italians, Spaniards and Frenchmen reached the Argentine coasts and from there settled in different provinces. Most of them came from European vinegrowing areas; they were knowledgeable in viticulture and were acquainted with winemaking procedures. This turned out to be a fundamental contribution to the Argentine development of viticulture and to the consolidation of practices rooted in a strong commitment to hard work.

Many of them knew how to take care of grapevines, were familiar with vineyard tasks and had learnt about wine elaboration processes, as they had been in viticulture in their mother countries. Their contribution was of capital importance in the development of viticulture in Argentina and the consolidation of an activity that was to become deeply rooted in the vital family commitment to the job. During the 20th century, this activity had various ups and downs until it found its path. On the basis of the local market and industry it grew in strength and became ready to conquer the world. Natural conditions were largely advantageous, but undoubtedly the effort made by men and women was the most important reason Argentine wines still have much more to offer consumers the world over.

WINE MUSEUMS

In a product so closely linked to culture, the memory is a great ally to understand the impact yesterday has on today and also on

Memory. *Façade of the Giol Museum, a matchless historic patrimony*

tomorrow. This spirit is present in places honoring the memory of wine, those special museums that can be found throughout the country.

The Felipe Rutini Wine Museum, located in Bodega La Rural -La Rural Winery- in Maipú District, Mendoza Province, shows the history of wine making from colonial times to the present displayed before the visitor's eyes. The pieces that Mr. Rodolfo Reina Rutini, a grandson of the winery's founder, kept for posterity are testimony to the effort made by those people who gave birth to the viticulture industry.

It is not a mere collection of machinery; it possesses, together with oenological art artifacts, an incredible collection of religious images of the Cuyo Region, domestic objects, weapons, and a great many valuable items -both for every day use and artistic expression- recreating the history of a century old activity. This story comes to a happy end: the museum's wine tasting is the perfect ending.

In Maipú District, as well, some minutes away from Mendoza City, is the Wine and Vintage Museum in the large manors once belonging to Italian businessmen Giol and Gargantini.

These manors were declared National Patrimony in 1988.

Another building whose original functionality was restored is the first Argentine model winery today: the Enoteca, the school where the first enologists in the country were trained. This 1902 building will be the first Wine Theme Center in Latin America. In Salta, the Wine Museum is a few steps away from Plaza Cafayate (Cafayate Square); in San Juan, the Graffigna Museum shows visitors the legacy of enterprising men from times gone: a collection of industrial antiques that together with the architectural and didactic design are enjoyable and admirable.

PRESENT AND FUTURE:

WINES WITH A COSMOPOLITAN TOUCH

By mid- 20th century, the Argentine winemaking industry became truly aware of the importance of gaining ground in the world wine business, without neglecting the domestic market. Beginning in 1990, Argentine wineries launched themselves on the world market with the firm decision of spreading their names beyond the great domestic market.

The complex reality forced vinegrowers and winery owners to adopt qualitative standards according to international consumer preferences. Changes, of course, began initially in the vineyards and involved better cultivation management practices and modernization of agrarian techniques. They continued in the wineries with the introduction of state-of-the-art technology allowing the enhancement of Argentine wines. These two factors helped strengthen the close relationship between field practices and oenological processes and resulted in designing each wine right from the vineyard. Nowadays, the agronomist can assess his/her practices in the winery while the oenologist in the vineyard can taste the quality of the raw material that will be transformed to a wine conceived with passion.

Today Argentine wines have a noticeable identity and clearly cosmopolitan style. Varietals stand out for their marked fruitiness, which is born in the vineyards and develops throughout the production process.

Together with some wineries that trace their history back to the pioneer days of Argentine viticulture, there are others newer, but equally successful. All of them reflect Argentina's uniqueness.

Projection. *Argentina is the winemaking giant of South America with a potential to surprise the world.*

Style. *The wineries' architecture is a plus when it comes to attracting wine lovers. The Salentein Winery's elegant lines are proof of this concept.*

ARQUITECTURE OF WINERIES

Architecture intermingles with art and science, drinking from the knowledge of man and nature. Hence the relevance of architecture when conceiving a winery, its response to the socio-cultural reality is inserted in, and its relationship with the landscape, the functionality of its space, assemblage with technology. Everything contributes to the expression of the company's philosophy and to making the meeting between visitors and wine most pleasant.

WINERY CHÂTEAUX

Different architectural styles give full expression to the symbolic universe typical of an age and also has a leading role in viticulture. In fact, Argentine viticulture history could be reconstructed from its architectural testimony. The first stage, from the end of the 19th century to the early 1900's, featured wineries reminiscent of colonial times, which displayed typical roofs. Later on, with the massive arrival of immigrants, winery châteaux mushroomed among the viticulture landscape.

Many of the buildings built then resembled the Italian Palladian style, featuring a façade in the classical temple style, gables typical of neoclassical constructions.

Adobe was the only material used at that time and a trademark of Latin American architecture. It offered the nobility and strength necessary for the founding wineries of Argentina.

Later bricks were used. The architectural mix-

Diversity. Stone walls, colonial style galleries, complement the landscape.
Carlos Pulenta Winery.

Materials. The nobility of adobe and
simple styles form the architectural base
of the oldest wineries.

ture was enriched with "quincha" roofs -a mortar made of adobe, clay and reed-.

Towards the beginning of the 20th century, wineries showed a significant conceptual change in their architecture, in contrast with more classical lines, buildings such as the Giol or Gargantine winery chalets (in Maipú, Mendoza) boast more organic and innovative features in harmony with Art Nouveau and Art Decó, displaying simpler lines.

THE POWER
OF PROGRESS

Since the Industrial Revolution, the whole world has enthusiastically supported the idea of achieving progress through technology. By the mid- 20th century, businessmen bet heavily on winery mechanization. Socially there was a strong tie between the future and the

Functional. *Equipped with the latest technology, Dominio del Plata Winery uses its architecture to unify its production plant, administration office and housing for its owners.*

possibilities opened up by technology. Driven by this concept of progress, huge structures spread to the wineries.

The new wine temples introduced gigantic structures on a monumental scale. The prosperity of an establishment seemed to be proportional to the size of its premises where Art Nouveau expressions survived amid more rationalistic features.

In the meantime, many more buildings began to show modernistic characteristics, though just a few reflect this architectural conception. They depict the absolute functionality of space.

HISTORICAL AND
CULTURAL HERITAGE

Searching for those features typical of regional identity, many companies were concerned with the refurbishment of old buildings. These initiatives permitted the recuperation of cultural heritage related to wine.

In the restored wineries, and even in renovated ones, the cultural bonds among the community and the building are sought. When the old and the restored must survive amid the new, architects attempt to unify the whole.

Moreover, the restoration of century-old constructions should make room for more tourists and more functional spaces to renew technological systems.

NATURE'S CELEBRATION

Since the late 20th century, the world of viticulture has seen a new trend related to sociability and tourism. It is a stage in which architecture supports the search for differentiation pursued by wine making establishments.

Framed by the well cared rows of vineyards, the Familia Schroeder Winery has simple lines offering harmony, sobriety and elegance.

Differences, regionalisms are given new value in contrast to homogenization and universal taste.

The benchmark of the new winery architecture is that, despite their being industrial constructions, it is fundamental for them to show they are an inviting venue, "livable" and capable of provoking curiosity in consumer-visitors. Hence the importance the surroundings acquire in the total design, the election of noble materials native to the area: rocks, plants, wood. Everything adds to the tour of the wineries and extra value given to the products.

In Mendoza, for example, new wineries are conceived in terms of a harmonious coexistence and continuity with imposing landscape shaped by the Andes mountain range, and trees, a typical picture of viticulture areas.

Wineries are the driving force of a geography lined with vineyards, poplars and hills. Following along this line are the Séptima, Tierras Altas, Hugo and Eduardo Pulenta and Dominio del Plata wineries.

Mendoza architect Mario Yanzón, of Bórmida & Yanzón, suggests that, even though some relatively similar features may occur, there is no unique winery architecture style. Instead, there are just as many styles as there are new enterprises. Each company wants to leave its mark on the building, its philosophy and way of making wine.

AVANT-GARDE
WINERIES

Fusion-contrast, tradition-modernity, balance-rupture, hot-cold, continuity-surprise are the principles underlying these new architectural complexes dedicated to the elixir of Bacchus. Stone from the mountain coexists with steel wood and glazed surfaces. This diversity sets a pace and personality that will hopefully be passed on with the wines. Technological functionality combines with architectural forms - which in turn accompany the production process-.

Avant-garde wineries are furthermore conceived in terms of gravitational concept to avoid wine displacements caused by brusque movements. Accordingly, the grape reception area is located on a higher level and de-stemmers are placed over maceration and fermentation tanks. This difference in levels is also used to transport wine to barrels for ageing. This way the wine does not suffer any rough pumping that could affect its qualities.

Among the functional requirements, attending tourists is fundamental. For this reason, an increasing number of wineries are designing comfortable tasting rooms, restaurants, inns and gift shops. This is the case of Salentein, Familia Zuccardi, Catena Zapata and Carlos A. Pulenta winery. In keeping with advanced architecture are the Schoeder, Bodega Fin del Mundo, Renacer, Monteviejo, O. Fournier, Andeluna, Ruca Malén, Tapiz, and NQN wineries, among others.

Supported by architecture, and along with oenologists, agronomists and other professionals, these "arts of making" outline the nature of a humanized wine culture integrating food, tourism and culture.

This new concept of winery architecture reasserts —as does an author's name on his writing— both the personality of wines along with the character of the land where they are produced.

Depth. *The NQN Winery Cellar in Patagonia gives a sense of intimacy thanks to its lighting system.*

Surprising. *Dolium's modern lines lead to an underground winery.*

CHAPTER 3

TRAVELLING ALONG, DISCOVERING, AND FALLING IN LOVE

"TOURISM BRINGS PEOPLE CLOSER TO THE ROOTS OF WINE"

BY MICHEL ROLLAND

There is strong interest all over the world in fostering wine-oriented tourism. Increasingly large numbers of people, when planning their holidays, take oenoturism into account as an alternative for coming closer to the sources of an increasingly prestigious product.

In Argentina, many people –both Argentineans and foreigners– travel to the viticultural provinces, mainly to visiting the wineries. Still, not many companies have fully developed the concept of tourism. In Mendoza a handful of wineries are slowly making some progress: they offer multilingual tours, tasting rooms and gift shops. Others provide lodging and meals along with their wines but, still, they are very few.

However, there are investment plans that may turn out to be attractive. Their implementation may be difficult, but, were I myself a major winery businessman, I would definitely have a stake in this field.

The clear definition the Americans have is still lacking. The United States is the country with the best tourist legislation the world over. Napa Valley is but one example of the perfect tourist organization. They would create the concept of a winery bearing tourism in mind. I personally saw businessmen in the United States create and develop the concept of tourism before building a winery. A winery cannot be planned without taking into account the fact that many people are going to walk through it. In France, this is poorly organized. Italy, in turn, hasn't made much progress. Burgundy has gone a step ahead with an interesting project along the road connecting Paris and the Mediterranean. Some small wineries offer a visit of the vineyards and sell their wines. This is an entirely new concept, something plainly unthinkable 15 years ago when such demand from the consumers was not present. Mondavi Winery, in the United States, where every detail is tailor-made for the tourist, receives over 4 million people a year! Tourist development is a company within the company. An enormous opportunity would be missed were this potential not exploited.

TRAVELLING ALONG, DISCOVERING, AND FALLING IN LOVE

AN AMAZING COUNTRY

Along its approximately 3.8 million square kilometers, the Argentine Republic embraces a wide range of landscapes and customs seldom found in one country. From the northern most province of Jujuy, to Tierra del Fuego in the far south, the visitor will discover Argentina's geography with extensive deserts, majestic Andes Mountain Range, marvelous lakes and Patagonian glaciers, small simple towns and bustling large cities, a true melting pot of the world.

Although the 23 provinces making up the republic, together with the Federal Capital share the same idiosyncrasies, they have somewhat different customs and ways of life resulting from different regional cultures.

San Telmo. *A typical Buenos Aires neighborhood.*

Large cities like Buenos Aires, Rosario, Córdoba or Mendoza, coexist with smaller towns where a picturesque and retrospective look survives amid a powerful present.

The country's huge extension makes it a never-ending trip. The nearly 5,000 meter view from the Clouds Train in Salta Province, the magnificent scene played by the Iguazú Falls in Misiones Province, the Aconcagua National Park in Mendoza Province, the impressive beauty of the southern lakes along with the infinite whiteness of the Perito Moreno Glacier, listen to the wonderful silence of the Northwest hills.

But it is not only about visiting tourist spots: Argentina also offers an enjoyable experience producing sensations that only felt in this latitude. Together with its natural wonders, the invitation is enriched by Argentine hospitality, the special ways of talking and passion in sharing tastes, rhythms and very own customs.

BUENOS AIRES
THE CAPITAL
OF TANGO

Buenos Aires, the capital city of Argentina, is one of the most densely populated urban areas in the world, with nearly 10 million inhabitants. It is 202 square kilometers and is about 12 hours by plane from New York, London, Madrid or Rome.

Buenos Aires City is the cradle of tango, of late-night bars, of street craft fairs but, above all, it is a major cultural center with an abundance of museums, theaters and shows. No wonder it is known as "the city that never sleeps".

Visiting Buenos Aires is about walking along its streets, talking with its people and being deeply charmed by its unique sites. The Caminito street museum, located in the color-

The Obelisk. *Its slim silhouette stands out.*

Two by four. *The Tango is a dance of feeling and embracing from the suburbs.*

ful "La Boca" Quarter, is one such site where drafts and antiques are fully displayed and professional artists sing and dance tango on weekends. Still, Buenos Aires hosts "a 100 neighborhoods". There are many other attractive sites to visit: San Telmo antique stores, the posh Recoleta neighborhood coffee bars, Palermo's restaurants (where the best beef in the world can be eaten), the emblematic Obelisk, the Colón Theater, the Latin American Fine Arts Museum (MALBA).

To prove that tango was born and lives here, one only needs to walk around the city. It is by no means unusual to run into a couple of entwined dancers offering a tango show on the street, or to enjoy a meal while an orchestra plays that blend of music and poetry born in the suburbs. Tango was born towards the end of the 19th century, on the outskirts of the Río de la Plata.

Although at the beginning it was a dance from the suburbs and thus only performed by men, it soon gained followers. The lyrics of those tangos always alluded to passionate fights, bad men, loners and bullies.

"Lunfardo" (slang) firmly established itself as the language of tango. It was the slang spoken on the street, the language of braggarts, a strange combination of the city bustle with the pidgin Spanish of Italian immigrants.

The Argentine Colonial North

Salta City was founded in 1582 and still maintains a Hispanic character that links it to the other northern provinces. Its urban profile displays colonial style houses and churches, framed by mountain ranges. Proud of its riches and traditions, amiable and friendly, Salta presents the tourist with innumerable entertainment and cultural events.

As part of the historical and religious circuit, the Museo of Arqueología de Alta Montaña (Upper Mountain Archaeology Museum) stands out because of its modern organization as a didactic and tourism tour. Located in the historical urban area, it houses testimonials of the discovery of mummified remains: one of its most significant possessions is a group of mummies preserved in exceptional condition, and related to Inca Culture. These mummies, which scientists from all over the world have come to see were found with their clothing and funeral objects. Part of the offerings made to the dead 500 years ago are also on display, such as ritual statuettes, and slingshots. The museum is open from Tuesday to Sunday and has an audiovisual room, as well as a nice café.

Churches. Salta has an important religious tourism circuit with buildings that have recuperated their original value.

THE NORTHERN DESERT
BEAUTIFUL SALTA

The provinces located in the northern boundary of the country reveal a landscape outlined by high plains, valleys, ravines, and colorful mountains. And it is precisely this view that can be seen during the crossing made by the Clouds Train in Salta Province. Salta City is located 1,625 kilometers north of Buenos Aires City. Air travel is the best way to get there, with regular flights from Buenos Aires airport.

Salta hosts one of the highest vineyards in the world. But to really experience altitude, the trip by The Clouds Train is the high point. It climbs to 4,200 meters above sea level. Condors can be seen from the train and the

Red road. *The road between Salta and Catamarca twists around natural curves bordered by red mountain peaks and vegetation particular to arid and desert areas.*

clouds seem to be within arm's reach. The Train travels along 217 kilometers while crossing valleys, ravines and Salta's puna. The journey starts at 1,187 meters above sea level and ends at La Polvorilla Viaduct, 4,220 meters above sea level. There is a stop at San Antonio de los Cobres, where a taste of the typical Andean cuisine can be quite rewarding.

Back in the capital Salta, traveling in this area, one comes across other villages, all of which are lovely. A few hours drive away, Catamarca, Jujuy and Tucumán also display the excellent cooking that is an important aspect of this culture: piping hot loaves of bread to be eaten just as they leave the creole mud oven, thick heavily laden stews, tamales with their characteristic corn, and the not-to-be-missed northern empanadas filled with mince chopped

Gauchos. *Men on horseback ride along the streets in a display of everlasting tradition.*

Popular art. *Typical mud piece made by hand and connected to the culture of wine.*

with a knife, seasoned with cumin, fresh pepper and chili, spices that are generously grown in the area. As for dessert, regional dulces (solid jellies made of fruit), several kinds of nuts, and the "cuaresmillo" (delicious peach that can be found only in the Argentine North).

Salta is a haven of the colonial past. The city has a circuit of ancient convents and cathedrals, a colonial town hall and a watch-tower which offers a view that is unique.

In the birthplace of the Torrontés varietal, the white stock that found the ideal place to grow, wine cellars are located in the south of the province, mainly in Cafayate (whose name means the pueblo that has everything), some 1,700 m above sea level. La Banda is the oldest winery in Cafayate, and it has been mak-

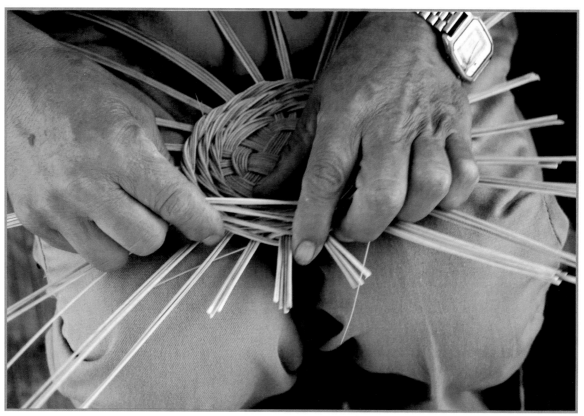

Hands. *The Northern art of weaving fabrics is based on techniques handed down from generation to generation.*

48

ing wine since 1857; it has a museum that is open to the public. At La Rosa, an estate belonging to Michel Torino, visitors can stay at a colonial style inn and try the wines as they eat a menu designed to give tourists a good impression.

In the very heart of an unequalled natural scenery stands Etchart, founded in 1850. If the objective is to visit an organic winery, the best thing to do is drop in at Nanni. Other places worth a visit are El Esteco, El Porvenir, Domingo Hermanos, Peñalba Frías , San Pedro de Yacochuya -8 kilometres from Cafayate-, Cavas de Santa María, in Tolombón, Los Parrales and Don Andrés in Animaná, Miralpeix, in Santa Rosa and Dávalos, in Tacuil.

REDISCOVERING
CATAMARCA

In Catamarca, the province adjoining Salta on the south, mountains and ravines turn into multicolored valleys. Owing to differences in relief and rainfall, fruit growing zones are clearly identified in Catamarca valleys. Traditional handicrafts, outlines an amazing profile where man and nature merge into one. Mud, leather, wood, alpaca, llama, vicuña weaves and other noble materials become "things of beauty" that keep the area's impressive cultural heritage.

The town colonial architecture is the ideal framework to try the delicious empanadas and Catamarca sweets, while listening to the music of the Argentine North, moving in its simplicity.

For wine lovers, the ideal destination is Colomé where viticulture has found new stimulus from companies that have faith in these lands generosity. Here the landscape shows low vines, testimony a historic viticulture, entwined with new plants that renew the fervor for the region's singular wines.

Up in the clouds. *Salta's roads follow the twisting form of the mountain peaks.*

Catamarca. *New impetus for viticulture.*

*La Garganta del Diablo. One of the breathtaking waterfalls visited by tourists from all over the world.
(Photo: Arturo Ballester Molina)*

A LITORAL PARADISE
IGUAZÚ FALLS

The Northeastern region features great rivers along with a subtropical forest, which has giant trees and exuberant vegetation typical of the Mesopotamian Region.

It contains one of the world's most spectacular waterfalls: the Iguazú Falls, located in Misiones Province, on the border with Brazil.

Posadas City, the capital of Misiones Province, is 1,060 kilometers from Buenos Aires.

Land transportation runs regularly from domestic and international airports to the waterfalls.

It is advisable to fly there since most airlines schedule regular flights and Puerto Iguazú town. Tourist infrastructure around this natur-al wonder is excellent. It hosts five-star hotels with a complete range of services so visitors can enjoy their stay to the utmost.

Iguazú falls -meaning "grand water" in Guarani language- have 275 falls up to 70 meters high. After crashing on the rocks below, the waters vaporize and form a fine drizzle that plays with the sun's rays, forming rainbows all around.

This site has been proclaimed a World Natural Heritage site by UNESCO. Its outstanding flora and fauna are protected by the Iguazú National Park.

Misiones province also hosts the San Ignacio Miní Ruins. They are an eloquent testimony to the Jesuits work in Latin America and the site has been pronounced a World Cultural Heritage by UNESCO.

Valle de la Luna (Valley of the Moon). Incredible volcanic formations resulting from erosion give this landscape a surreal look.

WESTERN WARMTH
MOON GEOGRAPHY

It is worthwhile touring San Juan province, an oasis of mountains and fertile valleys, as far as the Ischigualasto Provincial Park, better known as the Valley of the Moon (Valle de la Luna), 330 kilometers to the northeast of the San Juan capital. This fabulous place, with its incomparable scenery, takes visitors back to prehistoric times. UNESCO declared it a Natural Heritage in 2000 and amazes with its singular geography, mysterious volvanic forms no sculptor could ever imagine.

TALAMPAYA, NATURAL SCULPTURE

La Rioja has one of the most important reli-gious circuits in the country with buildings dating from the 18th century. One of the main attractions, and most beautiful in the province, is undoubtedly Talampaya National Park. The canyon of the same name is one of the natural wonders in the country that is visited the most. It has vertical walls almost 150 meters high and condors look out from the cliffs.

Never ending geography of red earth surprises visitors with curious natural formations resulting from erosion caused by wind and rain. It is possible to discover unique sculptures carved by time, with names like "The friar", "The family", "The Cathedral", among others. To visit this fabulous site, excursions can be arraigned with guides who specialize in geology and Talampaya history.

THE ANDES MOUNTAIN RANGE
MOUNT ACONCAGUA:
THE COLOSSUS OF THE AMERICAS

Mendoza Province has one of the most stately sceneries in Argentina: Mount Aconcagua, the highest peak in the Andes Mountain Range and in the Americas.

Mount Aconcagua, a term from the Quechuan language ackon-cauak -meaning stone watcher- rises 6,962 meters. It is in the middle of the Aconcagua Park, with 71,000 hectares and contains glaciers and sites of archaelogical interest.

From December to March, thousands of tourists and mountain climbers from all over the world arrive with the purpose of reaching the summit or trekking around Lake Horcones and Plaza de las Mulas.

International Route N° 7 connects Mendoza City and the Aconcagua Park. The Puente del Inca scenic site and border control can be reached both by car or by regular bus service. From there, access to the Park is on foot or mule as far as the base of the mountain where main camping sites are located.

The tourist is also offered snow from July until the end of August. The province has major winter sports centers, such as Vallecitos or Los Penitentes. The Las Leñas international ski center is located in Malargüe District, 440 kilometers south of Mendoza City and 1,180 kilometers from Buenos Aires City. Las Leñas Center can be easily reached by plane, since there are regular flights from Buenos Aires and Mendoza. This center also has top quality hotel infrastructure and is the site of many important ski, snowboard competitions, as well as other recreational and cultural activities.

Penitentes. This well-known international ski center is a few hours away from Mendoza city.

The Land of Dinosaurs

Patagonia is one of the main fossil fields in the world and Neuquén is recognized for the quality and variety of fossil animals and plants found in its territory. The most important institution in the recovery of Neuquén's fossil patrimony is the Comahue National University. Its work started in 1987 and has never been interrupted. Some of the places where the main discoveries have taken place are: Sierra del Portezuelo, where the fossil bones were found of a 90 million year old Unenlagia comahuensis, considered the missing link between carnivorous dinosaurs and primitive birds like the Archaeopteryx. Plaza Huincul, with the Argentinosaurus huinculensis, the largest herbivorous in the world, 90 million years old, which can be seen in the Museo Carmen Funes in that town. El Chocón where with remains of fossilized trees, tortoises and carnivorous dinosaur eggs were found. And the most important fossil found so far: the Gigantosaurus carolina, the biggest carnivore in the world. In Sierra de Auca Mahuida dinosaur eggs where found in nests, a phenomenon practically unheard of in science. The best specimen of the Titanosaurus was found in Rincón de los Sauces.

Fossils. *Argentina's Patagonia is one of the areas with greatest number of discoveries of dinosaur, fossilized remains and petrified forests.*

PATAGONIA:
WOOD, GLACIERS AND LAKES

The Argentine Patagonia is gifted with picturesque towns, thousand year old woods, mountains, glaciers, rivers and lakes, making up a unique landscape.

This southern region is a perfect place for those looking for a rest, contact with nature or adventure. The possibilities for enjoyment are infinite and only depend on imagination inspired by such beauty.

Neuquén province is the port of entry to the immense Patagonian geography, a fruit growing center, and currently one of the regions that has become an area of great viticulture potential.

Here too the promise of wine tourism can be

Patagonian lakes. *In the southern portion of the Andes Range, the hills are crowded with conifers.*

found, since the establishments in the province have the necessary infrastructure to offer visitors comfortable surroundings.

Beyond the Negro River is the natural border between the province of the same name and Neuquén. Here nature continues to offer interesting options, one of which is to drive the Seven Lakes Circuit. It connects Villa La Angostura and San Martín de los Andes, which is 110 kilometers away. Part of the native flora, conifers show off the relief of the mountains at the side of the road and around the lakes. Pines, araucarians, arrayanes and other species intermingle with the Patagonias steppe's tranquility.

Río Negro is also one of the tourist areas par excellence in the Argentine southern region. Its landscape combines mountains, woods and

Forests. *Native vegetation is a fabulous tree preserve.*

Bariloche. *This city's tourist infrastructure is a tribute its beautiful natural surroundings.*

ski centers in the west and beaches in the east on the Atlantic Ocean, attracting thousands of visitors every year. Viedma, its capital city, is 970 kilometers from Buenos Aires.

San Carlos de Bariloche city, which can be easily reached by plane from Buenos Aires, stands out for the architecture of its buildings, made of stone and wood, along with small scale non-industrial chocolate shops and its friendly people.

To the south of the Colorado River, the tourist has almost unlimited options: sport fishing, hunting, kayaking, rafting, snowboarding, skiing, hiking, camping, 4 x 4 adventures, religious and rural tourism, rock art, Paleontological routes, thermal waters, visits to native communities, mountain climbing and wine tourism.

During the colder months -June and July- the town is crowded with both Argentine and foreign visitors enjoying the ski centers. The main tourist attractions are Mount Catedral, Mount Otto, Piedras Blancas, Valle del Chalhuaco, Mount Tronador, and Chapelco International Ski Center.

THE COAST OF WHALES

Península de Valdés, in Chubut Province, is unique fauna post: sea lions, elephant seals and the Southern Right whales.

From May throughout December, an incomparable show takes place in the Nuevo and San José Gulfs where the whales arrive to bear their young. Magellan penguins and Punta Tombo sea birds also coexist here.

To follow these circuits, the traveler must first

White giant. *Tourists admire the magnificent texture of the Perito Moreno Glacier.*

reach Puerto Madryn and Trelew cities. From there, they can drive, and the most adventuresome tourists can see the whales from the coast.

THE FASCINATING PERITO MORENO GLACIER

One of the trips not to be missed on a visit to Argentina is the National Glaciers Park and its most important glacier: Perito Moreno in Santa Cruz province, 2,600 kilometers from Buenos Aires.

To admire this scenery, one must first reach El Calafate tourist village which has an international airport. Visitors can stay at either a five-star hotel, go camping or stay at an Alpine style cabin.

Marvelous. *Whale watching in southern Argentina attracts tourists from all over the world.*

Neuquén. *From the river that makes a natural border in Rio Negro province, Neuquén city rises as a point of reference in Argentina's Patagonia.*

The face of the Perito Moreno Glacier is 4 kilometers long and is 60 meters above the surface of Lake Argentino. Along with 12 other glaciers, it makes up the great sliding ice and snow masses of the National Park.

At any time of the year visitors -who come from all over the world- can admire the furious and exciting spectacle as ice towers soaring to 60 meters, collapse, breaking into fragments with an impressive thunderous noise.

Other minor glaciers can be seen, such as the Upsala, Onelli and Agassiz, by sailing along Lake Argentino.

Within this area is the Perito Moreno National Park, of great paleontological and archaeological value along with the Petrified Woods that have fossilized trees of up to 35 meters in height.

TIERRA DEL FUEGO:
AT THE END OF THE WORLD

This province is located at the extreme southern end of the republic and is separated from the rest of the country by the Straits of Magellan.

Its capital city, Ushuaia, is the southernmost city in the world, 3,194 kilometers from Buenos Aires. Ushuaia, meaning "bay penetrating to the west" in the native Yámana language, is the most suitable point of entry to the Antarctic. It has both a commercial and tourist harbor and a modern airport. The Tierra del Fuego National Park preserves several species of sub-Antarctic woodlands, where red foxes, guanacos, rabbits, beavers and condors co-exist. From there one has a panoramic view of the Beagle Channel.

A STROLL AROUND THE VINEYARDS

MENDOZA
HARVEST TIME IS A FESTIVITY

Dating back to ancient times, farm workers have celebrated the end of harvest time and their yearlong work by singing and dancing in the courtyards at the vineyards. The same joy is felt time and again in Mendoza Province when celebrating the "National Harvest Festival".

This celebration, which has gained international recognition, dates back to 1913. At that time, during a congress in Mendoza, a party was held to celebrate the harvest. However, this was not a popular festivity. Later on, in 1936, the celebration was given official and national status. It is the main popular festivity in Mendoza and encompasses a number of cultural and artistic activities.

The previous acts and the great festival, which has become an increasingly international tourist attraction over the years, impressive and world famous National Harvest Festival takes place the first week in March. However,

Coronation. *The party explodes with happiness when a new queen is crowned at the harvest Festival (Vendimia).*

several celebrations start in different districts much sooner with the selection of the queens who will represent each district. They choose a queen who represents the beauty of the place and who will participate in the finals.

Activities officially begin with the Blessing of the Fruit to thank the Virgin of Carrodilla, the Patron Saint of the Vineyards for the harvest's generosity. The night before the main celebration, downtown streets are alive with enthusiasm during the "Vía Blanca de las Reinas" -The Queens' White Way- parade. The young women chosen to represent each district ride on floats featuring both the district's distinctive culture and its economy.

At noon on Saturday, the "Carrusel de las Reinas" -The Queens' Carrousel- goes through the streets. The same floats parade, this time accompanied by traditional gauchos on horse-

The color of the vines. *After seeing the plants bursting with clusters, autumn in the vineyards is perhaps the most beautiful postcard.*

back, different communities, their dances, food and typical clothing.

The main celebration is held on Saturday evening at the Frank Romero Day Amphitheater. It is located to the west of the city in the heart of the mountains, and seats 22,000 spectators. Transportation to the celebration leaves from the main city hotels.

Music and lights lavishly bathe the huge main setting as well as the surrounding hills. Hundreds of dancers are on stage, offering a colorful and lively spectacle. Once the show is over, the election of the new queen begins. While votes are being counted, each candidate waves to the audience until the final decision is announced.

The crowning of the new National Harvest Queen and First Princess ends with a magnificent display of fireworks that light up the Mendoza night. During the harvest, there is street theater, painting exhibitions, wine tastings and other wine-related artistic and cultural activities.

The National Harvest Festival represents a toast to the cycle of nature, to popular culture and the festive spirits of those celebrating the harvest.

THE WINE ROUTE
OPEN DOOR WINERIES

In Mendoza , the heart of Argentina's viticulture where over 70% of Argentine wines are produced, there are many routes that always lead to a winery. The idea of tracing these routes is to exploit the potential of viticulture tourism and blend the unique landscapes

The Wine Routes. *A privileged path to enjoying culture through wine and music.*

flush with vineyards at the foot of the Andes Mountain Range.

This way, wine lovers will be able not only to taste wines from the different regions, alongside the casks, but also to hear exceptional stories about the typical cuisine of each terroir and those nuances that make Mendoza a privileged site in the wine culture.

"The Wine Route" is divided into different circuits relating to the province's oases where the most extensive vineyards are located. The visitor will understand during this tour that the best wine knows how to choose its birthplace; where the river, the aged groves mark the way and the stately mountain, as a great backdrop, combine.

As the city expanded, the wineries began to move away. Nevertheless, some remained in

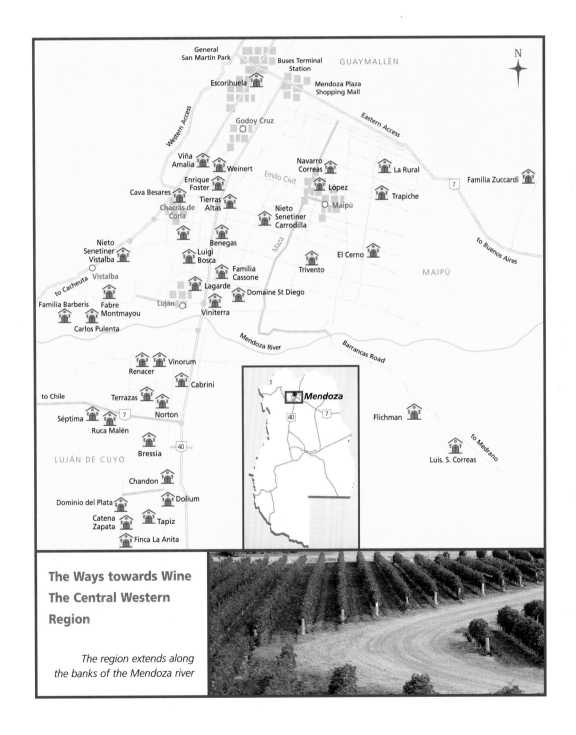

The Ways towards Wine
The Central Western Region

The region extends along the banks of the Mendoza river

the radius of Greater Mendoza and are nearby. Some good examples are Toso and González Videla wineries. The former has a very important production of sparkling wines, while the latter has one of the oldest viticulture building in the country and extremely valuable relics.

A few kilometers from Mendoza city, is the Upper Region of the Mendoza River that includes vineyards in Godoy Cruz, Guaymallén, Luján de Cuyo and Maipú districts. A large number of wineries as well as museums and historical sites are located in this region. It is also the area with the largest amount of Malbec, Argentina's great red wine stock.

The vineyards' altitude ranges from 650 to 1,100 meters above sea level, while the stocks are irrigated with water from the Mendoza river fed by melting snow.

Some of the wineries that can be visited are: Escorihuela, Santa Ana, Viña El Cerno, López, Trapiche, La Rural, Finca Flichman, Cruz de Piedra, Don Cristóbal, Dolium, Luigi Bosca, Viña Amalia, Chandon, Etchart, Norton, Cabrini, Viniterra, Lagarde, among others.

Besides wine tourism, those interested in local history and tradition ought to spend some time In Mendoza at the Museo del Área Fundacional -Foundation Area Museum-, which holds the ruins of the former city, founded towards the middle of the 16th century. To the south, they should not miss the Santuario de la Virgen de La Carrodilla -La Carrodilla Virgin Sanctuary- in Luján de Cuyo

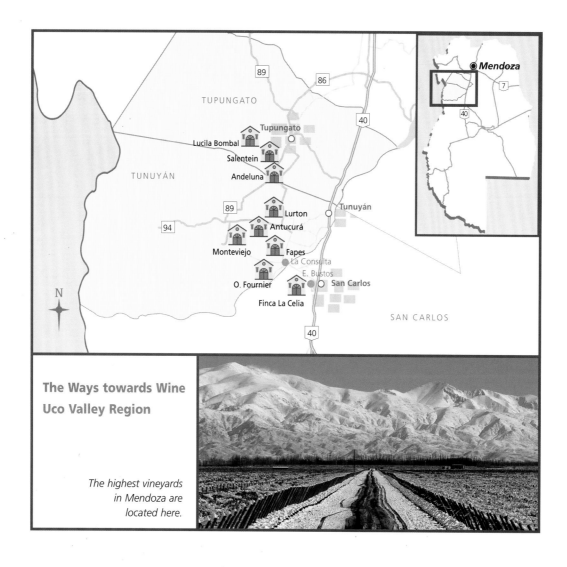

The Ways towards Wine Uco Valley Region

The highest vineyards in Mendoza are located here.

district or the two wine museums located in the Maipú district.

Towards the south, Valle de Uco (Uco Valley) includes San Carlos, Tunuyán and Tupungato districts.

This valley, with its magnificent landscape is also suitable for growing fruit, vegetables and garden produce as well as developing estancia tourism. Some of the wineries you can visit are: Salentein (which has an attractive inn with overnight accommodation), Lurton, Monteviejo, La Celia, Ortega Fournier, Estancia Ancón, among others. Besides being a notable winemaking region, it also has the Laguna del Diamante -Diamond Lake- a natural reserve renowned worldwide for its stately beauty. Expert guides can lead visitors to this area.

Discoveries. *From a vineyard in Lunlunta, Maipú, you can see the towers of an old church.*

Tupungato. *The Valle de Uco crosses the Mendoza landscape with the fertility of its extension and numerous green postcards that can be appreciated.*

Valle Grande. One of the favorite tourist destinations in San Rafael, Mendoza.

With the Southern Cross as a guide, this imaginary -or real- trip can include a tour around the dikes and dams in San Rafael and General Alvear where aquatic sports can be practiced. Some are considered excellent for trout fishing. Rafting along the Valle Grande and the Rio Atuel Canyon in San Rafael is a thrilling experience. The day can end with a visit to wineries like Bianchi, Jean Rivier, Goyenechea or Lávaque.

The great oasis located to the east of Mendoza's capital, is made up by the Junin, La Paz, Rivadavia, San Martín and Santa Rosa districts. It is a magnificent display of plains and desert sun. Some of the wineries to visit in this region are: Familia Zuccardi, Esmeralda, Fantelli, Tittarelli, Llaver, Crotta and the Don Bosco Enology Faculty, among others.

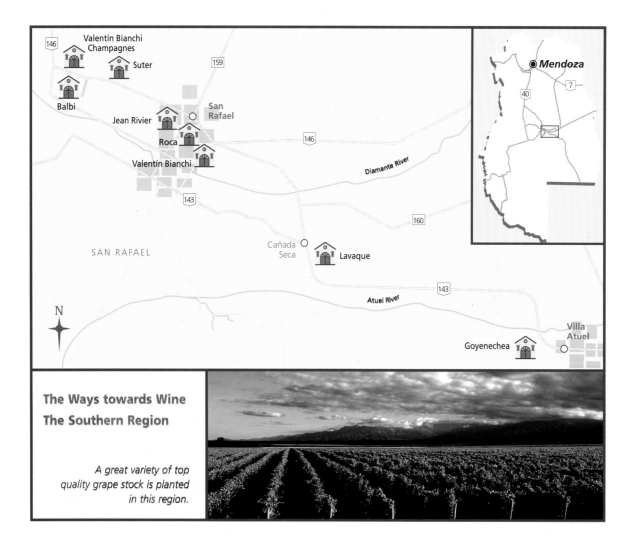

The Ways towards Wine
The Southern Region

A great variety of top quality grape stock is planted in this region.

CHAPTER 4

GRAPE
GEOGRAPHY

Colomé. One of the lands reincorporated to wine production. Its agro climatic conditions support
its wines singular expressions.

approximately 4,120 hectares of vineyards. The main variety is Torrontés followed by Cabernet Sauvignon and Malbec.

Tinogasta is a department that covers 70% of the vineyard surface of the province and in it most wineries are found.

Part of the crop goes to fresh consumption; nevertheless in coming years, new wineries will start producing beside the vineyards that have been recovered.

The Catamarca Valleys are being rediscovered by wine entrepreneurs although the area has traditionally been an oasis for vine growing.

It is worth noting the interest that Catamarca province has provoked as its terroirs are rediscovered for the notable expression they give the wine.

No doubt Catamarca will contribute high quality products since there are very promising endeavors there.

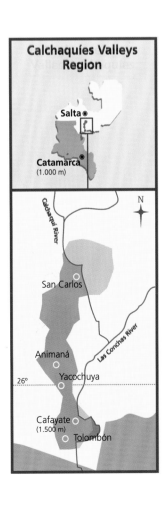

Calchaquíes Valleys Region

LA RIOJA PROVINCE

FAMATINA VALLEYS

The region is located at 20°10' South latitude with altitudes ranging from 935 m. to 1,170 meters above sea level. It has very low rainfall (130 mm per year) and is affected by moderate winds. Average temperature is 18 °C.

There are 7,000 hectares vineyards, most of it with Torrontés Riojano nutured by the generous sun of these valleys to express its deep floral and fruity aromas. Besides, in recent years, other red varieties have been grown, especially Syrah.

The most important terroirs are Chilecito, Nonogasta and Anguinan. Soils are predominantly pebbly and sandy.

La Rioja viticulture is carried out in small irrigated valleys in the west of the province, between Velasco and Famatina hills. Chilecito Department has the largest part of the vineyard surfaces (over 70%).

SAN JUAN PROVINCE

San Juan Province is the second most important in grape and wine production. The capital, San Juan City is 1,255 kilometers from Buenos Aires and its vineyards grow 650 meters above sea level.

Its viticulture oases are in the Tulum, Zonda, Ullum, Jáchal and Fertil Valleys, irrigated by the Jáchal and San Juan Rivers.

The Tulum valley is located between the Andes and the Pie de Palo hills on the left bank of the San Juan River. Average altitude is 630 meters above sea level, rainfall is scarce and the average temperature is 17 °C. Soils are stony.

This region produces very high quality typical sweet wines made from Moscatel de Alejandría, Torrontés, Chenin Blanc and Pedro

New impulse. San Juan's valleys display and interesting increase in viticulture production.

Mountain range. *New plantations rise among the peaks looking for altitude, sun and clear skies.*

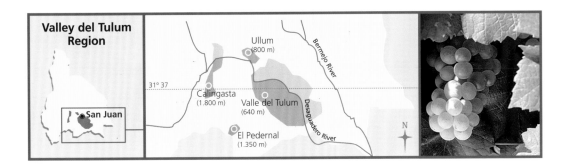

Ximénez varieties. The Angaco Moscateles together with the rich, fortified wines are also famous, a greatly appreciated local handicraft. These vineyards owe their high quality to state-of-the-art irrigation technology and improved agronomical activities.

The main viticulture terroirs are Rivadavia, Albardón, Angaco, San Martín, 9 de Julio, Caucete, Santa Rosa and Pocitos, all of them located on the right bank of the San Juan River. At an altitude of around 1,350 meters, the prestigious Pedernal valley stretches between Cerro Tontal and the Andean foothills. Crops are irrigated with water from springs. This area, ecologically suited for high quality wines, has been recently incorporated to the Argentine viticulture map. The varieties best adapted to this zone are Cabernet Sauvignon, Merlot and Chardonnay.

Chenin Blanc and Chardonnay are the varieties that adapt best to the traditional vineyards of the Ullum valley irrigated by the San

New and eternal. *The youngest vines reflect their promise in the Andes immutable greatness.*

Juan River. In the upper areas, Sauvignon Blanc and some reds such as Tempranillo find their finest expression.

The highest area in the region is the Calingasta District, located between the Andean foothills and the central Andean mountain range, some 1,800 meters above sea level.

MENDOZA
UPPER
MENDOZA RIVER AREA

The region is located at the Mendoza piedmont, at 30° south latitude. The average annual temperature is 15 °C and the altitude varies from 650 to 1,060 meters above sea level. The cultivated area is irrigated by the Mendoza River.

The appellations located in the higher area,

Nature. Mendoza's wines acquire singular expression from the landscape's generous wealth.

such as Vistalba, Las Compuertas or Perdriel, are the coldest and are particularly indicated for growing Malbec. Luján de Cuyo, Maipú and Panquehua (in Las Heras District) host the oldest vineyards of this variety. Going downhill, temperatures are higher giving origin to significantly different terroirs in relatively short distances (no more than 20 km). Climatic conditions foster the development of color and tannins, ideal traits in wines apt for being cellared. This region hosts 17% of the Mendoza vineyards, and is home to some 360 wineries.

Uco Valley

This region is located southwest of Mendoza City, between 33° 5' and 34° south latitude. The annual average temperature is 14 °C. Altitudes range from 900 m to 1,200 m above sea level.

This area has approximately 13,000 hectares

79

Future. New vineyards offer promising productive geometry.

East Mendoza Region

Mendoza

Montecaseros
Mendoza River
Buen Orden
San Martín
Los Barriales
Junín
(650 m)
Medrano
Reducción
Rivadavia
La Libertad
Santa Rosa
Las Catitas
Tumuyán River

N

of vineyards. The area is noted for the excellent quality of its grapes, resulting in wines apt for lengthy cellaring. At present, it has attracted strong investor demand, particularly due its capacity for high altitude viticulture.

Traditionally, the varieties grown in this area are Semillón and Malbec; together with Bonarda and Barbera in a smaller amount.

Among recently planted vineyards, vine growers have preferred medium cycle varieties, such as Merlot and Pinot Noir, since they reach optimum ripeness in this area.

Cabernet Sauvignon and Chardonnay are grown in the lower areas of the region. Chardonnay is harvested at an early stage, which ensures par excellence acidity levels in sparkling wines. The Syrah from this region is highly regarded.

MENDOZA'S EASTERN REGION

This region is the largest wine producer in Mendoza Province. It accounts for 50% of the area devoted to grapes and is the most impor-

A vineyard's palette. *The surprising color combinations in the viticulture landscapes.*

tant viticulture oasis in South America. This vast flat area is located at 33° south latitude and is irrigated by the Tunuyán River.

It covers the cultivated areas of Junín, Rivadavia, San Martín, Santa Rosa, La Paz and part of Maipú Districts.

Altitudes vary from 640 to 750 meters and are irrigated by the Tunuyán and part of the Mendoza Rivers. This area has deep, coarse soils with excellent drainage conditions.

In recent decades, improved vineyard management together with a significant modernization of winery technology have enabled the production of high quality, fruity, fully-bodied and structured wines with a delicate varietal expression.

These wines are typical of desert areas and display rich colors owing to the generous amounts of sunlight the grapes receive. Climate and soil combine for very good yields from the vineyards, while preventing the fruit/hectare equation from harming the wines typical distinctive features.

MENDOZA'S SOUTH REGION

Located between 34° 5' and 35° south latitude, the area covers the San Rafael and General Alvear District, at the foothills of the Andes main range.

This oasis is irrigated by the Atuel and Diamante Rivers.

The "San Rafael" DOC (Controlled Domination of Origin) was developed and excellent still and sparkling wines are produced here.

Vineyards are cultivates at altitudes that range from 450 meters (in Carmensa district, General Alvear) to 800 meters above sea level (in Las Paredes and Cuadro Nacional districts, San Rafael), the vines are irrigated by the Diamante River.

The annual average temperature is 15 °C. It is home to almost 22,000 cultivated hectares, (which represent 15% of the total viticulture area of Mendoza), and there are some 200 wineries, many of which are century old

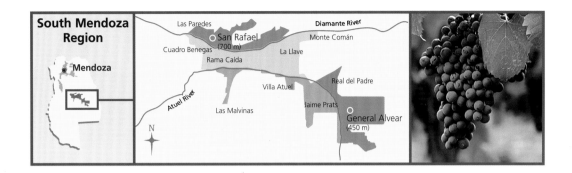

South Mendoza Region

Mendoza

Las Paredes · Diamante River · San Rafael (700 m) · Monte Comán · Cuadro Benegas · La Llave · Rama Caída · Villa Atuel · Real del Padre · Atuel River · Las Malvinas · Jaime Prats · General Alvear (450 m)

N

establishments founded by European immigrants.

This region is the main producer of Chenin Blanc, the basis for the freshness and vivacity of the area's white wines. The Chardonnay is remarkable and is one of the emblematic varietals of the region.

Noteworthy reds are also produced in this area; those made from Malbec and Cabernet Sauvignon are outstanding.

MENDOZA'S NORTH REGION

This region covers the lowest areas above sea level irrigated by the Mendoza River. It covers Lavalle (to the northeast of Mendoza city), Maipú, Guaymallén, Las Heras and San Martín Districts. The landscape is characterized by viticulture plots interspersed with typical Mendoza desert areas. The vineyards are located at altitudes varying between 700 and 550 meters above sea level.

In general terms, terrains are deep and slopes not pronounced. The average annual temperature is 16 °C. Fine soils are prevalent.

The region is characterized by the production of white wines such as Chenin Blanc, Pedro Ximénez, Ugni Blanc and Torrontés Riojano. Since the acidity in these varieties can be somewhat low, harvest must not be late. In any event, markedly fruity, floral and high performance wines are obtained, ideal for producing top quality base wines.

Though light, red wines display good varietal character. Malbec reaches exuberant color expression. Syrah, Bonarda and Barbera varieties are also noteworthy since they result in vividly colored and distinctively fruity wines. In general, they are fruity wines not apt for cellaring.

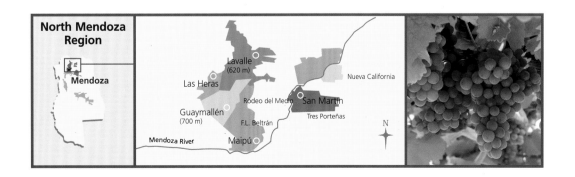

North Mendoza Region

Mendoza

Lavalle (620 m) · Las Heras · Nueva California · Rodeo del Medio · San Martín · Guaymallén (700 m) · F.L. Beltrán · Tres Porteñas · Mendoza River · Maipú

N

83

Patagonia. *On the banks of the Rio Negro, plateaus frame the wine growing area in the south of Argentina.*

RÍO NEGRO AND NEUQUÉN PROVINCES

UPPER VALLEY

This area is located in Patagonia, at 30° south latitude on the banks of the Limay and Neuquén rivers. It has over 32,700 hectares of productive vineyards.

San Patricio del Chañar in Neuquén is noteworthy for its quality, a true wine growing oasis with producing wines with outstanding notes.

It is the southernmost viticulture region, in Argentina and the lowest (around 400 meters above sea level). The climate is continental, dry, and temperate with remarkable temperature ranges and very windy.

Gusts of wind sweep the region. The region's ecological characteristics of the favor white wines such as Chardonnay and Sauvignon Blanc with the later, in addition to its regular features, displays exceptional smoky flavors difficult to find in other regions around the country. Great reds are also produced, particularly from medium cycle varieties. In this region Pinot Noir and Merlot find their most polished expressions, owing to the fact they are varieties with a short cycle that obtain full maturity.

CHAPTER 5

GRAPES AND WINES
WITH SOUTHERN STAMP

"ARGENTINA'S IDENTITY LIES WITH MALBEC"

BY MICHEL ROLLAND

Something good about Argentina is that it has a little bit of every single type of wine There are whites and almost all varieties of reds. However, a wine producing country should always have a distinctive personality, and when speaking about reds, Argentina's fame definitely lies with Malbec. No one will ever say that Malbec is doing badly in Argentina, even though not all Malbec wines are equally good. There is no doubt about Malbec's strong personality. Other varieties such as Merlot, Tempranillo, Cabernet and Syrah are also produced in Argentina, but Argentina's strength will always be Malbec.

Maybe one day Argentine producers will come to the conclusion that higher altitudes are better for Pinot Noir while Syrah is better suited to warmer areas. However, I think such a change will take time. Nowadays each winery wants to have a wide range of production, maybe not encompassing all varieties but having as many as possible. If a producer has a small plot of land,

he will plant everything in there. In my opinion, that is a mistake whose negative effects will be felt in the long term. It is necessary to reach an understanding of where each variety should be planted. There has been progress towards such a conviction, but there is still a lot to do. I do not mean to sound derogatory, but viticulture of opportunity still predominates over viticulture of interpretation. This situation, though, will not last longer than maybe 20 years. By then, we will find the right location for each variety.

Regarding blends, I think they are a better option than varietals, especially when it comes to making up for quality variations from year to year. Malbec may have one fantastic vintage but it is not possible to have the same quality every year with a single variety. A blend can be improved with each vintage: if one year Malbec is lean, a small percentage of a more robust Cabernet, Merlot or Tempranillo can do the trick of contributing a round body.

GRAPES AND WINES
WITH A SOUTHERN STAMP

VARIETIES

Diversity, originality of grape stock character and optimum agro-ecological conditions are some of the features that make Argentina one of the most attractive locations in the world to produce top quality wines. One of the most important strengths of this distinctly continental viticulture is the harmonious combination of three fundamental pillars: climate, soil and grape stock. A wide range of grape varieties planted on more than 210,000 hectares of vineyards have adapted and reached their full expression, thus offering the market memorable examples of the classical varieties. Along with them, a range of other grape stock varieties are being rediscovered and improved. Others promise "pearls" grown on Argentine soil in the coming years.

Vines grow in the desert and valleys.

Malbec

Leaf: Barely folded and twisted, medium-sized, dark green, unlobed and three-lobed.

Bunch: medium sized, conical, loose.

Berry: bluish-black, medium-sized, soft pulp.

Characteristics: deep red wine with plenty blue and purple tinges. Typical varietal flavours of plum, sour cherry and red fruit marmalade framed in sweet tannins. Good ageing potential.

Malbec

Although Malbec seems to have found the ideal terroir to express its full varietal prowess in Argentina, its birthplace is in France. There this grape is known as Cot or Auxerroir and is mainly grown in the Cahors region. Due to its intense color and dark tones, French Malbec wines were dubbed "the black wines of Cahors".

However, this variety never achieved greatness in Europe.

Undoubtedly, soil and climate conditions in Argentina are more favorable than in its homeland, the reason why Malbec has become Argentina's signature wine and its most planted red grape.

Argentina possesses both some of the highest vineyards in the world, at an altitude of 2,000 meters above sea level (Salta) and the southernmost vineyards in the world (Patagonia). Such comparative advantages are currently the basis of the quality that has gained world wide recognition for Argentine wines.

Here are Michel Rolland's remarks on grape stocks grown in Argentina:

RED VARIETIES
MALBEC

It is the signature grape of Argentina, the country with the largest area planted with Malbec in the world. Malbec seems to have found its home here.

Mendoza hosts many Malbec types that suit the diversity of soil-climate combinations.

When tasting a Malbec from Tupungato, San Martín or La Consulta, it is possible to discover different and distinctive personalities resulting from the different types of soil they grow in. By controlling yield and with favorable climatic conditions, it is possible to make good wine.

In order to develop its full potential, Malbec requires a wide variation of day and night time temperatures. Higher altitude terroirs, such as Vistalba, yield wines with optimum acidity, lots of color and sweet and abundant tannins, wines capable of aging wonderfully in barrels. In lower altitude areas, its concentration decreases and it ripens quickly. Malbec should be Argentina's flagship abroad because it is fantastic to have something original, whether a varietal or a wine with a Malbec base.

Every country always has some wines that are a local myth. Here, it could be Malbec.

CABERNET SAUVIGNON

This grape stock has spread to all Argentine viticulture areas. In order to take advantage of its full potential it must reach complete matur-

Diversity. The wide region offering optimum vine growth conditions has allowed a varied range of grape varieties.

ity. Otherwise, it may be flawed by herbaceous aromas or bitter tastes. It ripens late and under adequate conditions produces wines that are apt for lengthy macerations and aging in barrels.

It can make great wines but requires lots of work. It does not ripen easily and varies greatly from one year to the next because it is very sensitive to weather fluctuations. In the beginning it showed low density, had high production in overhead trellised vines and its tannins were somewhat rustic and aggressive. It is now improving; Mendoza and other regions are producing very good Cabernet with more finesse and elegance. I feel that the producers understood they could make a better effort with this wine. Everything indicates that maturity will be more easily reached; this is why very good Cabernet Sauvignons are produced, not tasting of green pepper any more, but of black fruit,

Cabernet Sauvignon

Total area: **15.440 ha**

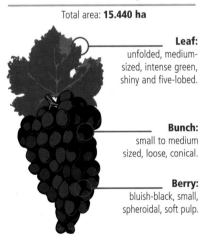

Leaf: unfolded, medium-sized, intense green, shiny and five-lobed.

Bunch: small to medium sized, loose, conical.

Berry: bluish-black, small, spheroidal, soft pulp.

Characteristics: this varietal wine develops aromas of black pepper, black olive, tobacco, red fruits and blackberries. More exotic flavour descriptors such as meat, smoked pepper and leather may also be associated with this varietal. Developed wines of this variety exhibit complex aromas.

Extremes. Argentine wines are children of the sun, but the plants resist the harshest winters in favor of quality.

spices and containing powerful round tannins. This is the way world consumers like it and Argentina is going to produce this type of Cabernet.

MERLOT

One of the more recently promoted varieties in Argentina, Merlot has a lot of potential. Some areas produce more concentrated wines that anticipate good aging provided vineyard has been controlled properly.

When I first arrived in this country, there was not a lot of Merlot, and what there was, was not located in ideal areas. Taking into account the diversity of terroirs in Argentina, very good Merlot wines could be made here, but this grape needs to be grown in cooler regions. Grape production control is essential for the fruit to achieve good maturity and thus produce deep wines, with important round and soft tannins. There is a lesson to be learnt from a bad experience. Twenty years ago the United

Merlot

Total area: **6.887 ha**

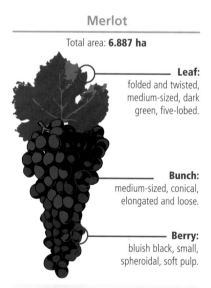

Leaf: folded and twisted, medium-sized, dark green, five-lobed.

Bunch: medium-sized, conical, elongated and loose.

Berry: bluish black, small, spheroidal, soft pulp.

Characteristics: ruby-coloured wine, with good intensity and deep red tinges. Its aromas are reminiscent of red fruit, tobacco, bell pepper, sour cherry, red currant, truffle and leather. It exhibits a pleasant attack in the mouth.

States underwent a "Merlotmania" because the market demanded it. Winegrowers began planting, but they did it badly. Today United States is a country where you can find good wines, but also some of the worst Merlots in the world; this cause the demand for this variety to decrease sharply. This variety has a promising future and can produce interesting blends with Malbec. The Merlot prevailing in Argentina now is not perfect, but an increasing number of interesting Merlot wines have been made in the last three to four years.

SYRAH

This variety ripens later than Malbec, and when the grape is overripe, the winemaking process becomes difficult and adversely affects the quality of the aromas. Colder Mendoza regions, such as Uco Valley, can yield wines with great structure, apt for aging. In the warmer regions, the wines have good color and a fruity taste.

Soil-climate relationship is fundamental to produce good Syrah. The problem with Argentina is that winegrowers do not have a great deal of experience with Syrah, since there are not many vineyards with this grape stock. We can see some now, but over time we have to analyze the soil where it grows, what type of wine it produces and what we need to do to attain a good level. We have identified a somewhat warmer region in San Juan where there is an important area devoted to Syrah. It seems to be a promising region, but it needs further study. Syrah requires considerable vineyard work because it is a high-yield variety and does not reach full ripeness easily, essential to producing a concentrated wine with ample tannins and typical Syrah fruit flavors.

PINOT NOIR

It was one of the varieties introduced by

Syrah

Total area: **10.212 ha**

Leaf: three-lobed, with a flat central lobe and folded side lobes, medium-sized, opaque green.

Bunch: medium-sized, compact to tightly full, conical and elongated.

Berry: bluish black, medium-sized, soft pulp.

Characteristics: berries tend to shrink and loose weight when overripe. It exhibits intense scarlet-red hue, spicy flavours and aromas of meat, sour cherries and fig. Pleasant tannins that develop quickly.

Pinot Noir

Total area: **1.140 ha**

Leaf: barely folded and slightly twisted, medium-sized, dark green, three- and five-lobed.

Bunch: small, completely full, cilindrical, with wings.

Berry: bluish black, small, soft pulp.

Characteristics: low-yield variety with aromas of raisin, licorice and violets framed in ample and slightly astringent tannins underlaid by coffee notes. It develops its full potential in cooler regions

Vineyards of high oenological quality

Around 10,000 grape varieties are grown throughout the world, the great majority of which belong to the "Vitis vinifera" species, whose name literally means varieties for making wine.

Many of the latter adapt well to Argentina, which is why the country's range of varietals is consi-dered among the most extensive in the wine world.

Towards the middle of the 19th Century, noble European varieties were introduced. During the 20th Century and especially after 1980, there was a renewed influx of European grape stock in order to incorporate selected virus-free clones.

During the 1960's, Argentina conducted an important survey of the country's existing varieties. Such research helped identify these varieties and determine their ampelographic characteristics and terroir requirements.

In the past few years, vineyard acreage of Cabernet Sauvignon, Chardonnay, Malbec, Merlot and Syrah has increased. Among the most recently planted varieties are Cabernet Franc, Viognier and Pinot Blanc. As for white varieties, Chardonnay and Sauvignon Blanc are increasing in vineyard acreage.

means of selected genetic material and some Argentine vineyards are quite old.

Although the area with this grape stock has increased in the last few years, the amount of Pinot Noir still wines in the market has not experienced a similar increase. A large percentage of this grape is used for making sparkling wines. The Argentine Patagonia produces wines capable of being cellared for several years.

It is a vividly red wine tending towards with ruby with burgundy tones. It shows seamlessly combined aromas of red and black fruit, especially cassis and cherry, along with raspberry, blackberry and plum marmalades. More complex aromas are reminiscent of cinnamon, coconut and smoked meat. In the mouth, tannins are not strong, but this wine exhibits elegant flavors, while its more concentrated versions offer a lingering finish.

Being French and originally from the famous Bordeaux region, it has become a well-known, highly-appreciated variety. However, it is hard to make great wines from Pinot Noir. More easily adapted to temperate zones, this stock develops especially in clay, lime soil.

Good Pinot Noir fruit typically has small clusters with small berries. This results in wines with fine aromas and texture that are delicate, yet vigorous; and in spite of their lighter color have a surprising aging capacity.

It is a delicate variety with great potential if grown according to irreproachable viticulture practices.

Sangiovese

It has been traditionally planted in Argentina, although not many wineries use it for varietal wines.

It is a difficult grape to grow since Argentine wine growers are not experienced with it. If it is planted only to claim that it exists in Argentina, it will not contribute to the

Care. In Argentina, vineyards are tended by hand, assuring grape quality.

Argentina's reputation as it is not easy to make a top quality Sangiovese. It should be grown with great care and not in large quantities. It is definitely not a recommended variety for Argentina.

BONARDA

This is the second most cultivated red grape in Argentina and one of the most traditional. A typical characteristic is its deep color. It is used in blends, to which it contributes color intensity and fruity notes.

There is plenty of Bonarda in Argentina, but I am not sure that great wines can be made from it. It is pleasant, fruity, with smooth tannins. Traditionally, Bonarda has never been that good and I believe that might be attributed to production problems, since in gener-

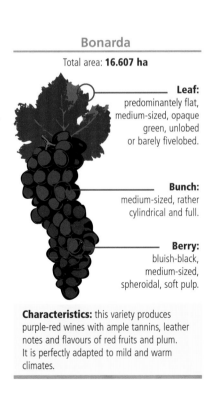

Bonarda

Total area: **16.607 ha**

Leaf:
predominantely flat,
medium-sized, opaque
green, unlobed
or barely fivelobed.

Bunch:
medium-sized, rather
cylindrical and full.

Berry:
bluish-black,
medium-sized,
spheroidal, soft pulp.

Characteristics: this variety produces purple-red wines with ample tannins, leather notes and flavours of red fruits and plum. It is perfectly adapted to mild and warm climates.

95

al, no one has been overly concerned with getting the best from this variety. I do not think Argentina's reputation will profit from it because it is a traditional Italian variety, but has never achieved much fame in its homeland either. Good wines always find a market, but I am not sure that producing great volumes of Bonarda will lead to good opportunities. Commercially speaking, I do not think it is very strong image-wise.

TEMPRANILLO

For several decades, this variety, which came to Argentina with the first Spanish settlers, has been overlooked. In the past few years, however, some wineries have decided to devote energy to developing this variety's potential. It is one of the first red grape varieties to ripen and has a large amount of tannins. It is a great red variety, but has not yet fully developed its potential in other regions of the world.

A somewhat rustic grape, it generally yields wines with good structure, color and tannins. It ripens early and sometimes lacks the desired acidity. Some of its virtues can disappear if overproduced.

PETIT VERDOT

It is not a widely planted variety, but the small area under cultivation has produced exotic wines used in blends, giving wines a distinct character.

It would be interesting to follow it little by little, to see if it can do something interesting to help the blend or even make a varietal wine. Further experience is needed before planting too many areas.

It is essential to experiment in order to have information about some new varieties, and very little information is available about this particular variety and nor are there old vineyards.

Tempranillo

Total area: **5.227 ha**

Leaf: folded and twisted, large size, opaque green, with five-lobes..

Bunch: large, tightly full, conical and elongated.

Berry: bluish black, medium-sized, spheroidal, soft pulp.

Characteristics: Vigorous wine, with ample tannins and exhibiting impressing colour dominated by bluish hues.

Surface planted per variety

Hectareas

Malbec	20.251,61
Bonarda	16.607,42
Cabernet Sauvignon	15.439,86
Syrah	10.212,16
Torrontés Riojano	7.944,09
Merlot	6.886,58
Tempranillo	5.227,21
Chardonnay	4.651,36
Pinot Noir	1,140,02
Semillón	977,35
Sauvignon Blanc	956,44
Viognier	183,84
Totales	**90.477,93**

Source: INV 2003

Torrontés Riojano

Total area: **7.944 ha**

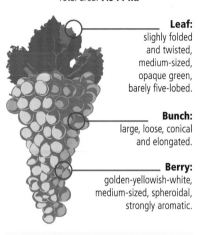

Leaf:
slighly folded
and twisted,
medium-sized,
opaque green,
barely five-lobed.

Bunch:
large, loose, conical
and elongated.

Berry:
golden-yellowish-white,
medium-sized, spheroidal,
strongly aromatic.

Characteristics: high-yield variety, early ripener, exhuberant aromas and flavours reminiscent of rose, orange rind, camomile, honey and Muscat grapes. Good balance between acidity and fruit.

This variety exists almost exclusively in Argentina, and due to its exclusiveness, it has become the typical Argentine white grape. Originally an indigenous Spanish grape, very little of it can be found in its homeland while there is a little; the only other country with a bit is Chile. In Argentina, the Torrontés Riojano is grown in several provinces: Mendoza, Catamarca, La Rioja and Salta. In my opinion, the region of Cafayate has great potential for producing the best Torrontés. This variety has a strong and interesting personality. I am convinced that it can produce good wines, distinct from any in the world. Argentina must make an effort to develop it and position it as the country's signature wine. However, the country is on its own in such an endeavor. Torrontés can become an appealing product in the inter-

national market because of its unique characteristics. From the enological point of view, it is not very complex with very expressive and pleasant fruit; it is fresh, with good balance between acidity and fruit, making it agreeable to drink. This variety's image needs to be developed in international markets. It is a complicated task with uncertain results.

CHARDONNAY

This is the best-known white variety in the world and adapts very well to all sites. In Argentina we have seen some very good wines, but the only problem is that it faces very strong competition. Planting it in cooler areas allows a slow ripening process and better acidity.

Argentine Chardonnay has enormous potential, and attention should be focused on the evolution of consumer tastes because it may change. Ten years ago we were talking about a strong, full bodied, perhaps a little heavy Chardonnay. Nowadays preferences are changing towards a more fruity style. The consumer wants more freshness and a little less wood. Chardonnay can be changed and adapted to meet the market's demand for something a little different.

SAUVIGNON BLANC

This could become an appealing variety in Argentina. There are not a lot of good ones but there are some. Together with Viognier, this grape stock generated enthusiasm when consumer trends began shifting towards fresh and more fruity white wines. It could adapt well to high-altitude, cool regions, where it is possible to develop intense aromas. I believe that this variety might be interesting as part of a winery's range of products. The growing international market is demanding a fruitier Sauvignon Blanc, with typical slightly vegeta-

Chardonnay
Total area: **4.651 ha**

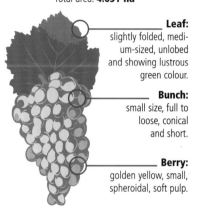

Leaf: slightly folded, medium-sized, unlobed and showing lustrous green colour.

Bunch: small size, full to loose, conical and short.

Berry: golden yellow, small, spheroidal, soft pulp.

Characteristics: It displays pineapple, apple, ripe banana and linden flower aromas. When submitted to malolactic fermentation, it develops honey, nutty, toasted bread and vanilla aromas.

Sauvignon Blanc
Total area: **956 ha**

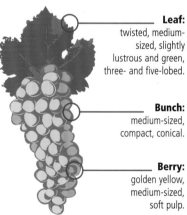

Leaf: twisted, medium-sized, slightly lustrous and green, three- and five-lobed.

Bunch: medium-sized, compact, conical.

Berry: golden yellow, medium-sized, soft pulp.

Characteristics: rather high-yield variety. It shows pineapple, mango and pink grapefruit aromas with herbaceous touches of eucaliptus. Grapes grown further south yield wines with enhanced smoky and gunpowder aromas.

Semillón

Total area: **977 ha**

Leaf: unfolded and twisted, medium-sized, opaque green, moderately five-lobed.

Bunch: medium-sized, full, short and conical.

Berry: golden yellow, medium-sized, spheroidal, soft pulp.

Characteristics: ripe peach and apricot syrup aromas. Wines from Patagonia show subtle smoke. Unctuous and pleasantly acid palate.

Break. *After harvesting, a well-deserved rest next to some bins.*

tive aromas, good acidity and freshness in the mouth. I have found some examples of such a style in Argentina.

When comparing Chile's and Argentina's versions of this varietal, the former's are undoubtedly more stylish, higher quality wines, whose evolution will certainly be something to talk about.

SEMILLÓN

Semillón is a variety traditionally planted in Mendoza, used as a base for white wines produced in the Uco Valley and Upper Mendoza Valley. Unfortunately, its sensitivity to rot and easy oxidation discouraged growers and now only a few hectares remain. Nevertheless, the wines from Mendoza's Uco Valley and from Patagonia have outstanding characteristics. In warmer areas, they lack acidity, have a light, greenish-yellow color wand in some cases occasional golden flashes. Its aromas are reminiscent of honey, apricot and peach, wild herbs and some citrus. In the mouth, it reveals great personality, and though sometimes it may appear light, it is pleasantly balanced. It is also used in blends for sparkling wines, while some wineries produce it as a varietal.

To achieve maximum quality, it is necessary to make sure the plant is balanced to avoid developing herbaceous aromas and favor the formation of fruity flavors such as pear and citrus as well as toasted bread.

Originally from Bordeaux (France) this grape stock variety is in constant decline, however there are still 15,000 hectares in that country.

In general, it has large berries, so yield must be controlled by shoot thinning after pruning. It is not a very vigorous variety, but produces plenty of fruit, which increases its good qualities.

The wines are generally powerful and fleshy, with low acidity and apt for barrel aging. Proper vinification increases its aptitude for aging.

VIOGNIER

Along with Sauvignon Blanc and Torrontés, Viognier is one of the varieties deemed to have the greatest potential for producing young, very fruity and refreshing wines. It has only recently been introduced in Argentina and although the area with Viognier is small, some wineries are already producing it as a varietal and it is sometimes barrel-aged. It yields very fruity, aromatic and fresh wines.

Viognier has been grown for a long time on the southern coast of the Rhône (Condrieu), in France and exhibits high quality aromas of apricot and peach along with balanced citrus notes.

With good exposure to sunlight, it ripens well. It usually produces wines of good alcoholic strength, but can sometimes lack acidity, especially when yield and irrigation have not been perfectly controlled.

Viognier

Total area: **184 ha**

Leaf:
Large size, five-lobed, light green.

Bunch:
Small, compact, conical.

Berry:
Yellowish-green, medium-sized, soft pulp.

Characteristics: medium-yield variety, difficult to grow, aromatically flavoured, with low acidity and producing highly alcoholic wines. It exhibits delicate floral aromas combined with melon, peach and subtle spices.

CHAPTER 6

INVESTMENTS.
BETTING ON THE FUTURE

"ARGENTINA HAS IT ALL"

POR MICHEL ROLLAND

Investors are coming, and that is a good thing. Argentina has it all. It is a huge, rich country so spacious that there are no risks of being overcrowded. This country has so much, that almost everywhere there is the possibility of doing something different, and I am not talking only about wines.

In Argentina there are fewer obtacles than in some other countries. There is no need to request permits. If you want to plant Cabernet Sauvignon and it does not work, it is your problem. Administration officials do not decide which variety to plant in your vineyard. If you want to have your property planted with 60% Malbec vines or else 20%, you just do it. Because, unlike France, there are no strict regulations in force. In France, we started to regulate a century ago, and now we have to comply with more and more rules. Today, the game has become so complicated that nothing can be done. In contrast, Argentina offers its most positive asset: complete freedom.

However, freedom is not the only advantage. This country can offer competitive prices. The place is fantastic: the Andes are superb, the climate is good —there is hail, of course, but problems exist everywhere— and Argentines are very nice people. There is good food, excellent beef and one can always listen to or dance a tango.

A far more significant advantage, however, is the quality of human resources. There are people with a tradition and knowledge of wine who are capable of successfully undertaking any project. This fact is particularly true in this new generation of agronomists, oenologists and technicians who are very well trained, willing and very eager to learn.

Investors come to a country where they like the people, the friendly atmosphere, and the food. And, if all the minor details have already been taken care of, they can focus on important issues. That's why I say interest rates are not the problem, that requesting a loan at those rates is not an issue because in France things are not too different, and there are always some obstacles.

Investors will continue to come, and we can attract many more, though they disembark with some caution, given that they want to generate business with some degree of security. Little by little, Argentina seems to be grasping this concept.

INVESTMENTS.
BETTING ON THE FUTURE

THE WORLD'S EYES ON ARGENTINA

Since 1990, there has been significant investment in the viticulture industry, particularly with capital investments from the U.S., Chile, France, Spain and the United Kingdom, and, to a lesser extent, from the Netherlands and Portugal. This first wave of investments was concentrated mainly in Mendoza, particularly in the Luján de Cuyo, Maipú, Tupungato, Tunuyán, San Rafael and San Martín districts. This phenomenon, which placed Mendoza at the center of investors' attention, demonstrated viticulture's qualitative potential and its competitive capacity.

According to estimates by the Research

Passionate. "*The Argentina of wine captivated me*".

Contemporary Visionary

Jean Michel Arcaute was a true pioneer among the foreigners who offered their expertise to Argentine viticulture in recent years. Nominated many times by Robert Parker as "Wine Man of the Year", he gained well deserved prestige with the celebrated Château Clinet wine in Pomerol region of France.

Shortly before his early death in Arcachon, France, he recalled how he discovered Argentina: ..."My friend Michel Rolland encouraged me to visit South America in 1991. We were coming back from Chile, and I was enthusiastic, but my encounter with the wine of Argentina captivated me: the diversity of varieties, the climate, its huge stretches of land, and above all, its people, wise in vine growing. I saw the enormous potential, especially in Mendoza, where the finest Malbec in the world finds its home."

Arcaute, a man of great personality and a visionary entrepreneur, managed to convince several qualified European investors from the wine world. And this group brought significant projects to a successful conclusion, such as Bodega Alta Vista and the business endeavor Clos de los Siete, in Vista Flores, in the Valle de Uco, Mendoza.

Many businessmen from all over the world have followed Jean Michel to Argentina.

Center for Production of the National Industry, Commerce and Mining Secretariat, transactions were over U$S 500 million during the 90's. If statistics from the Secretariat are taken into account, U$S 398 million was invested and projected for the 1990-1996 period, and U$S 125 million for the 1997-1999 period. Investments for viticulture businesses were about U$S 120 million for the 2000-2005 period.

The major share of these investments was destined for the purchase, construction, refurbishment and equipping of wineries. A smaller percentage was devoted to new plantings. Specialists agree that transactions in this sector experienced a peak between 1992 and 2000, when the majority of the operations for purchasing and construction of new wineries took place. During 2001, however, businesses dropped off, and a more cautious trend concentrated on strengthening companies' operating and technical development.

Broadly speaking, it is possible to verify that the arrival of capital investments brought about a series of changes focused on the acquisition of new technology both in the industrial and the primary productive sectors.

In the area of marketing significant improvements were achieved not only in the exploitation of vacant market niches and in the offer for the domestic segmentation, but also in production quality.

Without considering the type of investments, all these transactions share common characteristics such as the purchase of existing companies as a strategy for capital investments, an objective of breaking into the top quality wine niche, supplying raw material from estate-owned vineyards, technological restructuring, and export oriented production.

According to information from the Department of Investment Promotion of Mendoza's Economy Ministry, U$S 50 million was invested in the private viticulture industry

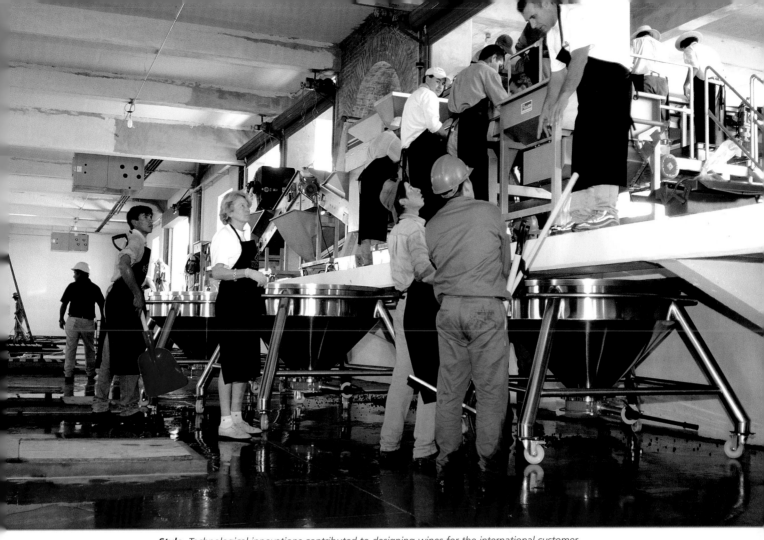

Style. *Technological innovations contributed to designing wines for the international customer.*

during the 1999 - 2001 period in the Province. By the mid 90's, foreign investment transactions spread to the remaining viticulture provinces: Salta, Catamarca, San Juan and Neuquén.

Together with investments devoted to the acquisition of wineries, vineyards or joint ventures with local companies, there have been mergers strengthening wine distribution logistics and marketing mechanisms.

IMPROVEMENT PROGRAMS

Consultants for the Latin American and Caribbean Economic Commission divided the investments according to the origin of the capitals.

The first large group are investments by foreign companies that set up in Argentina by purchasing shares in existing wineries and

Stone and vineyard. *Despite their coarseness, terroirs appeal for their capacity to yield superb grapes.*

Selling and Buying

Interestingly enough, in recent decades the trend was to reinvest part of the profits made from selling a winery in new viticulture businesses. Such is the case of Adriano Senetiner, who after selling the traditional Bodega Nieto Senetiner to the Pérez Companc holding, reinvested a portion of the capital in his new business Viniterra.

Carlos Basso, former director of Bodegas y Viñedos Santa Ana, who transferred the company to the Chilean company Santa Carolina, reinvested part of the resources from the transaction in the acquisition of a small winery: Viña Amalia. Most cases involve U$S 2 or 3 million investments devoted to producing premium and ultra premium wines in limited volume under one million bottles.

vineyards with the intention of implementing modern technology programs and had a strong interest in exporting.

Some Examples:
- Concha y Toro, Chile: the vinegrowing firm established their Trivento company in 1996. They acquired 150 hectares of vineyards in Maipú and then 150 more in Tupungato, Mendoza. They invested over 8 million dollars in technology. In 2005, they began to expand the winery, adding a line of sparkling wines and improving their bottling. In addition that year, they acquired a winery in San Martín (Mendoza).
- Santa Carolina, Chile: in 1996 they purchased the Santa Ana Winery (with an investment of over 25 million dollars), one of the four largest in the country for its storage capacity. In 2000, Santa Carolina sold its shares to Peñaflor for 73 million dollars.
- Pernod Ricard, France: bought Etchart Winery in Mendoza and Salta. In 1992, it bought 50% of the shares and in 1996 took complete control with an investment of 7 million dollars. In 2005, this multinational bought all the wineries owned by Allied Domecq, the most important of which was Graffigna.

Destination. *A great part of the new wineries are focused on the international markets.*

Innovation. Investments stimulated technological modernization in all the processes.

- Sogrape Vinhos, Portugal: purchased the majority (60%) of Finca Flichman. As part of its initial investment plan of 15 million dollars, the company improved the building and planted vineyards.
- Gernot Swarovsky, Austria: in 1992, this group bought the Norton Winery in Luján de Cuyo, Mendoza. It made a new section and a 3,000 square meter building to bottle its wines.
- Marubeni Corporation, Japan: spent 16 million dollars to buy 40% of the stock of Viñas Argentinas (formerly Resero) to develop exports, mainly concentrated grape juice destined for the Asian market.

NEW WINERIES

This group is made up by the investors who chose to build new wineries. The following are noteworthy:

- Codorniú, Spain: bought 320 hectares in Luján de Cuyo, Mendoza. With an inicial investment of 2.5 million dollars, they built their Séptima Winery.
- Lurton, France: bought land and built its winery in Valle de Uco (Uco Valley), Mendoza.
- Codorniú, Spain: Acquired 320 hectares in Luján de Cuyo, Mendoza, and invested U$S 2,5 million to build the Séptima winery.
- Lurton, France: Acquired land and built a winery in Valle de Uco, Mendoza.
- Domaine Vistalba, France: Arrived in 1992 and acquired 85 hectares in Luján de Cuyo where they planted Malbec and later, in Río Negro Province. They own two wineries: Fabre Montmayou, in Mendoza, and Infinitus, in Río Negro.
- Salentein, Holland: In 1999, settled in Mendoza, and in 2000, they opened a winery in Valle de Uco, whose construction cost

Chile in Mendoza

After the U.S., Chile is the second largest investor in Mendoza. Chilean viticulture business in Argentina was over U$S 60 million in 2004. It is estimated that this amount will increase in coming years.

The first Chilean investors to arrive were Concha y Toro (in 1996), followed by Santa Carolina, Viña Carmen (with its Doña Paula brand), Viña San Pedro (controlling Finca La Celia), Montes and Tarapacá. Together these wineries combine 2,000 hectares of vineyards in Mendoza and play a significant role in exports.

For Chilean companies, investing in Mendoza vineyards and wineries is a way of increasing their product portfolios. Furthermore, Argentine prices are very competitive for exports, particularly to key markets such as Brazil.

around 10 million dollars. Later, Salentein added El Portillo, also in Mendoza. In 2003, the group built its new winery Callia in San Juan.

WORTHWHILE RENOVATION

Some longstanding multinational companies established in the country have made significant investments.

The most notable example is Chandon. The French company, currently a multinational holding, invested over U$S 10 million, as part of a U$S 50 million program, to enlarge the productive capacity of its winery that produces sparkling wine in Luján de Cuyo, in Mendoza. In 1999, the company opened a new winery, Terrazas de Los Andes, where they concentrat-ed their entire production of still wines to expand exports.

The participation of Argentine investment has been fundamental. A clear example is Perez Companc that took control of the Nieto Senetiner winery and vineyards. First it invested 30 million dollars to buy 45% of the shares and later through the Mercosur Private Equity Fund (a fund controlled by Perez Companc and the Brazilian bank Bozano Simonsen).

Commitment. *Demanding quality standards imply meticulous attention to all the process stages.*

112

Modernization. *The proposal is to optimize technology in order to assure international quality standards.*

Viticoles investments in Argentina* (in millions of U$S).

Capital	Type of Operation	1998	1999	2000	2001	2002	2003	2004	2005 (1)
Foreign	Mergers and Acquisitions	40,0		25,0			7,7	5,0	
	Capital Formation	29,3	28,9	41,0	64,8	66,5	25,0	24,7	7,5
Total Foreign		69,3	28,9	66,0	64,8	66,5	32,7	29,7	7,5
National	Mergers and Acquisitions	45,0	16,0	45,0			11,7		
	Capital Formation	30,3	3,3	0,3	21,8	51,5	19,4	36,8	7,2
Total National		75,3	19,3	45,3	21,8	51,5	31,1	36,8	7,2
TOTAL		**144,6**	**48,2**	**111,3**	**86,6**	**118,0**	**63,8**	**66,5**	**14,7**

* Investments registered here come from announcements by the companies in newspapers, surveys and information supplied directly by the companies themselves. Investments made in expansion, greenfield, mergers andacquisitions are listed. (1) Projects from previous years to be done in 2005 and announcements made in the first quarter of the year are included. Temprorary data.

Source: Production Studies Center(CEP) - Ministry of Economy, Investment Database. Argentina.

ADDITIONAL WINERIES

- La Azul winery owned by Shirley Hinojosa: this Argentine family owned company built its winery in Valle de Uco, Mendoza.
- Velasco de Baquedano Winery: in 1912 the La Navarra, a Spanish group that makes wines and liquors bought 70 hectares of vineyards with Malbec grape stock, in Agrelo, Luján de Cuyo. On the same estate, it built a winery with a production capacity of 1.5 million liters. Taking into account, the land and winery, the group, which belongs to Spanish businessman Juan Ignacio Velasco, has invested 6 million Euros in Mendoza. It is the first project Navarra has undertaken outside of Spain; 90% of its production goes to the United States and European markets.
- O. Fournier: of Spanish origin, this company opened its winery in 2004. The project stands out for its important investment in constructing avant garde works, both in

113

Differentiation. *One of the Argentine wine industry features is the care of the grapes that are harvested manually.*

architectural design as well as in technological infrastructure.

- Ruca Malén Winery: owned by Jean Pierre Thibaud (an Argentine whose parents were French) and Jacques Louis de Montalembert, born in France. The winery is located in Luján de Cuyo, Mendoza.
- Clos de los Siete: this group of French origin, headed by Michel Rolland, opened its first winery, Monteviejo, in 2003, which is owned by Catherine Péré Vergé. The group's investments have continued with the construction of Flechas de los Andes.
- Antucurá: a family business owned by French businesswoman Anne Caroline Biancheri and her husband Carlos Cartellone, from a traditional Mendoza family. The winery is located in Vista Flores, Tunuyán, Mendoza.
- Cursor: this new winery in Mendoza

belongs to the Mayol family and concentrates on producing top quality wines.

- Andeluna: it is a joint venture between the Reina family, well-known for producing grapes and making top quality wines in Mendoza, and businessman Walter Lays of the United States. It is located in Valle de Uco, Mendoza.
- Walter Bressia: began building a boutique winery in Agrelo, Luján de Cuyo, Mendoza. It is a family endeavor that aims to produce premium products: still wines, sparkling wines and grappa.
- Fin del Mundo Winery: a pioneer in the development of viticulture in the Neuquén province, in Patagonia. This winery made an important investment in technology for its vineyards, production and expansion of its installations.
- Schroeder Family Winery: located in San

New plantings. *Recently planted, these vine plots decorated the mountain scenery.*

Patricio del Chañar, Neuquén. In 2002, it began building the winery that was finished two years later. It stands out for its architectural and technological innovation.

- Sophenia Estate: finished building its winery in Valle de Uco, Mendoza.

- Tapaus Winery: opened in 2004, this Mendoza company is dedicated to making fine wines, distilled beverages and premium liquors. Located in Lunlunta, Maipú, Mendoza.

- Carlos Pulenta Winery: winery construction in Vistalba began in 2002 and finished in 2005. The investment included an exclusive restaurant.

- NQN (Patagonia Vineyards): the winery in San Patricio del Chañar was finished in 2004. The company displays important technological development in its vineyards and production plant.

Technological shine. *Stainless steel structures shine in the majority of the new wineries.*

115

Quality. *The quest for excellence begins the initial production.*

- Andean Wineries: a joint venture in 2003 between Argentine and foreign investors involving boutique wineries dedicated to producing premium and ultra premium wines for export and in limited amounts. Located in Rodeo del Medio, Mendoza on an 80 hectare estate.

- Tittarelli: in 2003 it joined other local wineries that received Chilean capital. Pucosol, an investment fund, owns shares together with Ecipsa (a real estate developer). The fund has investors connected to vine growing, especially must production.

- Tapiz (Fincas Patagónicas): in 2003 Kendall Jackson sold Tapiz to the Argentine company Fincas Patagónicas, owned by the Ortiz family. Investment added to the vine growing business, the creation of its Club Tapiz, with an inn and restaurant, one of the best tourist endeavors. Located in Agrelo, Luján

de Cuyo, Mendoza.

- Carinae: a project by Philippe Subrá who opened his winery in 2003. Located in Cruz de Piedra, Maipú, Mendoza.

- Enrique Foster Winery: owned by the Spanish businessman of the same name living in the United States. Located in Luján de Cuyo, Mendoza. Investment included building the winery and updating the vineyards.

- Navarro Correas Winery: the new plant opened in 2004 and shows important invest-ment in the renovated technological infra-structure and improvement of the tourist facilities. It is located in San Francisco del Monte, Godoy Cruz, Mendoza.

- Renacer Winery: with Chilean capital, this company, managed by Patricio Reich, is located in Agrelo, Luján de Cuyo. Investment concentrated on a modern architectural concept.

Monteviejo (Valle de Uco). The first winery built by the Clos de los Siete French investment group.

Salentein (Valle de Uco), the construction built with Dutch investment reflects the new trend in architectural design for wineries.

Séptima (Luján de Cuyo). Spanish capital focused particularly on producing Malbec and Tempranillo.

Catena (Agrelo). Surprising architecture among a landscape of vineyards producing internationally acknowledged wines.

Andeluna (Uco Valley). A winter scene of this new
enterprise by the Reina family and US businessman Walter Lay.

Carlos Pulenta (Luján de Cuyo). The building took into account the
harmony of the landscape and an exclusive restaurant.

Renacer (Luján de Cuyo). Chilean investors have
bet heavily on innovation.

NQN (Neuquén). Endeavors on the Patagonian steppes have made
the austral area valuable.

Del Fin del Mundo (Neuquén). Architecture and innovation in ecological machinery are two strong points of this Neuquén winery.

Trivento (Maipú). Chilean investment capital located in the Mendoza River's upper region.

Norton (Luján de Cuyo). Austrian capital has improved the establishment and wagered on exporting.

Fabre Montmayou (Luján de Cuyo), French investors determined to bet on Malbec.

CHAPTER **7**

WINERIES
& WINES

Walter Bressia, Roberto González and Jorge Riccitelli tasting Michel Rolland's wines.

"252 WINES"

BY MICHEL ROLLAND

When I was asked to write a book about the wines of Argentina, I wanted to have a personal and updated view of what was being produced to convey more precise information about the wines' quality to consumers around the world.

The principal exporting wineries were selected and invited to send their wines for us to taste and describe. I do not intend to assign a score because I am not a judge. I am simply and oenologist commenting on the wines he tasted. In this new edition, 105 wineries were chosen and sent their wines to the tasting which I carried out the first week in January 2004.

The venue chosen for the tasting session was the Mendoza Park Hyatt Hotel. During that long day, I tasted 252 wines which were served in OEnologue glasses by a team of professionals from the Park Hyatt and I was accompanied by French specialist Jacques Begarie. My work was observed by a significant number of oenologists, winery owners and journalists from Argentina and abroad, all of whom were later invited to enjoy the wines. The following pages contain a listing of the major Argentine wineries, their background and other pertinent information, together with my comments and impressions of their wines.

The description of the wines from the Monteviejo, Valdeflores and Yacochuya wines, to which I am connected as an owner or a direct consultant, were written by the prestigious Argentine enologists Jorge Riccitelli (Norton) Roberto González (Nieto Senentiner) and Walter Bressia.

ACHAVAL-FERRER

Santiago Achaval.

WINERY HISTORY

The Achaval-Ferrer winery produces only top quality red wines in limited volumes. A dream, rather than a project, the idea of gathering together friends from Argentina, Italy and the world to express the nobility of a native wine.

The members of our enterprise are intent on producing high quality wines, with outstanding style and character that deserve a place among the topmost wines in the world.

We choose the best combination of soil, climate and stock to achieve maximum accrual of land and vineyard which, together with our excellent elaboration processes allow us to discover and taste the soul of wine.

Achaval-Ferrer's goal is to accomplish a territorial expression through wines of limited production featuring an unequalled concentration of taste, color and bouquet.

WINERY LOCATION
Azcuénaga 475, Luján de Cuyo, Mendoza, Argentina (5507)
Tel. 0261 498 4874
Business Address: Azcuénaga 475, Luján de Cuyo (5507) Mendoza
Tel.: 0351 422 4347
Fax: 0351 425 3812
Web Page:
www.achaval-ferrer.com
e-mail: ventas@achaval-ferrer.com

VINEYARDS
Finca Altamira, at La Consulta, 5.5 ha of Malbec.
Finca Bella Vista, at Perdriel, 11.5 ha, Malbec, Merlot and Syrah.
Finca Mirador, at Medrano, 5 ha, Malbec and Cabernet Sauvignon.
Finca Diamante, at Tupungato, 16 ha, Merlot, Cabernet S. and Cabernet F.
Third party vineyards: 27 ha.

VAT CAPACITY
214,.000 liters.
Storage capacity:
430 casks, 200,000 bottles

BRANDS
Domestic and Foreign Market:
Achaval Ferrer Quimera
Achaval Ferrer Finca Altamira
Achaval Ferrer Finca Mirador
Achaval Ferrer Finca Bella Vista
Achaval Ferrer Malbec Mendoza
Exports to: Canada, USA, Mexico, Panama, Korea, Ecuador, Puerto Rico, Costa Rica, Peru, Colombia, Brazil, Uruguay, Czech Rep., United Kingdom, Germany, Netherlands, Belgium, France, Italy, Spain, Switzerland, Sweden, Denmark, Norway, Russia, Ireland, Austria, Cyprus and Malaysia.

STAFF
Winemaker: Roberto Cipresso
President: Santiago Achaval Becú
Vice president:
Manuel Augusto Ferrer Minetti
Business Manager:
Marcelo D. Victoria
Operations Manager:
Diego Rosso
Agronomist: Juan P. Calandria
Visits: Monday to Friday preferably in the morning.

QUIMERA 2002

Intense red fruit aroma. Steady, with quality tannins, good fairly smooth finish.
The fresh fruit taste remains, and acidity is well-balanced: excellent.

FINCA ALTAMIRA MALBEC 2002

Aroma with lots spice, wood well consolidated, some notes of anis, lots of very ripe fruit. Tastes a bit heavy, slightly oily in the middle. A good finish with silky tannins. Fairly smooth, a well balanced wine with great potential for ageing.

ADUNKA

Elaboration shed.

WINERY HISTORY

ADUNKA Company began its activities in 1963. It has 150 ha in three estates in different zones: Barrancas (Maipú), in Plumero (Costa de Araujo) in Lavalle, and Las Margaritas in Fray Luis Beltrán (Maipú); to raise red grape varieties: Cabernet Sauvignon, Malbec, Merlot, Bonarda, Tempranillo, Sangiovese, and white: Chardonnay, Torrontés, Riesling, Chenin Blanc and Pedro Ximénez.

The winery has a storage capacity of 3,500,000 liters, with technology, epoxy resin pools, stainless steel tanks, 225 liter casks and wood vats of various capacity.

Wines are produced from grapes grown on their own estates. The quality philosophy of these wines is based on the virtues of their stock.

WINERY LOCATION
Calle Las Margaritas s/n, Fray Luis Beltrán, Maipú, Mendoza.
Business Address: San Juan 991, 5500, Mendoza, Argentina
Tel./Fax: +54 261 4201356
e-mail: adunkasa@nysnet.com.ar

VINEYARDS
Barrancas, Maipú, Mendoza: 40 ha.
Fray Luis Beltrán, Maipú, Mendoza: 68 ha.
Costa de Araujo, Mendoza: 15 ha.
Varieties: Cabernet Sauvignon, Malbec, Bonarda, Sangiovese, Tempranillo, Torrontés, Chenin and Riesling.

VAT CAPACITY
3,500,000 lts.
Storage capacity:
300,000 bottles

BRANDS
Domestic Market: Adunka, Fray Luis Beltrán, Trepac
Foreign Market: Adunka
Exports to: England, Switzerland, Panama, U.S.A.

STAFF
Ingeniero Guillermo Adunka
Licenciado Guillermo Stahringer

ADUNKA CABERNET SAUVIGNON 1999

It has a fairly well developed nose with notes of good quality wood, but also touches of brettanomyces, leather, almost horse sweat. A little carbonic at first. A wine with an interesting structure and good finish.

COLECCIÓN ADUNKA TEMPRANILLO 2002

Pleasant with a fruity attack. Needs density and volume, but is fairly well balanced. Could be classified as elegant with somewhat hard tannins at the finish, giving it an almost lineal aspect.

ALTA VISTA

Patrick d'Aulan.

WINERY HISTORY

Alta Vista is a family winery with a philosophy in search of quality and pleasure in an international framework. Its wines are the product of a Franco-Argentine cultural fusion. It is part of the Edonia Group belonging to the French d'Aulan family, with their own distribution in Bordeaux, Buenos Aires and Tokyo, as well as other estates in the world: Château Sansonnet (Saint-Emilion), Château Valrose (Saint-Estèphe), Champagne Becker (Reims), Calvados Marquis d'Aguesseau (Calvados) in France and Château Dereszla (Tocaji, Hungary). The d'Aulan family, the former owners of Piper-Heidsieck champagnes, well known the world over, was a pioneer in Argentina in the 80's when they started a joint-venture to produce wines under the Henri Piper brand. In 1999, they joined the Alta Vista project. The company owns four "terroirs" in Luján de Cuyo and Valle de Uco, Mendoza. The winery, located in Chacras de Coria, can produce 1,500,000 premium bottles. Our "terroir management" and production methods are those used in our French "Grands Crus", adapted to the characteristics of the Mendoza "terroirs".

WINERY LOCATION
Alzaga 3.972, Chacras de Coria, Luján de Cuyo, Mendoza.
Tel.: 54 261 4964684
Fax: 54 261 4964683
Business Address: Scalabrini Ortiz 3355, piso 5° K, Buenos Aires.
Tel.: 54 11 4809 3535
Fax: 54 11 4809 3939
Web Page: www.altavistawines.com
e-mail: altavista@altavistawines.com

VINEYARDS
Mendoza: 348 ha. Salta: 1,220 ha.
Varieties: Syrah, Malbec, Cabernet Sauvignon, Merlot, Chardonnay, Tempranillo and Bonarda.
Third party vineyards:
Mendoza: 10.5 ha Malbec and Pinot Noir. Salta: 9 ha Torrontés.

VAT CAPACITY
700 French and American oak barrels
Storage capacity:
350,000 bottles.
Quality Norms: HACCP /ISO9000

BRANDS
Domestic Market: Alta Vista Alto, Alta Vista Grande Reserve, Alta Vista Premium, Atemporal, Finca Monte Lindo.
Foreign Market: Alta Vista Alto, Alta Vista Grande Reserve, Alta Vista Premium, Finca Monte Lindo, Finca Navarrita.
Exports to: 30 countries.
Main markets: United States, United Kingdom and Brazil.

STAFF
President: Juan Antonio Argerich
General Director: Philippe Rolet
Commercial Director:
Benoit Berneron
Viticulture Production Manager: Juan Antonio Argerich (Jr.)
Production Manager:
Didier Debono (Red varieties Oenologist); Rubén Sfragara (White and sparkling varieties Oenologist).

Visits: October to April: everyday; May to September: Monday to Saturday from 9 a.m. to 4:30 p.m.
Gift Shop: Yes.

ALTA VISTA ALTO 1999

Wine still full of fruit with aromatic expression. Good evolution, the vanilla of the maturing process is well integrated. elegant, balanced, very round, good firm tannins. It is a wine that is going to age very well.

ALTA VISTA GRANDE RESERVE MALBEC 2002 SINGLE VINEYARD ALTO AGRELO

Balanced, charming, lots of fruit and very fresh. Agreeable in the mouth, round and structured. Good tannins at the finish. A very pleasant wine.

ALTA VISTA GRANDE RESERVE MALBEC 2002 SINGLE VINEYARD LAS COMPUERTAS

High concentration of ripe red fruti, good extraction. Fairly oily and fleshy with a well balanced tannic finish. An easy pleasurable wine. Good for drinking right now.

ALTUS

Altus vineyards.

WINERÝ HISTORY

The Group Vitivinícola de Tupungato (Tupungato Viticulture Group) was created as part of excellence project in Argentina's new viticulture industry in producing top quality wines for the most demanding markets. For this purpose, they have highly qualified personnel, the latest wine technology and the best terroirs in the central western region of Argentina, at the foot of the Andes. All the wines are made at the Altus winery where nearly 1,300 hectares have been selected to grow their vineyards in the Tupungato Valley, in Mendoza province, at an altitude ranging between 900 m and 1,425 m above sea level in addition to 300 ha in the 25 de Mayo desert, Tulum Valley, San Juan.

The wines' high quality find its expression in the Altus Gualtallary. The premium Altus Grand Vin, is the house blend, together with a Grand Chardonnay. The varietal line includes Merlot, Malbec, Tempranillo, Cabernet Sauvignon, Syrah, Chardonnay and Torrontés, Finca Los Algarrobos offers the Grand Syrah (Black label) and the line of lively young varietals of the Agliánico, Montepulciano, Cabernet Sauvignon, Syrah, Chardonnay and Malbec.

WINERY LOCATION
La Vencedora and Las Costas, Tupungato s/n, Mendoza
Business Address:
Paseo Colón 505, 2° floor, Buenos Aires (1063), Argentina.
Tel.: 54 11 4110 5142
Fax: 54 11 4110 5151
Web Page: www.gvt.net.ar
e-mail: export@gvt.net.ar / vinos@gvt.net.ar

OWN VINEYARDS
Malbec: Finca San José: 11 ha in Tupungato, at 1,200 meters.
Cabernet Sauvignon: Finca Las Costas: Tupungato, 8 ha.
Merlot: Finca Gualtallary: 8.5 ha at 1,550 m altitude. Chardonnay is grown here.
Finca Los Algarrobos: 200 ha (700 m altitude). Cabernet Sauvignon, Syrah, Malbec, Aglianico and Montepulciano are grown here.
Third Party Vineyards:
Over 60 ha Tempranillo, Merlot and Torrontés. Vineyards are located at an altitude ranging from 900 to 1,200 meters.

VAT CAPACITY
Total: 1,000,000 liters.
Storage capacity:
600,000 bottles.

BRANDS
Domestic Market: Finca Los Algarrobos, Altus Varietales, Altus Grand Vin and Gualtallary.
Foreign Market: Finca Los Algarrobos, Altus Varietales, Altus Grand Vin and Gualtallary.
Exports to: United States, Russia, Brazil, Spain and Germany.

STAFF
Tourism Manager: Karen Noval
Exportation Manager: Carolina Ranftl.
Agronomist: Ricardo García
Oenologist: Alejando Colombi

Visits: By previous appointment.
Gift shop: In "La Tupiña", outside the winery, a sales room offers T shirts, corkscrews, engraved glasses, decanters, etc..

ALTUS CABERNET SAUVIGNON 2003

Medium intense color, not very with orange tones. Ripe fruit aromas, slight vanilla flavor. Round and soft with pleasant tannins. The wine has a certain harmony and elegance.

ALTUS MALBEC 2001

Brilliant color, fairly neat. Good fruity nose, suggestive of ripe red fruit. Slight vanilla flavor. Middle of the mouth is interesting, with volume and texture. The finish leaves pleasant tannins. Too strong for such a young wine, but balanced and harmonious.

ANDELUNA CELLARS

Ricardo Reina Rutini and Ward Lay.

WINERY HISTORY

At an altitude of over 1,300 m and at the foot of the Andean range lie the 80 ha vineyards belonging to this winery, which also has stainless steel tanks, state of the art technology machinery and a cellar with a capacity for 1,200 casks. The imposing vineyards and a volcano, the Tupungato, create an ideal atmosphere to enjoy a drink in the wine-tasting room, the bar, the cellar and the exclusive restaurant. Andeluna cellars is a joint venture involving part of a traditional Argentine family of winemakers and an American partner, Ward Lay.

Ricardo Reina Rutini, a pioneer in the Tupungato Valley has devoted his life to vitiviniculture. At present, the property extends over 250 ha of low yield, which contributes excellent raw material to the project. Oenologist Silvio Alberto is responsible for the elaboration and storage of wines, while the prestigious consultant Michel Roland does the tutoring.

Andeluna is the trademark chosen for the American and European market. In the Latin American market the brand names are Andeluna and Familia Reina.

WINERY LOCATION
Ruta Provincial 89 S/N, Gualtallary, Tupungato, Mendoza.
Business Address: Sarmiento 250, 5to piso "B", Ciudad, Mendoza, 5500. Tel.: 54 261 4299299.
Web Page: www.andeluna.com
e-mail:
andeluna@familiareina.com.ar
info@andeluna.com

VINEYARDS
250 ha at the Alto Valle de Tupungato, from 1,000 to 1,300 meters high.
Varieties: Chardonnay, Traminer, Malbec, Merlot, Cabernet Sauvignon, Cabernet Franc and Syrah.
Third party vineyards:
15 ha at Luján de Cuyo, Mendoza. Varieties: Malbec.

VAT CAPACITY
1,000,000 liters in stainless steel and 1,200 225 liter barrels.
Storage capacity:
720,000 bottles.

BRANDS
Domestic Market: Andeluna & Familia Reina.
Foreign Market: Andeluna.
Exports to: USA 70%, rest of the world 30%.

STAFF
Presidents: H. Ward Lay and Ricardo Reina Rutini
Business Management and Marketing: Mike Kenter and Rodrigo Reina Rutini
Wine Production: Francisco Reina
Winemaker: Silvio Alberto
Adviser: Michel Rolland

Visits: restaurant, guided tastings. Advanced reservations required.
Wine Merchandising: Yes.

ANDELUNA RESERVE MERLOT 2003

Good color and freshness. Pleasant fruit aromas. Balanced wine, harmonious with an interesting texture, fairly silky. Elegant and well made wine.

ANDELUNA GRAND RESERVE PASIONADO 2003

Pretty color, fruit, good aromatic intensity with a mixture of cedar and ripe fruit. Good density, lasting, the tannins are still very noticeable. The wood overpowers the wine a little, but will blend, leaving an elegant wine with great potential.

ANDELUNA RESERVE LIMITADA CABERNET FRANC 2003

Attractive color, lots of aromatic intensity with notes of spice and pepper. Intense. Taste is smooth, pleasant, with good staying power. The finish is agreeable, smooth with good tannins.

ANTUCURA

Anne-Caroline Biancheri.

WINERY HISTORY

The communion of this land, its people and its vineyards, create the ideal place to obtain the best grapes, essential to the quality of our wines. Antucura is a true family project. A dream we share with our children and with all those who love wine and Mendoza. In Vista Flores, Tunuyán, conditions are optimum for the growth of the vines that produce our best wines. The cool star-studded nights and the gloriously sunny days accompany the ripening process of grapes we select later by hand. Our winery is very respectful of the land, the historic viticulture traditions and the new winemaking technology. Originally conceived to produce super premium and ultra premium wines, the winery has maximum standards of quality care and control.

Antucura means Sun Stone in Mapudungun, the ancient language of the Pehuenches, the first inhabitants of the area. We chose this name for our winery and inn in Vista Flores where our beloved grapevines grow naturally, among rocks and stones.

WINERY LOCATION
Barrandica s/n, Vista Flores, Tunuyán (5565), Mendoza.
Business Address:
Nicolás Avellaneda 550, Ciudad (5500), Mendoza
Tel./Fax: 54 261 4255324/ 4231076
Web Page: www.antucura.com
e-mail: info@antucura.com
prensa@antucura.com

VINEYARDS
Vista Flores, Tunuyán, 98 ha.
Varieties: Malbec, Cabernet Sauvignon, Merlot, Pinot Noir, Syrah.

VAT CAPACITY
220,000 liters.
Storage capacity:
100,000 bottles.

BRANDS
Domestic Market:
Antucura, Calvulcura.
Foreign Market:
Antucura, Calvulcura.
Exports to: Brazil, United States, European Union and Switzerland.

STAFF
Owners: Anne-Caroline Biancheri and Gerardo Cartellone.

ANTUCURA 2003

Nose is complex, fruity with a note of wood and some hints of spice. Pleasant, dense with good texture, interesting tannins. The finish is still tannic, somewhat narrow, but top quality, with volume. A wine that should age very well.

CALVULCURA 2003

Nose of ripe fruit, plums with notes of vanilla and spice. It has good concentration in the mouth, nice balance; tannins still need a little time to round out. Long lasting and tannic finish.

BALBI

Balbi's house façade.

WINERY HISTORY

Bodegas Balbi is located in San Rafael, 37° 4' South Latitude, 240 km from Mendoza City. San Rafael's altitude and its excellent climate are the perfect conditions for growing top quality grapes. At the foot of the Andean Range, the zone is irrigated by crystal clear meltwater, of utmost purity.

San Rafael enjoys low humidity, perfect luminosity and an important temperature range. This climate is especially suitable for completing the grapes ripening process, and then, the harvest. Bodegas Balbi was founded in 1929 by Don Juan Balbi, who started a prosperous family business. Their wines gained rapid recognition for high quality and soon became quite popular in the Argentine market.

In 1992, the Allied Domecq Group bought their total ownership and started an investment plan aimed at producing only high quality wines, modernizing both the winery and vineyard and developing solid brands for local and export markets.

WINERY LOCATION
Jensen and Sarmiento, Las Paredes, (5601) San Rafael, Mendoza.
Tel.: 54 2627 430027
Fax: 54 2627 420001
Business Address: Jujuy 1197, Bella Vista. B1661KTA Buenos Aires, Argentina.
Tel: 54 11 4469 8000
Fax: 54 11 4469 8023
e-mail: balbi@adsw.com

VINEYARDS
101 hectares.
Third party vineyards: 600 ha.
Vineyard location:
San Rafael and Tupungato (Valle de Uco), Mendoza
Varieties: Chenin Blanc, Chardonnay, Sauvignon Blanc, Torrontés, Pinot Noir, Malbec, Merlot, Cabernet Sauvignon and Syrah.

VAT CAPACITY
Total 6,500,000 liters.
American and French oak casks: 815 of 225 liters.
Storage capacity:
6,500,000 liters
Quality Norms:
ISO 9002

BRANDS
Domestic Market: Sparkling Mumm, Wish, Calvet.
Foreign Market: Balbi, Sparkling Mumm, Sparkling Balbi, Wish, Timara.
Exports to: 30 countries on five continents.

STAFF
Wine Division Director:
César Azevedo
Winery Manager: Angel Riva ·

BALBI
MALBEC 2003

Aromatic intensity with a great deal of small red fruit; interesting color and fairly intense; while not too complex, it has good harmony. A pleasant wine, especially for drinking now.

BANFI

Rubén and Genoveva Banfi.

WINERY HISTORY

Bodega Banfi started in mid 2001, as a personal project supported by Rubén Banfi, his wife and their 3 children.

At an altitude of 1,070 meters in the best viticulture area in Mendoza: Vistalba, Las Compuertas, Luján de Cuyo, the winery has a simple design and was conceived to produce personal top quality wines.

The establishment is equipped with the latest technological developments.

At present, production is 150,000 bottles and their wines are sold under two brands: Cinco Tierras (Five Lands) and Sorbus. Eighty percent of the production is exported to various countries.

WINERY LOCATION
Roque Sáenz Peña s/n, Las Compuertas, Luján de Cuyo
Business Address:
Laprida 1024, Buenos Aires, CP 1425
Tel.: 54 11 4104-2089/2021
Web Page: www.bodegabanfi.com
e-mail: ventas@simmetry.com.ar

VINEYARDS
Agrelo, 22 ha.
Varieties: Malbec.
Third party vineyards:
La Consulta, Agrelo, Vistalba, Medrano: 30 hectares
Varieties: Malbec, Merlot, Cabernet Sauvignon, Cabernet Franc, Petit Verdot and Chardonnay.

VAT CAPACITY
780,000 liters..

BRANDS
Domestic Market:
Cinco Tierras and Sorbus
Foreign Market:
Cinco Tierras and Sorbus.
Exports to: United States, Brazil, France, Spain, Uruguay, Peru and Belgium.

STAFF
Director: Guillermo Banfi
Director: Ruben Banfi
Visits: Not open to visitors.

CINCO TIERRAS MALBEC 2003

Lots of wood. Very strong notes of vanilla with some red fruit in the background. Rather pleasant in the middle of the mouth, well balanced; powerful tannins at the finish, whether they are from the wood or their own nature. Could use a bit more volume.

CINCO TIERRAS RESERVA CABERNET SAUVIGNON 2002

The fruit is correct and also has some noticeable hints of wood. Good balance in the middle of the wood, good persistence of the wine, with tannins from the wood that always appear at the finish. They are wines with a high acidity, fairly noticeable, which makes them fresh.

CINCO TIERRAS RESERVA FAMILIA 2002

Fruit is fairly noticeable, with good freshness and very clear. The middle of the mouth always tends towards the wood, with powerful tannins. It can achieve even more charm and roundness. The wine is solid and has good dimension, the acidity can be somewhat noticeable.

BENEGAS

Federico Benegas Lynch.

WINERY HISTORY

The Benegas family has a long tradition with wine. Tiburcio Benegas, together with Silvestre Ochagavía in Chile and Agoston Harszthy in California, are considered fundamental in American viticulture. In Argentina Tiburcio Benegas, one of the founders of this industry in the country, bought a vineyard in 1883 he called "El Trapiche". This led him to gain world recognition as a forerunner of high quality wines in Argentina. Federico J. Benegas Lynch was born in 1951 at "El Trapiche", his great grand-father's establishment. He grew up alongside his father, tasting wines and walking the vineyard. In 1998, Federico Benegas Lynch renewed his winery activity, buying 40 hectares of Finca Libertad, an old family property, and an exclusive centennial winery -under the French châteaux concept, where the vineyard and the fact he has his own property, allowed him to produce excellent wines. For his first vintage, in 2000, Federico Benegas Lynch worked with Daniel Llose, oenologist from Lynch Bage, to set the quality basis of his wines. After that, he was tutored by Michel Roland, currently the winery consultant.

WINERY LOCATION
Carril Aráoz (Ruta 60), 300 meters from the intersection with the Southern Access, Luján de Cuyo, Mendoza.
Tel./Fax: 54 261 4960794.
Business Address:
Ortiz de Ocampo 3050, Third floor Office 304, Buenos Aires
Tel./fax: 5411 4806-6577/8393
Web Page:
www.bodegabenegas.com
e-mail: info@bodegabenegas.com

VINEYARDS
Finca Libertad, 40 hectares, Cruz de Piedra Southern East corner, Maipú.
Varieties:
Cabernet Franc, 100 year old vineyards.
Samgiovese, 55 year old vineyards.
Syrah, 30 year old vineyards.
Chardonnay, 30 year old vineyards.
Merlot, 30 year old vineyards.
Petit verdot, 5 year old vineyards.

VAT CAPACITY
1,500,000 liters
Storage capacity: 200,000 bottles, 1,000 French oak casks.

BRANDS
Domestic Market: Benegas Lynch Meritage, Benegas Lynch CS-CF, Benegas Lynch FBL Barrica, Benegas Lynch Cabernet Franc; Benegas Blend, Benegas Sangiovese, Benegas Syrah, Benegas Malbec, Benegas Chardonnay and Bautista Heguy, Carmela Benegas, Clara Benegas, Don Tiburcio and Juan Benegas.
Foreign Market: Benegas Lynch Meritage; Benegas Blend, Benegas Sangiovese, Benegas Syrah, Benegas Malbec, Benegas Chardonnay, Bautista Heguy, Carmela Benegas, Clara Benegas, Don Tiburcio and Juan Benegas.
Exports to: England, U.S.A., Switzerland, Belgium, Mexico, Brazil and Uruguay.

STAFF
President and Winemaker:
Federico Benegas Lynch
Marketing Director:
Carmen Burone
Enologist: Juan Manuel González.
Visits: By previous appointment.

BENEGAS BLEND 2000

Hints of dry flowers where wood is also present, Remains balanced, very fresh and good acidity. A bit languid, more volume and thickness are advisable. Very subtle and elegant.

BENEGAS MALBEC 2002

Pleasant color, lots of fruit, expressive nose. Many spices also characteristic of the combination of grapes. Subtle, elegant wine with a good finish and balanced. Still a bit tannic, normal for a young wine. Pleasant and very lively.

BENEGAS LYNCH MERITAGE 2002

Red fruit, hints of vanilla and wood on the nose. A lot of aromatic expression, fairly complicated. Good density and finish. Appears to have great potential, though still young. Quality tannins will be more rounded and voluptuous in a few years.

BOMBAL

Lucila Bombal.

WINERY HISTORY

The Bombal family, originally from France, have lived in Mendoza since 1760 and are one of the pioneers in the wine making industry. The first winery was built in 1914 by Lucila Barrionuevo de Bombal. Her son, Domingo Lucas Bombal carried on with the tradition taking charge of the development of vineyards and the inauguration of a new winery in Estancia Ancón. Her daughter, the present owner, Lucía Bombal, at the beginning of this century built a modern winery for producing the highest quality wines.

In 1995, work was started on recycling the existing vineyards, planting fine grapes and adapting to coming technological changes.

In 2000, Ancón was reopened by Lucía Bombal, the current owner, as a high-tech wine boutique, producing with no more than 70,000 bottles of premium wines a year under the label of Bodega Bombal. Estancia Ancón wines compete with the best wines worldwide and have won silver and bronze medals in various competitions.

WINERY LOCATION
Estancia Ancón s/n, (5561) San José, Tupungato, Mendoza.
Argentina +54 2622 488245
Business Address: Peatonal Sarmiento 250, 4° piso dpto A, (5500) Mendoza, Argentina +54-261 4235843
Web Page: www.estanciancon.com
e-mail: bombal@arnet.com.ar

VINEYARDS
100 ha located at an altitude between 1,100 and 1,400 meters, at San José, Tupungato.
Varieties: Malbec, Bonarda, Sangiovese, Pinot Noir, Cabernet Sauvignon, Chardonnay, Sauvignon Blanc.

VAT CAPACITY
150,000 liters
Storage capacity:
90,000 bottles

BRANDS
Domestic Market: Estancia Ancón and Bombal
Foreign Market: Estancia Ancón
Exports to: England, Switzerland, Scotland.

STAFF
President: Lucía Bombal
Foreign Commerce Manager: Carlos Vissio
Oenologist: Gonzalo Ruiz

Visits: Tuesday and Thursday from 10 a.m. to 12 noon and from 3 p.m. to 6 p.m.; Saturdays, Sundays and holidays from 11 a.m. to 6 p.m.
Gift Shop: yes, at the winery.

ESTANCIA ANCÓN CHARDONNAY 2003

Dark golden color. Aromas that bring pears, peaches and flowers to mind. Not very dense, but well balanced with good freshness.

BOMBAL GRAN RESERVA 2001

Attractive color. Nose with good intensity of fruit and floral notes. Not very dense, but good texture. Finishes with fairly powerful tannins. A pleasant wine with good presence and long lasting.

BRESSIA

Bressia family.

WINERY HISTORY

At the beginning of 2003, Walter Bressia, together with his wife and children, started an endeavor along the lines of the "Original Wines" concept. This is a result of his vast experience and background as an enologist in Argentina and abroad. The main objective is personalized and limited sales of top quality wines and grappa. Each bottle is unique, offering exclusive pleasure.

The "Winery Boutique and House of Wines", located in Agrelo, Luján de Cuyo, in its final stage will have a building for wines carefully made with the special "pissage" technique. It is an innovative concept to meet the requirements of knowledgeable and demanding consumers.

The first wine was called "Bressia Profundo" (Deep Bressia), a name born from a passion for blends, the perfect combination of grapes to produce a complete, singular and well-defined wine.

The "House of Wines" reproduces an old railroad station with ceiling decorations brought from England at the end of the 19th Century. All the details have been carefully looked after so that a visit to the winery will be unique and memorable.

WINERY LOCATION
Calle Cochabamba 7752, Agrelo, Luján de Cuyo, Mendoza.
Business Address: Cartagena 1188, Godoy Cruz, Mendoza.
Tel/Fax.: 54 261 4393860
e-mail: wbressia@ciudad.com.ar

THIRD PARTY VINEYARDS
In Agrelo and Pedriel (Luján de Cuyo); Tupungato, Mendoza
Varieties: Malbec, Merlot, Syrah and Cabernet Sauvignon.

VAT CAPACITY
30,000 liters in stainless steel
30,000 liters in French and American oak barrels
Storage capacity: 20,000 bottles

BRANDS
Domestic Market: Bressia Profundo, Bressia Conjuro, Grappa Bressia Dal Cuore
Foreign Market: Bressia Profundo, Grappa Dal Cuore
Exports to: Switzerland, Holland, Belgium, Peru, Brazil, Uruguay, Panama and the United States.

STAFF
Director and Winemaker: Walter Bressia
President: Marita Illanes de Bressia
Director and Manager of Domestic Market and Exports: Marita Bressia

Visits: By previous appointment

BRESSIA PROFUNDO 2002

Very fresh, lots of fruit, a very elegant wine. Interesting features, good tannins, a bit harsh, but good quality at the finish. I really like the harmony and finesse of the very fresh red fruit. Wood is not too noticeable. It is elegant.

BRESSIA PROFUNDO 2001

Rather intense color, aromas with lots of fruit, freshness harmony and persistence. Good tannins appear in the mouth. Very good blend. An elegant wine.

CALLIA

Vineyards and winery.

WINERY HISTORY

It is located in the Valle de Tulum (Tulum Valley) enclosed by the Cerro Pie de Palo, on the North, and the Chico del Zonda on the South, in the foothills of the Andean Range in the province of San Juan. The valley average altitude is 630 m above sea level with an annual mean temperature of 17 °C, low annual rainfall and torrential soil. This valley has the necessary characteristics to produce intense, ripe tasting wines with unique style and personality.

The 241 hectares devoted to their grapevines share an ideal climate. The trickle irrigation system extends to all the farms and supplies the quantity of water every plant needs to fully develop the canopy.

The area has a desert climate. Day temperatures from January to March vary between 30° and 34.6 °C, with a range of some 15 °C, which insures very good ripeness of the grapes. Scarce rainfall and low relative humidity are excellent sanitary qualities. They make this zone exceptionally satisfactory from the sanitation view point and very easy to qualify organically.

WINERY LOCATION
Address: Av de los Ríos y San Lorenzo, Pozo de los Algarrobos, Caucete, San Juan. CP 5442.
Tel/fax: 54 264 496 1940
Business Address:
Av. Leandro N. Alem 855, 6°. piso, Buenos Aires, Argentina. CP 1001
Tel: 54 11 4131 1100
Fax: 54 11 4131 1199
Web Page: www.bodegascallia.com
e-mail: info@bodegascallia.com

VINEYARDS
241 hectares at Caucete, Valle de Tulum, San Juan.
Varieties: Syrah, Malbec, Bonarda, Chardonnay, Cabernet Sauvignon, Viognier, Merlot, Sauvignon Blanc, Pinot Gris, Tannat.

VAT CAPACITY
4,360,000 liters
Storage capacity:
200,000 bottles
Quality Norms: ISO 9001 and HACCP certification pending

BRANDS
Domestic Market: Callia Magna, Callia Alta and Signos.
Foreign Market: Callia Magna, Callia Alta and Signos.
Exports to: United States, United Kingdom, Ireland, Switzerland, Netherlands and Brazil.

STAFF
Oenologist:
Oscar Biondolillo
Business Manager:
Alejandro Panighini

Visits: Tuesday to Friday, 9 a.m. to 4 p.m.
Gift shop: Yes.

CALLIA MAGNA VIOGNIER 2004

Pale yellow. Not much wood, but balanced with good notes of pear and peach. To be enjoyed.

CALLIA ALTA SYRAH / TANNAT 2004

Attractive color. Pleasant nose with hints of fruit and simple wood. Fairly delicate, almost sugary, smooth. Not much consistency and with very smooth tannins. To drink and enjoy.

CALLIA ALTA SYRAH 2003

Fruity with fairly fresh floral notes, a great deal of freshness and subtlety. Needs a little more volume in the middle of the mouth. A simple, but balanced and pleasant wine. To drink cool and easily.

CAMPO NEGRO

Pedro and Ricardo Rosell.

WINERY HISTORY

Pedro Rosell Boher and his wife Celia Navarro Correas, started this new project at their Cruz de Piedra property togehter other young partners, among them their son Ricardo, in charge of management. The boutique winery has a 230,000 liter capacity in stainless steel tanks, with the latest equipment imported from Italy. In addition, the first stage of construction of the underground cellar -where the French and American oak casks are placed- has already been completed.

The project aims towards the precise boutique cellar concept with 300,000 liters of top quality wine previously placed in casks.

A young line is now being launched with "Finca El Reposo" trademark. The product quality is determined by the Malbec vineyards in La Consulta (San Carlos) and Cabernet Sauvignon in the same estate Cruz de Piedra (Maipú). In addition to Cabernet Sauvignon another variety grows there: Saint Jeannet, a white grape that matures late and produces a wine with lots of body, with good acidity and a fine bouquet, not as strong as the Chardonnay, but less tiring and very noble. We currently export to Belgium, Poland and Colombia.

WINERY LOCATION
Callejón Zapata S/N in the corner with Calle Nueva, Cruz de Piedra, Maipú, Mendoza.
Business Contact:
Tel.: 54 261 4242590
Web Page: www.camponegro.com
e-mail:
ricardorosell@supemet.com.ar

VINEYARDS
11 ha. Cruz de Piedra, Maipú and 10 ha. at La Consulta, San Carlos, Mendoza.
Varieties: Malbec, Cabernet Sauvignon and Saint Jeannet.

VAT CAPACITY
230,000 liters in stainless steel tank. 8,100 liters in barrels.
Storage capacity: We stow in frigorific.

BRANDS
Domestic Market: Finca El Reposo (Young line with 20% in barrels)
Foreign Market: Finca El Reposo
Exports to: Belgium, Poland and Colombia.

STAFF
President and General Manager: Ricardo Rosell
Oenologist: Ing. Agr. Pedro Rosell
Second Oenologist:
Ing. Agr. Cristián Allamand

Visits: Not currently open to tourists; only special visits are permitted.

FINCA EL REPOSO MALBEC 2003

Attractive color fairly intense. Red fruit and floral notes. Good density, finishes with firm tannins. A wine with medium power. Still lacks a bit of harmony, but it is a well made wine, fairly agreeable.

FINCA EL REPOSO CABERNET SAUVIGNON 2003

Good intense and bright color. Bouquet of red fruit and cassis. The wine has good density, agreeable texture, tannic, a bit firm, but with good aromatic freshness. Easy to drink, with good acidity, fairly elegant and harmonious.

FINCA EL REPOSO SAINT JEANNET 2002

Notes of dry grass, honey and beeswax are noticeable in its aromas. A very special style.

CARINAE

Philippe Subra.

WINERY HISTORY

CarinaE Vineyards and Winery was created by Brigitte and Philippe Subra, in their 80 year old vineyards in Cruz de Piedra, Maipú. They also have 3 hectare 85 year old vineyards in Perdriel. In this area, they also manage 4.5 hectare vineyards belonging to relatives who are partners. The winery was rebuilt on pre-existing concrete vats. The "boutique winery" has a 260,000 liter capacity and a cellar that holds 6,500 liters in French oak barrels. Here tradition and technology combine to produce only top quality wines made from Malbec, Syrah and Cabernet Sauvignon grapes from their own vineyards.

WINERY LOCATION
Videla Aranda 2899, Cruz de Piedra, Maipú, Mendoza, 5517.
Tel.: 0261 499 04 70
Fax: 0261 499 06 37
Business Address:
Videla Aranda 2899, Cruz de Piedra, Maipú, Mendoza, 5517.
Tel.: 0261 499 04 70
Fax: 0261 499 06 37
Web Page: www.carinaevinos.com
e-mail: carinae@carinavinos.com

VINEYARDS
12 ha at Cruz de Piedra, Maipú.
Varieties: Malbec, Cabernet Sauvignon, Syrah.
At Perdriel (Luján de Cuyo), they have 3 hectare Malbec.
Third party vineyards:
4.5 ha. Malbec at Perdril (Luján de Cuyo).

VAT CAPACITY
260,000 liters
Storage capacity:
60,000 bottles.

BRANDS
Domestic Market:
CarinaE, Octans, El Galgo.
Foreign Market:
CarinaE, El Galgo.
Exports to: United States

STAFF
President: Philippe Subra
Manager: Brigitte Madaule de Subra
Oenologist: Gabriela Celeste
Oenologist (in training):
Martín de Marchi

Visits: Daily from 10 a.m. to 6 p.m.
Gift Shop:
Daily from 10 a.m. to 6 p.m.

OCTANS MALBEC 2004

Frank color, fairly bright. Nose of fresh first fruit, good intensity. Balanced wine, harmonious, not very long lasting, but very agreeable.
To drink now.

EL GALGO MALBEC 2004

Pretty color. Good nose, fruit and hints of wood. Pleasant texture, dense, good persistence; too young. Tannins still firm, but the texture will enable it to age well.

CARINAE RESERVA MALBEC 2004

Seductive color. Good aromas of small red fruit and good complexity. Elegant wine, medium concentration, balanced, pleasurable. Still too young, reason why the tannins are a little firm at the finish. To drink within a year.

CARLOS PULENTA

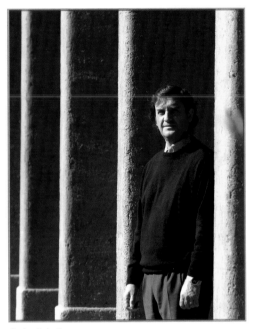

Carlos Pulenta.

WINERY HISTORY

Construction of the winery started in 2002 and finished in 2005. The estate has belonged to the Pulenta family since 1970.

The winery is essentially devoted to the production of red wines with the Malbec as the flagship.

The wines produced by the winery are Vistalba Corte A Cosecha 2003; Vistalba Corte B Cosecha 2003 and Vistalba Corte C Cosecha 2004.

One of the characteristics that distinguish BVCAP is that the wines are produced exclusively from grapes from the Vistalba vineyards.

La Bourgogne restaurant, open from Tuesday to Sunday at midday, is located in the winery.

The winery has a multi-space room, called Lounge, for special events, with capacity for 100 persons. There are also two double rooms for guests.

WINERY LOCATION
Roque Sáenz Peña 3531, Vistalba, Luján de Cuyo, Mendoza.
Tel.: 54 261 498 9400
Fax: 54 261 498 9406
Business Address:
Roque Sáenz Peña 3531 Vistalba, Luján de Cuyo, Mendoza.
Web Page:
www.carlospulentawines.com
e-mail: info@cpwines.com

VINEYARDS
Located in Vistalba, near the Mendoza mountain range, with a wide range of temperatures. The soil is alluvial and lies on a bed of gravel which offers good drainage. It has a low amount of organic material and is fairly fertile. The estate has 58 hectares, 53 of which are cultivated.
Malbec: 35 cultivated ha (1948)
Merlot: 5 ha (1999)
Cabernet Sauvignon: 5 ha (1999)
Malbec: 5 ha (1999)
Bonarda: 3 ha (1999)
Vines per ha: 5,500
Method: pruning mixed with python and loader, with shoots positioned vertically.

VAT CAPACITY
1,160,000 liters.
Storage capacity:
450,000 bottles

BRANDS
Domestic and Foreign Markets:
Vistalba Corte A, Vistalba Corte B.

STAFF
President: Carlos Pulenta
Oenologist: Alejandro Cánovas
External Consultant:
Alberto Antonini
Local Consultant: Luis María Cano

Visits: By telephone appointment to 54 261 498 9400
La Bourgogne Restaurant, open Tuesday to Saturday, midday and evening, and midday on Sunday.
Reservations: 54 261 4989400

VISTALBA CORTE A
2003

Deep color. Good red and black fruit, well integrated with the wood. Agreeable texture, silky, fine, elegant; tannins at the finish give the wine power and general harmony. It is a very good quality wine, well balanced.

VISTALBA CORTE B
2003

Interesting color, good aromas of small red fruit, with interesting maturity of the fruit. Balanced, medium density. Finishes with tannins still a bit compact. Harmonious wine and a correct finish that will improve much more as it ages.

CASA MONTES

Dr. Francisco Baltazar Montes.

WINERY HISTORY

Bodega y Viñedos Casa Montes, a viticulture establishmen, is located 700 meters above sea level, at Pozo de los Algarrobos, Caucete, San Juan province.

It covers over 176 hectares, of which 150 have 11 varieties of vinestock imported from Italy, on American foot. On Smart- Dyson (VSP) design trellis, with trickle irrigation fed from a 33 million liter reservoir of meltwater from the Andean Range, healthy growth and perfect ripening is ensured of the grapes with which the wines are made.

The winery is equipped with the very latest technology in the wine world. The building stands beside the vineyard, which permits the planning and control of harvesting and production times at an ideal pace. The advanced development of grape growing methods is combined with the careful use of production techniques, choosing the best stocks from top quality wines will come after duly maturing in French oak barrels.

Bodegas y Viñedos Casa Montes sells Ampakama and Don Baltazar and Casa Montes oak matured wines.

WINERY LOCATION
Calle Colón y Caseros, Pozo de los Algarrobos, Caucete, San Juan.
Business Address:
Av. Libertador 2399 (Oeste), C.P. (5400), Ciudad de San Juan.
Tel/Fax: 54 264 4236632
Web Page:
www.casamontes.com.ar
e-mail:
esavastano@casamontes.com.ar

VINEYARDS
150 ha located at Pozo de los Algarrobos, Caucete, San Juan.
Varieties: Cabernet Sauvignon, Malbec, Merlot, Syrah, Tannat, Cabernet Franc, Petit Verdot, Tempranillo, Nero Davola, Chardonnay and Viognier.

VAT CAPACITY
2 million liters.
Storage capacity: 2 million liters and 30,000 boxes.
Quality Norms: ISO 9000 and HACCP in process of being certified.

BRANDS
Domestic Market: Ampakama, Don Baltazar and Casa Montes.
Foreign Market: Alzamora Grand Reserve, Ampakama and Don Baltazar.
Exports to: Brazil, United States, Belgium, Canada, Sweden, China, Switzerland, Luxemburg and the Russian Federation.

STAFF
President: Lic. Francisco J. Montes
Commercial Manager: Eduardo Savastano.
Administrative Manager: Carlos Pujador
Oenologist: Lic. Gustavo Bauzá
Purchases and Logistics: Mauricio Colomé

Visits: Monday to Friday from 10 a.m. to 4 p.m. During holidays, daily from 10 a.m. to 4 p.m.

DON BALTAZAR CABERNET FRANC 2003

Pretty color, fruity, elegant, fresh, with smooth tannins. Easy to drink, but a well made wine, very pleasant.

CASA MONTES SYRAH ROBLE 2001

Nice color, bright. Red fruit and spice, intense middle. Elegant wine, finishing with powerful tannins. A fresh wine, a very lively acidity and rather pleasant.

DON BALTAZAR PETIT VERDOT 2003

Good color, fairly intense, good fruit, minty notes. Very fresh, medium density that finishes with delicate tannins and pleasant acidity. A fresh wine, easy to drink.

CATENA ZAPATA

Nicolás Catena and Laura Catena.

WINERY HISTORY

Catena Zapata is a family enterprise, led by Nicolás and Laura Catena, third and fourth generation wine-growers. The winery was founded by Nicola Catena, who came to Argentina in the 1800's with the dream of starting his own vineyard.

In the early 1980s Nicolás Catena was invited, as a visiting lecturer, to give classes on Agricultural Economy at Berkeley University, California. Stimulated by the energy and ambition shown by Napa wine-growers at the time, he returned to his country for the purpose of producing quality wines on a par with the best worldwide. He introduced French and Californian clones, small French oak barrels, trickle irrigation system and other breakthrough technologies. Although Catena wines became popular first through their classic Chardonnay and Sauvignon styles, during the last decade the winery was recognized as a Malbec pioneer in Argentina. Its research team, with Dr. Laura Catena's leadership has developed the first clone selection of native Malbec and defined the best areas in Mendoza to grow Malbec.

WINERY LOCATION

Cobos St., Agrelo, Luján de Cuyo, Mendoza. Tel.: 54 261 490 0214. Fax: 54 261 490 0217.
Business Address: Cochabamba s/n (5519) Agrelo, Mendoza, Argentina
Web Page: www.catenawines.com
e-mail: jeffm@catenawines.com

VINEYARDS

425 ha located in Maipú, San Carlos, Luján de Cuyo and Tupungato, Mendoza.
Varieties: Malbec, Petit Verdot, Cabernet Sauvignon, Chardonnay, Merlot, Sauvignon Blanc, Semillón, Syrah, Sangiovese, Cabernet Franc, Pinot Noir, Viognier and Tannat.

VAT CAPACITY

2.9 million liters in stainless steel and 5,000 casks.
Storage capacity: 2 wine cellars with 25,000 bottles each and a 500,000 bottle refrigerated warehouse
Cold Storage: 2,300,000 bottles.
Quality Norms: ISO 9000.

BRANDS

Domestic Market: Saint Felicien, Estiba SF, Angelica Zapata and Catena Zapata.
Foreign Market: Alamos, Catena, Catena Alta and Nicolás Catena Zapata.
Exports to: Brazil, Peru, Mexico, Puerto Rico, Canada, England, Netherlands, Japan, Denmark, Norway, Finland, Sweden, Switzerland, Germany, France, Austria, Hong Kong, South Korea, U.S.A., China, Singapore, Vietnam, India, Malaysia and Taiwan.

STAFF

Owner: Nicolás Catena.
Research & Development Director: Laura Catena
Winemaker: José Galante.
Vineyard Director: Alejandro Sejanovich.
Exportation Managers: Cecilia Razquin/Leandro Juarez.
Public Relations Manager: Jeff Masbach.
Visits: By previous appointment.
Gift Shop: Yes.

CATENA ALTA CHARDONNAY 2003

Attractive golden color. Flower and peach aroma. Elegant, balanced, pleasant fresh finish. A great Argentine Chardonnay.

CATENA ALTA MALBEC 2002

Pleasant color, fresh, lively. Fruity nose, ripe red fruit. Well balanced and harmonious with an extremely agreeable texture.

CAVA BESARES

Juan Carlos Ubriaco.

WINERY HISTORY

This family winery was built between 1902 and 1904. In the early days it only did transportation. In the 90's, the founder's daughter María Antonieta Mariani and her husband Juan Carlos Ubriaco, bet on bottling wine, creating the Araoz and Vieytes brands.

This family-owned establishment only produces top quality premium wines that are aged for a lengthy period in the bottle. The intention is that when the consumer buys the wine, it is the perfect moment for drinking it.

WINERY LOCATION
Besares 397, Chacras de Coria, Luján de Cuyo, Mendoza.
Tel/Fax: 54 261 496 0043
Business Address:
Besares 397, Chacras de Coria, Luján de Cuyo, Mendoza.
Tel/Fax: 54 261 496 0043
e-mail:
cavabesares@hotmail.com

VINEYARDS
3 hectares in Luján de Cuyo, Mendoza.
Third party vineyards:
Tupungato-Merlot and San Carlos and Agrelo-Cabernet Sauvignon.

VAT CAPACITY
1,000,000 liters

BRANDS
Domestic Market:
Araoz and Vieytes
Foreign Market: Araoz, Vieytes, Lanyeni and Ayentlac
Exports to: Great Britain

STAFF
Owners: Juan Carlos Ubriaco and María Antonieta Mariani
Visits: By previous appointment. Call 54 261 4960043.

CAVA BESARES CABERNET SAUVIGNON 2003

Good color. Interesting nose with fruit, wood, some notes of dried herbs, slightly vegetable. Powerful wine, fairly dense with lots of tannins, somewhat rustic. An intense wine that should gain qualities with aging.

CAVA BESARES MALBEC 2002

Nose of ripe fruit, somewhat overripe. Medium concentration, fairly good with intense tannins.

CICCHITTI

José Antonio Cicchitti and his sons José Antonio, Ignacio and Augusto.

WINERY HISTORY

Our winery is a family company, oriented to making products in limited quantities, high quality, healthy and ecology friendly.

The nobility of our wines starts in the grapevine and continues in our installations until it reaches the consumer. With this aim in mind, this lengthy process is carefully tested daily.

Bodegas Cicchitti has been exporting to the US, Switzerland, Belgiuim, Germany and England since 1992.

With our various options we serve our demanding consumers, with excellent wines for daily consumption and others for special occasions.

The full line ranges from our sparkling Soigne (the name means made with careful attention, which can be proven), to the passionate Reserva Cicchitti, Colección Cicchitti, Cicchitti Blend, and to Cicchitti Néctar, perfect for surprising guests.

Our greatest commitment is to making the sparkling Soigne and the exciting task of producing surprising wines.

WINERY LOCATION
Buenos Vecinos, 57, Rodeo de la Cruz, Mendoza.
Tel.: 54 261 4913139 / 4910845
Business Address: at winery
Web Page:
www.bodegacicchitti.com
www.brutsoigne.com
e-mail:
ventas@bodegacicchitti.com
silviam@bodegacicchitti.com

VINEYARDS
36 ha vineyards at Vista Flores, Tunuyán, 22 ha at Agrelo, Luján de Cuyo, and 24 ha at Medrano.
Varieties: Semillón, Chardonnay, Cabernet Sauvignon and Malbec. At Medrano, Sangiovese, Torrontés and Malbec.
Third party vineyards:
Medrano 10 ha, San Carlos 12 ha, Tupungato 22 ha.
Varieties: Malbec, Cabernet Sauvignon, Pinot Noir, Sangiovese, Merlot and Chenin Blanc.

VAT CAPACITY
1,000,000 liters.
In the winery: 300,000 bottles.
In climate controlled storage: 200,000.

BRANDS
Domestic Market: Reserva Cicchitti, Colección Cicchitti, Cicchitti Blend, Néctar, Soigne Champaña.
Foreign Market: Cicchitti Vinos, Soigne Sparkling Wine.
Exports to: United States, Germany, Switzerland, England, Belgium, Chile and Mexico.

STAFF
President: José A. Cicchitti (jr.)
Oenologist: Rafael Cicchitti
Advertising: Carlos E. Ruberto
Foreign Commerce:
Silvia Marti de Cicchitti
Finance Advisor: A. Scocco
Commercial Advisor:
Prof. José Cicchitti.
Marketing: José A. Cicchitti (III)

Visits: By previous telephone appointment.

COLECCIÓN CICCHITTI TORRONTÉS 2004

Pretty yellow color with green hues. Very pleasant, smooth, round, a wine with a good mouth.

CICCHITTI CABERNET SAUVIGNON 2002

Interesting color, fairly intense. Fruit is expressed in a delicate manner. A simple wine, but balanced with lots of harmony and good Cabernet Sauvignon character.

CICCHITTI MALBEC 2002

Interesting color, fruit is ripe, with a slightly overripe character. Good harmony in the mouth, tannins are fine and elegant with good texture. A good example of wine making.

CLOS DE LOS SIETE

Michel Rolland.

WINERY HISTORY

Clos de los Siete is a viticulture project by a group of French investors in the foothills of the Andean Range, Vista Flores, Tunuyán, 120 km south of Mendoza City.

The history of Clos de los Siete closely linked to oenologist Michel Rolland, for years a consultant to prestigious wineries around the world, really started in 1998. It was Rolland's influence that grouped together these French investors, all members of families traditionally linked to wine, and to the internationally famous Châteaux de Bordeaux.

Clos de los Siete wine is made with the best grapes grown and vinified in each terroir.

At first it was in Monteviejo (2002 and 2003), the pioneer winery of Catherine Péré Vergé. Then, Flecha de Los Andes, belonging to Laurent Dasseault and Benjamin Rothschild, the third to join was the Cuvelier family. All focused on making a unique wine that became their benchmark. Production started in 2002.

WINERY LOCATION
Vinification in wineries: Monteviejo, Flechas de Los Andes and Cuvelier Los Andes.
Tel 54 261 4234230
Fax: 54 261 4234486
e-mail:
Closdelossiete@clos7.com.ar

VINEYARDS
Clodomiro Silva s/n Vista Flores, Tunuyán, Mendoza, Argentina
Total surface: 850 ha
Planted surface: 350 ha
Varieties:
Malbec, Merlot, Syrah and Cabernet Sauvignon.

VAT CAPACITY
Total: 2,500,000 liters in steel tanks
Barrels: 2,200

BRANDS
Clos de los Siete
Exports to: France, Germany, UK, Canada, USA, Switzerland, Japan and 37 other countries.

STAFF
Majority shareholders:
Catherine Péré Vergé,
Benjamin Rothschild, Laurent Dasseault, Bertrand Cuvelier and Jean Guy Cuvelier
Consultant: Michel Rolland
General Manager:
Carlos Tizio Mayer
Agronomist:
Ing.Marcelo Canatella
Oenologists: Marcelo Pelleriti, Pablo Richardi and Adrian Manchón.

Visits:
Reservations: turismo@clos7.com.ar (Sofía Dalvit)
Gift Shop: Yes

CLOS DE LOS SIETE

A beautiful purple red color, very intense and bright. The nose is elegant and consistent. Very good tertiary aromas combined with red fruit and spices. A bit of vanilla can be noticed. In the mouth, it is pleasant, with good tannins and great quality. A great wine for many years.

COLOMÉ

Donald and Ursula Hess.

WINERY HISTORY

In 2001, the Swiss Group Hess bought the Colomé Winery, in the Valle Calchaquí, Salta. The Group also owns other vineyards: The Hess Collection, Napa (USA); Glen Carlou (South Africa); Peter Lehmann (Australia). The establishment's 39,000 hectares are irrigated by melt water. The estates in Colomé, El Arenal and Río Blanco, lie at altitudes that range between 2,200 and 3,015 meters. Ten hectares are dedicated to pre-phylloxeric vine cultivation; 4 of those varieties (Malbec, Cabernet Sauvignon among them) were brought from France in 1854. The Colomé and Río Blanco vineyards are cultivated bio-dynamically and are undergoing the certification process. El Arenal will start the bio-dynamic program in 2006. In the Colomé Estate and Reserva wines Malbec predominates by 85 and 90% respectively. Cabernet Sauvignon and Tannat are also combined. The Torrontés is 100% varietal. The Amalaya wine from Colomé combines with Malbec, Bonarda and Cabernet Sauvignon. The original establishment dates from 1831. The new winery has a visitor center and an estancia (large ranch) luxury hotel that offers a lot of activities such as massage, horseback riding, swimming, tennis, golf, and hikes, among others.

WINERY LOCATION
Ruta Prov. N. 53 km N. 20, (4419) Molinos, Salta
Tel.: 54 3868 494044 /494043
Business Address:
San Juan 277 (4400), Salta
Tel.: 54 387 422271171
Web Page:
www.bodegacolome.com
e-mail:
estancia@bodegacolome.com
bodega@bodegacolome.com

VINEYARDS
106 ha in Valle Calchaquí, Salta.
Varieties: Malbec, Cabernet Sauvignon, Tannat, Torrontés, Syrah and Bonarda.

VAT CAPACITY
1,300,000 liters
Storage Capacity:
1,570,000 bottles

BRANDS
Colomé Reserva, Colomé Estate, Colomé Torrontés and Amalaya de Colomé.
Exports to: Brazil, Switzerland, Austria, United States and England.

STAFF
President and Ad interim Manager:
Donald M. Hess.
Business development Wine Manager of the Hess Group: Jean-Marc Amez-Droz
CFO: Bernardo Jarabroviski
Oenologists: Steve Galvan and Thibaut Delmotte
Vineyard Manager: Javier Grané

Visits and Gift shop:
By previous appointment, from 11a.m. to 7 p.m.

COLOMÉ TORRONTÉS 2004

Plenty of aromatic finesse, balance, charm. A true Torrontés, fresh and harmonious.

COLOMÉ ESTATE 2003

Excellent color, intense and dark. Good quality fruit, strong, complex, with a good bit of red fruit. In the mouth, it is fine and elegant; good concentration, ending with pleasant tannins, that are young, still strong, but of good quality. A good wine, strong and elegant.

COLOMÉ RESERVA MALBEC 2003

Black, deep, intense. Nose of very ripe fruit, almost overripe, suggestive of black fruit such as blackberries, excellent quality. Plenty of volume and powerful in the mouth, round, lots of tannins but with finesse and harmony. A wine that is powerful and at the same time refined.

CUVELIER LOS ANDES

Jean-Guy Cuvelier and Bertrand Cuvelier.

WINERY HISTORY

Specialists in producing French "Grands Crus" wines, the Cuvelier family has owned Château Leoville-Poyferre in Saint-Julien and Château Le Crock in Saint-Estephe since 1903.

In 1999, Bertrand and Jean-Guy Cuvelier were impressed and seduced by the quailty of wines from Mendoza. Advised by Michel Rolland, they installed and created a new vineyard in Vista Flores, Tunuyán. The property is located at the side of the Andes Mountain Range, in the well-known Uco Valley region of Mendoza, at an altitude of 1,000 meters. The company built its Cuvelier Los Andes Winery in this fabulous setting.

The winery is part of the prestigious Clos de los Siete group.

WINERY LOCATION
Clodomiro Silva s/n, Vista Flores, Tunuyan, Mendoza. Tel/Fax: 54 2622 425688
Business Address: Sarmiento 250, 2nd floor, "B", Mendoza
Tel.: 54 261 4234230/4234833
Fax: 54 261 423 4486
e-mail: amanchon@clos7.com.ar
ctizio@clos7.com.ar
turismo@clos7.com.ar

VINEYARDS
Clodomiro Silva s/n, Vista Flores, Tunuyán, Mendoza, 43 hectares
Varieties: Cabernet Sauvignon, Malbec, Merlot, Syrah and Petit Verdot.

VAT CAPACITY
3,400 hl. in stainless steel tanks, 990 hl in casks (440 casks)
Storage capacity: 350,000 bottles

BRANDS
Domestic Market: Cuvelier Los Andes Colección and Grand Vin
Foreign Market: Cuvelier Los Andes Coleccçion and Grand Vin
Exports to: United States, Europe and South America

STAFF
Owners: Bertrand Cuvelier and Jean-Guy Cuvelier
Agronomist: Engineer Marcelo Canatella
Oenologist: Adrián Manchón
Consultant: Michel Rolland

Visits: By previous appointment, Monday to Friday, 9 a.m. to 3 p.m.

CUVELIER COLECCIÓN 2003

Beautiful dark red color with purple glints. Brilliant. Complex aromas, capturing ripe fruit spice, vanilla and black pepper. Sweet first taste in the mouth with great structure and oily tannins. Good wood. A wine with great potential.

CHAKANA

Juan Pelizzatti.

WINERY HISTORY

Chakana is a modern endeavor that renews an old family legacy. At present, the Pelizzatti family produces in Argentina wines of excellent quality and international style, focusing its development on foreign markets. Chakana produces farm wines from grapes coming exclusively from the family farm in Agrelo, Luján de Cuyo, 34 km south of Mendoza city. In order to attain these high quality standards, special emphasis is placed on the care of the grape and the utilization of practices that yield great results on the varieties that adapt best to the farm soil and climate. To the ancient inhabitants of the Andes, la Chakana -the Square Cross- was a symbol of their universe. The Sun and Earth creative forces inspired the Andean world, its four cardinal points and three life elements: air, soil and water. The Southern Cross established a stellar calendar that governed the dynamics of the agricultural cycle. All these elements are represented in the holy cross, which takes its name from a simple but powerful object: the Chakana, a stone used to send water to the irrigation canals.

WINERY LOCATION
Ruta Provincial No. 15, Km. 34 Luján de Cuyo, Mendoza
Tel.: 54 261 410 6002
Business Address:
Cerrito 1070, Piso 9, C1010AAV
Ciudad Autónoma de Buenos Aires
Tel.: 54 11 4811 7559
Fax: 54 11 4811 7559
Web Page:
www.chakanawines.com.ar
e-mail:
info@chakanawines.com.ar

VINEYARDS
Finca 300 ha: 100 planted at Agrelo, Luján de Cuyo, Mendoza.
Varieties: Cabernet Sauvignon, Cabernet Franc, Merlot, Malbec, Bonarda, Shiraz, Tannat, Petit Verdot, Sauvignon Blanc and Chardonnay
Third party vineyards:
We make only farm wines.

VAT CAPACITY
600,000 liters
Storage capacity:
500 casks
Quality norms: Certification pending ISO 9001-2000 and HACCP for winery processes and EUREP-GAP for farm processes.

BRANDS
Domestic and Foreign Market:
Chakana
Exports to: U.S.A., Netherlands, Belgium, Denmark, Italy., England, Mexico, Peru and Brazil.

STAFF
General Director: Juan Pelizzatti
Oenologist: Lic. Liliana Iannizzotto
External consultant:
Dominique Delteil
Agronomist:
Ing. Santiago Mayorga
Business Manager:
Santiago Bernasconi
santiago@chakanawines.com.ar

Visits: By previous appointment.

CHAKANA BONARDA 2003

Good color and fruit, although not explosive. Very smooth, totally harmonious; a wine to be enjoyed. Well made, clean with a nice fullness.

CHAKANA CABERNET SAUVIGNON 2003

Good color, pleasant fruit, a touch of vegetable. Its texture is agreeable; needs a bit more harmony at the finish because of its harsh tannins that are a bit austere; a somewhat young wine. It should be kept a while before drinking.

CHAKANA MALBEC 2003

Lots of fruit, and spice. An expressive wine on the nose. It has good concentration that is not enormous in the middle, but with lots of tannins. Time will lead to harmony between the mouth and the tannins, resulting in a good quality Malbec.

DEL FIN DEL MUNDO

Julio Viola.

WINERY HISTORY

Until a short time ago, no one could imagine Neuquén as a producer of top quality wines, but the region has now proven the aptitude of its climate and soil for grapevines. With the planting of its first vineyards in 1999, Bodega Del Fin Del Mundo changed the map of Argentine viticulture. As it was the first winery in Neuquén, it was the founder of this new region that rapidly gained prestige in the country.

After four years of work, Bodega Del Fin Del Mundo inaugurated the first of the four modules that make up its winery and produced its first vintage to be sold.

With 800 hectares of its own and a modern winery, Bodega Del Fin Del Mundo is already in more than ten international markets and throughout Argentina.

Neuquén, as a province that produces high quality wines is already a reality and Bodega Del Fin Del Mundo, a pioneer in this new region, is beginning to be seen as one of the great Argentine wineries in future years.

WINERY LOCATION
Ruta Pcial. 8, Km. 9, San Patricio del Chañar, Neuquén.
Tel.: 54 299 4855004
Web Page:
www.bodegadelfindelmundo.com
e-mail: info@bdfm.com.ar
Neuquén Offices:
J.B. Alberdi 87, 1° piso, Neuquén (Q8300HLA), Tel.: 54 299 4424040
Buenos Aires Offices:
Juncal 3490, 2° piso. (C1425AYV)
Tel.: 54 11 5787 1287.

VINEYARDS
850 ha, San P. del Chañar, Neuquén.
Varieties: Cabernet Sauvignon, Cabernet Franc, Malbec, Merlot, Pinot Noir, Syrah, Petit Verdot, Chardonnay, Sauvignon Blanc, Semillón and Viognier.

VAT CAPACITY
4.2 million liters, with capacity for 8.5.
Storage capacity:
1,000,000 bottles.
Quality Norms: BPA and BPM. HACCP being certificated.

BRANDS
Domestic and Foreign Market:
Postales, Newen, Reserva Del Fin Del Mundo, Special Blend.
Exports to: England, United States, Denmark, Holand, Belgium, Luxemburg, Korea, Ireland, Finland, Sweden, Russia, Brazil, Uruguay, Cyprus, Italy, Mexico, Canada and Colombia.

STAFF
President: Julio C. Viola
Vicepresident: Graciela P. de Viola
Director: Lic. Julio Viola (jr.)
Director: Dr. Ana Viola
Bs. As. Manager: Lic. Pedro Soraire
Commercial Manager:
Carlos Fernández
Country Manager:
Ing. José Barria
Oenologist: Lic. Marcelo Miras

Visits: Everyday from 10 a.m. to 4 p.m. Sunday and holidays from 10 a.m. to 5 p.m. Gift Shop.

DEL FIN DEL MUNDO PINOT NOIR 2003

Fairly intense color for a Pinot. Good fruit, ripe, good quality of typical aromas. The wine is powerful, fairly tannic but with lots of charm and harmony. Interesting wine in its category.

DEL FIN DEL MUNDO MALBEC 2003

Good color, fruity, elegant, charming. Harmonious and medium persistence. A pleasing wine, easy to drink with good balance.

DEL FIN DEL MUNDO MALBEC RESERVA 2003

Very agreeable color. Good nose of fruit and spice with good intensity. Wood dominates a little and the middle of the mouth has correct volume. It is a young wine that with cellaring will achieve more harmony and has very good potential.

DOLIUM

Emma and Ricardo Giadorou.

WINERY HISTORY

The winery was conceived by its founder, Engineer Mario Giadorou, who, after an important career in the private sector, took up an old family tradition as his ancestors used to produce wines, grappa and maraschino in Italy during the 17th century. The winery started operating in February 1998. The name "DOLIUM" comes from Latin, meaning amphora and takes us back to the ceramic flask the Greeks and Romans used to store wine underground and let it age, maturing at an ideal temperature.

DOLIUM is the first winery totally underground in Argentina. This produces a "natural" temperature throughout the year ranging between 12° and 18° C, the optimum temperature for the wine conservation and storage. The majority of the production ages in French or American oak barrels.

Dolium produces only varietal wines in three lines: Clásico, Reserva and Gran Reserva; each of which uses grapes from selected plots of land, and has been aged in oak barrels for the right amount of time.

WINERY LOCATION
Ruta provincial 15, km 30 s/n Agrelo, Luján de Cuyo, Mendoza, Argentina.
Tel.: 0261-4900190; 0261-4900200; 0261-15 6627 111
Web Page: www.dolium.com
e-mail: dolium@dolum.com

VINEYARDS
Located around the winery at Agrelo, Luján de Cuyo.
Varieties: Cabernet Sauvignon, Tempranillo, Syrah, Malbec and Merlot.
Third party vineyards: Perdriel, Chacras de Coria and Lunlunta.
Varieties: Malbec, Cabernet Sauvignon and Sauvignon Blanc.

VAT CAPACITY
220,000 liters in 225 liter barrels.
Storage capacity:
400,000 liters in stainless steel tanks.

BRANDS
Brands in Domestic Market:
Dolium
Brands in Foreign Market:
Dolium, Andes Peak, Doña Cristina and Doña Emma, Cumbre Andina
Exports to: United States, England, Brazil, Germany, Australia, Colombia, Canada, Mexico, Denmark, Belgium, Hong Kong, Japan and Switzerland.

STAFF
Owners: Giadorou Family
CEO: Ricardo Giadorou
Oenologists: Andrea Marchiori, Luis Barraud and Sergio Montiel
Consultant: Paul Hoggs

Visits and Gift Shop: By previous appointment with the owners, Monday to Friday from 10 a.m. to 5 p.m. Inquire about tastings or special events.

DOLIUM CABERNET SAUVIGNON RESERVA 2002

Bouquet of red fruit with wood very well integrated. The middle of the mouth has medium volume. Tannins are delicate and quite harmonious. It is a well made pleasurable wine.

DOLIUM MALBEC RESERVA 2002

Agreeable color, good fruit in harmony with the wood. Red ripe fruite. Good texture, fleshy with a tannic middle of the mouth. Intense wine, fairly dense with ripe tannins. Very good quality.

DOLIUM TEMPRANILLO 2004

Attractive color, bright and frank. Nose of cacao, red fruit, toasted spice. Good texture, pleasant; ends rather quickly with tannins that are still firm.

DOMADOS

Fernando Spigatin, partner and manager of Domados.

WINERY HISTORY

Domados was born from the dream of small wine growers, Italian immigrants who arrived at the beginning of the last century and settled in southwest Mendoza, in the Valle de Uco.

Don Giocondo Ficcardi and Humberto Spigatin cultivated Malbec for the first time in 1923 at La Consulta (San Carlos), one of the best terroirs in the world for this variety.

The care their children took of those vineyards allowed their grandchildren to make grapes into wine now and gave origin to Domados.

The name refers to "taming a wine". The Indian way of taming a wild colt was similar to that practiced by gauchos, but the Indians were gentler with their horses, hence their taming was a better process.

Knowledge, patience and infinite care were the qualities Indians displayed while breaking their horses. Similarly, every instant in the process of making wine, knowledge, patience and infinite care of the raw material are fundamental to achieving a successful result.

WINERY LOCATION
Callejón Zapata s/n, Cruz de Piedra, Maipú, Mendoza.
Tel/Fax: 54 261 4362755
Business Address:
San Martín 7933, Carrodilla, Luján de Cuyo, Mendoza.
Tel/Fax: 54 261 4362755
Web Page:
www.domadoswines.com.ar
e-mail: info@domadoswines.com.ar

VINEYARDS
40 hectares at La Consulta, San Carlos, Valle de Uco, Mendoza.
Varieties: Malbec, Merlot, Cabernet Sauvignon and Bonarda.
Third party vineyards:
25 hectares at La Consulta, San Carlos, Valle de Uco, Mendoza.
Varieties: Syrah, Pinot Noir, Chardonnay, Semillón and Sauvignon Blanc.

VAT CAPACITY
100,000 liters in steel tanks
Storage capacity:
120,000 bottles

BRANDS
Domestic Market:
Domados, Tobiano, Gateado.
Foreign Market:
Domados, Tobiano.
Exports to:
Belgium, Luxemburg, Netherlands, Switzerland and China.

STAFF
President: Bruno Spigatin
Manager: Fernando Spigatin
Agronomist: Ricardo Gattoni
Oenologist: Pedro Rosell

Visits: Monday to Saturday, from 10a.m. to 3 p.m.

TOBIANO CABERNET SAUVIGNON 2003

Good color, expressive fruit, good maturity with some notes of spice. A little earthy in the aroma, but good maturity of the fruit. Elegant, the persistence in the mouth is correct with robust tannins that need a little time to become harmonious. A good Cabernet Sauvignon, just a little bit aggressive at the finish.

TOBIANO MALBEC 2003

A lot of fruit, very fresh, memories of red fruit with floral notes. Medium complexity in the mouth, elegant. Correct finish with fairly silky tannins. In the elegant range and smooth. A good Malbec.

TOBIANO MERLOT 2003

Attractive color with beautiful hues, intense. Lots of ripe fruit, important floral notes and good aromatic intensity. Powerful wine, fleshy with a lot of tannin. Needs to become harmonious over time. A wine with lots of expression, typical of the variety: a very good wine.

DOMAINE ST. DIEGO

Juan Manuel, Lucas and Ángel Mendoza.

WINERY HISTORY

In 1988, Ángel A Mendoza, a well-known Argentine oenologist, suggested his family start a small enterprise to develop a winery and be passionate wine growers.

With their savings and free time on the week-ends, the family succeeded in recycling and designing a viticulture domain in the magical "Lunlunta" lowlands to the south of Maipú, Mendoza.

The splendid climatic conditions favorable to ripening grapes, combined with the family's university knowledge, love of nature, passion for winegrowing and unity, are reflected in the taste of wine from Domaine St. Diego belonging to Ángel A. Mendoza and his family.

Their Pura Sangre red wine won three gold medals in international competitions: Vinandino 1999 and Malbec al Mundo 2000-2002.

Since 2003, Ángel and sons have designed a new top quality red wine, Paradigma.

WINERY LOCATION
Franklin Villanueva 3821, Lunlunta, Maipú, Mendoza.
Tel.: 54 0261 4990414
Business Address: Laprida 479, Portal del Sol, La Puntilla, Luján de Cuyo, Mendoza.
Tel.: 54 0261 4395557
e-mail:
juanmmendoza@sinectis.com.ar

VINEYARDS
3.5 ha planted with Chardonnay, Cabernet Sauvignon, Cabernet Franc and Malbec.

VAT CAPACITY
In stainless steel: 25,000 liters
50 225 liter barrels
Storage capacity:
30,000 bottles per year.
Quality norms: we have no certified quality norms. But all our members are oriented towards a philosophy of quality.

BRANDS
Ángel A. Mendoza, Lucas Mendoza, Pura Sangre, Brut Xero and Paradigma.
Foreign Market:
We do not export at the moment.

STAFF
Family enterprise, led by Ángel Mendoza and his wife Rosalía Emilia Pereyra. Their sons, Juan Manuel and Lucas Nicolás are in charge of administration and operations.
María Laura, the youngest daughter, still in school, collaborates with Lucas Nicolás in making the sparkling Brut Xero.

Visits: By previous appointment, Monday to Friday, from 9 a.m. to 12 noon and from 3 p.m. to 6 p.m.
Gift Shop: Products are sold at the winery only on Saturdays, Sundays and holidays from 9 a.m. to 1 p.m.

PURA SANGRE 2001

Fairly pretty color with somewhat orange notes. Fruity nose, fresh, good expression of fruit. Elegant wine, but at the same time tannic at the finish. Tannins are still rather young and will age with time. A classic wine, well made that reflects the soil's expression.

PURA SANGRE 2002

Lots of fruity expression with good quality fruit, very fresh, agreeable aroma. The mouth is always elegant with finesse and persistence; the tannins at the finish are still young, but with lots of aroma. an elegant wine, great finesse and good concentration. A pleasurable wine.

DOMINIO DEL PLATA

Susana Balbo and Pedro Marchevsky.

WINERY HISTORY

Susana and Pedro met in 1994. Their interest in making quality wines drew them together at once and a year later they decided to join their lives and families.

In 1999, searching for an expression of their love and devotion to viticulture, they started a project of their own at Agrelo, Luján de Cuyo, Mendoza. This is not only the establishment where they make the wines, with the latest technology, but also the site chosen for their home and family.

Susana Balbo is one of the best-known oenologists in Argentina. She graduated with honors as an oenologist in 1981 and worked at Michel Torino (Cafayate, Salta province) where she succeeded in transforming regular regional wines into the famous Torrontés, the variety recognized as the emblem of Argentine wine industry.

Pedro is well-known because of his expertise in the management of quality grapevines. He has developed methods called "precision viticulture" to obtain the best grapes of each variety.

WINERY LOCATION
Cochabamba 7801, Agrelo, Luján de Cuyo, Mendoza.
Tel: 54 261 4986572 / 4982934
Business Address:
Cochambamba 7801, Agrelo, Luján de Cuyo, Mendoza.
Tel: 54 261 4986572 / 4982934
e-mail:
info@dominiodelplata.com.ar
Web Page:
www.dominiodelplata.com.ar

VINEYARDS
66 ha.
Third party vineyards: 35 ha.

VAT CAPACITY
1,242,000 liters
Storage capacity:
600,000 bottles.
Quality Norms:
ISO 9000 in process, HACCP.

BRANDS
Domestic Market: Anubis, Crios, BenMarco, Susana B.
Foreign Market: Anubis, Crios, BenMarco, Susana Balbo.
Exports to: United States, Canada, Puerto Rico, Mexico, Colombia, Portugal, Sweden, England, Austria and Ireland,

STAFF
1st Oenologist Owner:
Susana Balbo
Viticultor Owner:
Pedro Marchevsky
Logistics Department:
Laura Santi
Export Department:
Juan Ruiz and Federica Alvarez
2nd Oenologists:
Pablo Peralta and Oscar Goslani
Laboratory: Carina Daguerre
Accounting Department:
Carlos Hernandez
Accounting Assistant:
Daniel Farias

Visits: Only by previous appointment.

BENMARCO MALBEC 2003

Intense, very thick color. Nose is powerful with red fruit and a markedly smoky background, characteristic of the casks. The wine is smooth, silky with good volume, delicate tannins at the finish and well balanced. It is powerful and should be aged a bit before drinking.

CRIOS CABERNET SAUVIGNON 2003

Good color. Aroma of small red fruit, correct maturation and silky texture. Medium persistence; it is an agile wine and easy to drink. Balanced.

SUSANA BALBO CABERNET SAUVIGNON 2002

Pleasant color. Good nose of ripe fruit with hints of dry grass and dried fruit. Good medium in the mouth, fairly smooth with good density and lasting persistence. A young wine to be enjoyed in awhile

DON CRISTÓBAL

Eduardo Lapania.

WINERY HISTORY

Don Cristóbal owns 150 ha that are exclusively devoted to vitiviniculture, 95 ha are already being cultivated at their three vineyards: Finca La Niña, La Pinta and La Santa María.

Don Cristóbal 1492 is 20 km south of Mendoza City, in the Cruz de Piedra district, Maipú department.

Don Cristóbal red and white wines are made in their own winery, with a 1,000,000 liter capacity, in stainless steel tanks and epoxipated cement. The winery has state of the art equipment, with a thermo-regulation automated system, and powerful cold temperature units (350,000 cbu) that optimize fermentation and elaboration processes.

Every year, between 60 to 70 thousand liters of choice wines are put in French oak casks to mature for a 12 month or longer period.

The Don Cristóbal 1492 team, of 25 people, strive to satisfy wine lovers who can have the opportunity to appreciate their products: Chardonnay Verdelho, Viognier, Merlot, Malbec, Cabernet Sauvignon, Shiraz, Bonarda and Sangiovese.

WINERY LOCATION
Videla Aranda 361, Cruz de Piedra
Maipú M5586BQG, Mendoza.
Tel.: 54 261 4990003
Business Address: Pacheco de Melo 1869 PB "B", C1126AAA, Buenos Aires. Tel.: 54 11 48078484.
Fax: 54 1148018827
Web Page:
www.doncristobal.com.ar
e-mail: exportaciones@doncristo-bal.com.ar

VINEYARDS
Finca La Santa María: Ugarteche, Luján de Cuyo, Mendoza
Planted Area: 52 ha
Varieties: Cabernet Sauvignon, Malbec, Merlot, Shiraz and Bonarda.
Finca La Niña: Rodríguez Peña, Junín, Mendoza.
Planted Area: 17 ha.
Varieties: Malbec, Merlot, Shiraz and Sangiovese.
Finca La Pinta: Los Campamentos, Rivadavia, Mendoza.
Planted Area: 39 ha.
Varieties: Chardonnay, Verdelho, Viognier, Cabernet Sauvignon, Merlot and Shiraz.

VAT CAPACITY
900,000 liters in concrete vats and stainless steel. 420 oak barrels.
Storage capacity:
200,000 bottles.

BRANDS
Domestic Market: 1492; Finca La Niña, Cristóbal 1492; Cristóbal Oak Reserve.
Exports: Brazil, United States, Sweden, France, Iceland, Italy, Denmark, Belgium, United Kingdom, Korea, Japan, Germany.

STAFF
Oenologist: Juan Bruzzone
Business Administration: Laura Gutierrez
Agronomist:
Andrés Méndez Casariego.

Visits: by previous phone appointment: 54 261 4990120.

CRISTÓBAL 1492 VERDELHO 2004

Fresh, balanced with good acidity and fruity. Very refreshing, a thirst-quencher. Very agreeable.

CRISTÓBAL 1492 OAK RESERVE SHIRAZ 2003

Pretty color, fairly deep. Good fruit bouquet, fresh and with an elegantly aromatic taste. Very silky and smooth with good persistence. An extremely elegant wine. Pleasant for drinking now, not very complex, but most pleasurable.

EL ESTECO

Winery entrance.
Vina y la bodega.

WINERY HISTORY

Cafayate is a premium area in the north of Argentina, 1,700 meters above sea level. It is where the sun lives and the wine shines. Thanks to a wide range of temperatures and the dry sunny climate, the region is especially apt for producing wines with highly concentrated colors, aromas and taste, powerful red wines with intense personality and flowery white wines like the well-known Torrontés.

Cafayate's excellent "terroir" (soil) and microclimate convinced brothers David and Salvador Michel to create a winery there. In 1892, they planted the first grapevines and built the winery, which was called El Esteco after the legend of El Esteco town in the province of Salta, that was destroyed in an earthquake in 1600, but whose riches survived and have been rediscovered in our vineyards. We make premium wines under the "Estate" concept, with preferential positioning in the gastronomy segment, top wine stores and retail chain chains.

Michel Torino will certify 100% organic vineyards in 2005, and the same year they will open their Hotel Wine-Spa, the most important in South America, with 35 rooms and a thematic look.

WINERY LOCATION

Ruta 40 y 68, Cafayate, Salta. CP. 4427
Tel/Fax: 54 3868 421139
Business Address:
Arenales 460, 4° Vicente López, Buenos Aires. CP (1638).
Tel.: 54 11 5198 9018/08
Web Page: www.elesteco.com.ar
e-mail: ncornejoelesteco.com.ar

VINEYARDS

400 ha. at Cafayate, Salta.
Varieties: Malbec, Cabernet Sauvignon, Tannat, Syrah, Merlot, Tempranillo, BonardaTorrontés, Chardonnay, Sauvignon Blanc and Chenin Blanc.

VAT CAPACITY

5,500,000 liters.
Storage capacity: 200,000 bottles.
Quality Norms: BPM (Buenas Prácticas de Manufactura) and HACCP in process. Organic farming certification in 100% of the vineyards.

BRANDS

Domestic Market: Elementos, Don David, Ciclos, Altimus.
Foreign Market: Colección, Don David, Ciclos, Altimus.
Exports to: European Union, Switzerland, Scandinavia, Russia, United States, Canada, Colombia, Peru, Brazil, Costa Rica, Paraguay, Taiwan, Hong Kong, Korea, Vietnam and Australia.

STAFF

Production Manager: Andrés Hōy
Oenologists: Alejandro Pepa and Fabián Miranda
Viticultor: Maximiliano Lester
Exportation Manager: Nicolás Cornejo
Marketing Manager: Juan Manzioni
House Manager: Florencia Perkins

Visits: Monday to Friday, from 8 a.m to 5 p.m. Saturday, 9 a.m. to 1p.m.
Gift Shop: Yes. Visits will be reasumed once construction is finished.

ALTIMUS 2003

Intense and singular color. Good nose, complex. Powerful, elegant with good tannins. Needs some time in the bottle to reach its full potential.

CICLOS MALBEC- MERLOT 2003

Striking black color. Intense fruit aroma, fairly strong. Abundant and concentrated tannins. A good wine.

DON DAVID RESERVE MALBEC 2003

Attractive color. Wood still a little noticeable, has good ripe fruit. Good structure with the firm tannins of a young wine.

EL PORVENIR DE LOS ANDES

Vineyards and winery.

WINERY HISTORY

Late in the 1890's, this winery had its origin in Cafayate, Salta. A second foundation took place in 1999 and a new profile soon began to take shape under the influence of the new owner, a family with good knowledge of the region that was determined to develop a vigorous vitiviniculture project. The process got underway with important investment in infrastructure and fresh vineyards.

The advice of a prestigious Spanish oenologist, Isabel Mijares, and the international quality certification of the vineyards and the production plant are attributes that place it in a privileged position to export. As do the awards won by their Laborum brand in national and international competitions.

The professional team is committed to the challenge of producing premium wines with the best technology and methods that guarantee quality production, with a strict control not only of the production, but also of the bottling and storage of the wines.

The original building has been restored, preserving the old adobe walls that maintain the charm of Salta's colonial architecture.

WINERY LOCATION
Córdoba 32, Cafayate, Salta.
Business Address:
Cerrito 348, 3° B, Buenos Aires.
Tel.: 54 11 51999747/48
Web Page:
www.bodegaselporvenir.com
e-mail:
info@bodegaselporvenir.com

VINEYARDS
At Cafayate, 100 ha.
Varieties: Torrontés, Mallbec, Cabernet, Sauvignon.
Third Party Vineyards:
Santa María, 100 ha.
Varieties: Merlot, Syrah, Tannat and Tempranillo.

VAT CAPACITY
220,000 liters
Storage capacity:
In bottles: 100,000 liters
In barrels: 90,000 liters
Quality norms:
In process Hazard, and ISO Norms being implemented

BRANDS
Domestic and Foreign Markets: Laborum, Maximum, Amauta.
Exports to: United States, Europe and other American countries.

STAFF
Executive Director:
Marcelo Romero
Commercial Director:
Juan Carlos Solari
Internal Oenologist: Luis Asmet
External Oenologist: María Isabel Mijares y García Pelayo.

Visits: By previous appointment
Gift Shop: Yes.

LABORUM MALBEC-CABERNET 2002

Good color, with good aromatic intensity, notes of spice, ripe fruit, red and black fruit. Smooth, silky, very round and pleasurable. Tannins have good concentration. A well-balance wine, with a good future.

LABORUM CABERNET SAUVIGNON 2002

Interesting color. Notes of eucalyptus and ripe grape appear on the nose. The middle of the mouth is fairly correct, not too oily with a good finish of powerful tannins.

LABORUM TORRONTÉS 2004

Good aroma of the variety. With those notes of moscatel and oil that characterize it. Agreeable, rather refreshing. Different and aromatic.

EL PORTILLO

Main entrance to El Portillo's vineyards.

WINERY HISTORY

At the foot of the Andes perennial snows, El Portillo creates wines expressing the terroir's character. At this altitude, the sun is closer, nights are cooler and the soil is irrigated by melt water. That is what nature is like in Valle de Uco, where fresh fruity wines are produced, a veritable varietal expression. El Portillo is a unique winery because of its gravity flow irrigation. Gentle handling of the fruit is the main principle that guides level disposition; this architecture, with subtle inclinations, melts into the landscape, gravity flow substitutes juice and wine pumping, and prevents seeds from breaking and generating phenolic bitterness in the wine. This technology also reduces oxidation risk. At El Portillo, technology and tradition merge to insure the highest quality fruit which is used to create world-class wines.

The winery was built using innovative masonry techniques with local stones from the thick sedimentary layers of the mountain valley: materials that harmonize with the landscape. El Portillo is designed to blend harmoniously with the surroundings

WINERY LOCATION
Ruta 89 s/n, Los Árboles, Tunuyán, Mendoza.
Tel.: 54 02622 425544
Fax: 54 02622 429000
Business Address:
Av. Leandro N. Alem 855, 6° Piso, (C1001AAD) Ciudad de Buenos Aires, Argentina
Tel.: 54 11 41311100
Fax: 54 11 41311199
Web Page:
www.bodegaelportillo.com
e-mail:
info@bodegaelportillo.com

OWN VINEYARDS
455 ha in Valle de Uco, Mendoza.
Varieties: Merlot, Malbec, Cabernet Sauvignon, Tempranillo, Syrah, Chardonnay and Sauvignon Blanc.

VAT CAPACITY
5,600,000 liters
Storage Capacity:
2,000,000 bottles
Quality Norms: ISO 9000 and HACCP being implemented.

BRANDS
Domestic Market: Finca El Portillo, Pasos del Portillo and El Portillo Raza.
Foreign Market: Finca El Portillo, La Pampa Estate and Finca San Pablo
Exports to: Europe, United States, Canada, Brazil, Japan, China and Hong Kong.

STAFF
Commercial Manager:
Alejandro Panighini
Agronomist:
Ing. Gustavo Soto

Visits: Monday through Sunday, 10 a.m. to 4 p.m, with previous reservation.
Gift Shop: Yes.

FINCA EL PORTILLO MALBEC 2004

Fairly vivid color, violet notes and good black, similar to the color of blackberries. Pleasant texture, soft, good tannins. A balanced wine, for instant pleasure (not to be stored).

FINCA EL PORTILLO MERLOT 2004

Neat color, not very deep. Good nose, fruity and floral, somewhat toasted. Simple and balanced; pleasant texture. With still very young tannins.

FINCA EL PORTILLO SAUVIGNON BLANC 2004

Pretty pale yellow. Good floral nose. Elegant, simple, refreshing, not complex, but agreeable.

ENRIQUE FOSTER

Enrique Foster.

WINERY HISTORY

In the 90's, an American born in Spain, planted Primitivo and Cannonnau in his native land of Mallorca, in hopes of producing a wine similar to Zinfandel, his favorite then. In 2001, he tasted Argentine Malbec for the first time. This led him to Mendoza, where he bought a vineyard planted in 1919, in Luján de Cuyo. The winery was built there to produce only Malbec wines from grapevines that were old enough to guarantee the quality of future wines, using modern technology and the latest oenological methods and respecting the gravitational concept throughout the process.

Equipped with the latest technological developments, with a bridge crane and a winch especially designed for the purpose, the winery has a 260,000 liter capacity in stainless steel tanks and 90,000 liters in oak barrels. In addition a 6,000 m3 cellar was built 7 meters underground, which allows storage of up to 1,000 casks and 300,000 bottles. Thus, in 2002 this company, unique in the country and created for the sole purpose of producing exclusively high quality Malbec wines, was born in homage to the Argentina's signature variety.

WINERY LOCATION
San Martín 5039, Luján de Cuyo, Mendoza. Tel.: 54 261 4961579 Fax: 54 261 4961240.
Business Address:
San Martín 5039, Luján de Cuyo, Mendoza. Tel.: 54 261 4961579. Fax: 54 261 4961240.
Web Page:
www.bodegafoster.com
e-mail:
contact@bodegafoster.com

VINEYARDS
Mayor Drummond, Luján de Cuyo, Mendoza.
Varieties: 12 ha Malbec
Third party vineyards:
Las Compuertas, Luján de Cuyo, Mendoza.
Varieties: 7 ha Malbec.

VAT CAPACITY
260,000 liters in stainless steel tanks and 90,000 liters in oak barrels.
Storage capacity:
300,000 bottles.
Quality Norms: GMP (in process of certification).

BRANDS
Domestic and Foreign Markets:
Ique, Enrique Foster Reserva, Enrique Foster Limted Edition.
Exports to: United States, Germany, England, Brazil, Peru, Colombia, Switzerland, Mexico, Austria, Canada, Puerto Rico and El Salvador.

STAFF
Oenologist and General Manager:
Mauricio Lorca
Marketing and Sales:
Julián Gómez
Administration:
Jorge Macchiavello
Public Relations:
Verónica Vázquez

ENRIQUE FOSTER
EDICIÓN LIMITADA
MALBEC 2002

Medium intense color, bright, fairly sustained. Aromas are fine, discreet with notes of fruit and good wood. Notable for its elegance. A good wine

ENRIQUE FOSTER
RESERVA MALBEC
2003

Very good color, fairly intense. Nose of fruit, hints of leather, wood that stand out a bit and lightly pass through the wine. Nevertheless, the combination shows good complexity. It has good density in the mouth.

ERAL BRAVO

Matías Sánchez Nieto.

WINERY HISTORY

Eral Bravo is a new wine growing endeavor by the Sanchez Nieto family. They have been connected with the production of top quality wines for over 30 years since Don Nicanor Nieto founded the Nieto Senetiner Winery, one of the most prestigious in Argentina.

Eral Bravo has a clear objective: produce top quality wine in limited amounts, in an effort to express intense sensorial richness. The winery does this by using grapes from their vineyards in the privileged areas of Agrelo, Luján de Cuyo and Eugenio Bustos, San Carlos, in Mendoza.

The name Eral Bravo was inspired by another family tradition: raising bulls in the Salamanca region of Spain. There a bull between two and three years old is called "Eral". At that age, the bull begins to show its essential charactristic: bravery.

The traits looked for in raising courageous bulls, very much respected in this noble and elegant animal, coincide with the concept identifying the Sanchez Nieto Family wines.

WINERY LOCATION
Calle Pública s/n, Agrelo, Mendoza.
Business Address: Primitivo de la Reta 1010, 3rd fl. "B", Mendoza City (5500)
Tel/Fax.: 54 261 429 6864
Web Page: www.eralbravo.com
e-mail: info@eral bravo.com

VINEYARDS
In Agrelo, Luján de Cuyo, Mendoza; 48 ha. In Eugenio Bustos, San Carlos, Uco Valley, 24 ha.
Varieties: In Agrelo: Malbec, Cabernet Sauvignon, Syrah, Pinot Noir, and Chardonnay.
In Eugenio Bustos: Malbec, Cabernet Sauvignon, Sauvignon Blanc and Viognier.

VAT CAPACITY
65,000 liters
Storage capacity: 80,000 bottles

BRANDS
Domestic Market: Eral Bravo and Urano
Foreign Market: Eral Bravo and Urano
Exports to: Holland, Colombia, United States and Brazil

STAFF
General Director:
Matias Sanchez Nieto
Administrative and Financial Director: Luis Danti
Oenologist: Luis Barraud

URANO CABERNET SAUVIGNON 2003

Attractive color, fairly deep. Nose has a bit of bruised fruit. There are notes of ripe fruit and also vegetables, a bit shredded. The middle of the mouth is fairly full and round. Finish is tannic and powerful.

URANO MALBEC 2003

Rather intense color. Aroma with touches of algae and notes of the sea. The tannins are still a bit dry. The wine has good potential, but needs time in the bottle to harmonize better.

ESCORIHUELA GASCÓN

Lic. Gustavo Marín, oenologist.

WINERY HISTORY

Escorihuela Gascón, founded in 1884 by Don Miguel Escorihuela Gascón is one of the oldest and most traditional wineries in Mendoza. Only three kilometers from Mendoza City, in Godoy Cruz Department, it is an obligatory place to visit for tourists and wine lovers.

In 1910, when the May Revolution's first centennial was celebrated, Don Miguel ordered from France a 63,000 liter barrel carved entirely in Nancy oak, whose central image represents Dionysius. The spectacular work is considered one of the most important viniculture relics in Argentina. In 1992 a group of shareholders headed by Dr. Nicolás Catena Zapata, bought the enterprise and introduced important technological changes but did not interfere with Escorihuela tradition and architecture.

Guided visits always close with a tasting of excellent varietal and generic wines.

Inside Escorihuela is the 1884 Restaurant, owned by prestigious international chef Francis Mallmann. In 1997 Escorihuela began producing the Escorihuela Gascón line and a Premium, Miguel Escorihuela Gascón.

WINERY LOCATION
Belgrano 1188, Godoy Cruz, Mendoza. Tel.: 54 261 4242282
Fax: 54 261 4242857
Business Address: Rivadavia 413, Piso 7. (C1002AAC), Buenos Aires. Tel.: 54 11 52385050
Web Page: www.escorihuela.com
e-mail: fpriori@escorihuela.com.ar

VINEYARDS
At Agrelo, Luján de Cuyo, at 950 meters altitude. And at La Consulta, San Carlos, at 1,000 meters.
Varieties: Malbec, Cabernet Sauvignon, Merlot, Syrah, Sangiovese, Barbera, Chardonnay, Viognier, Sauvignon Blanc and Semillón.
Third party vineyards: Malbec at La Consulta (San Carlos) and at Las Compuertas (Luján de Cuyo).

VAT CAPACITY
8.5 million liters, 800,000 in stainless steel tanks.
Storage capacity: 1,300,000 bottles.
Quality Norms: Administrative registration of winery tasks.

BRANDS
Domestic Market: Escorihuela Gascón, Familia Gascón, 1884, Carcassonne, Pont L'eveque and Pinar del Río.
Foreign Market: High Altitude, Don Miguel Gascón, Candela and Sol Amante.
Exports to: United States, Europe and Latin America.

STAFF
Director: Ricardo G. Villanueva
Agronomist: Ing. Gonzalo Videla
Administration: Fanny Priori, Miriam Flores and Jorge Bonello.
Tourism: Cristina G. Villanueva and Sabrina Facchin.
Exports: Alfredo Matilla and José Saravia.
Laboratory: Gabriela Orozco
Oenologist: Lic. Gustavo Marín

Visits: Monday to Friday. Bilingual. By previous appointment. tour&events@escorihuela.com
Gift Shop: Yes.

ESCORIHUELA GASCÓN SANGIOVESE 2003

Suggestive color. Pleasant aromas, although wood is very present. It could have a more fruity expression. Elegant, fine, agreeable to drink. A pleasurable wine to drink almost daily, enjoyable, fairly balanced.

ESCORIHUELA GASCÓN SYRAH 2003

Deep color. Good aromas with noticeable smoked notes that dominate the red fruit aromas a little. Balanced, silky middle of the mouth and smooth. Ripe tannins, good finish. a young wine that deserves to age for some time. Elegant with lots of finesse.

ESCORIHUELA GASCÓN CABERNET SAUVIGNON 2003

Sustained and intense color. Lots of red fruit with vanilla and good aromatic complexity. Interesting aromatic flow with good middle of the mouth, balanced, powerful tannins still too noticeable, but fine. With time, it will be a wine that has very good expression and great finesse.

ESTEPA

Michael Lean Cole and María Teresa Prieto.

WINERY HISTORY

Bodegas y Viñedos Estepa is a young company that produces high range Patagonian wines in small amounts.

The area has a number of favorable conditions: excellent vineyards that have grown there for over 45 years: the soil of torrential origin, adequately stony, the dry climate with a wide range of termperatures and the Estepa inhabitants, who give a craftman's touch to all their products.

The winery, located in the heart of the Alto Valle, north of the Río Negro, is small, has been recycled and has lined concrete vats and stainless steel tanks. The "La Antigua" estate with a 45 hectare vineyard is close to the winery, and the vines grow on the traditional low trellis. "La Agreste", with 8 hectare being cultivated, is quite an original under staking, lying outside the valley, on the bank of the Río Negro, in a desert-line area. There our vines grow among with the native vegetation.

WINERY LOCATION
Ruta 22, km 1208, Fernández Oro, Río Negro.
Business Address:
Colón 60, (8300) Neuquén.
Web Page: www.bodegasestepa.com
e-mail: info@bodegasestepa.com

VINEYARDS
Finca La Antigua: Contraalmirante M. Guerrico, Río Negro, 45 ha.
Varieties: Malbec, Merlot, Cabernet Sauvignon, Pinot Noir, Torrontés, Trousseau and Semillón.
Finca La Agreste, located in semidesertic zone, on the southern bank of the Río Negro, 15 km from Cipolletti. 8 ha.
Varieties: Malbec, Merlot and Cabernet Sauvignon.

VAT CAPACITY
600,000 liters.
Storage capacity: 300,000 bottles.
Quality Norms: HACCP, in process.

BRANDS
Domestic and Foreign Markets:
Estepa Línea Clásica
2 Trivarietals: Malbec-Merlot-Syrah and Torrontés-Semillón-Trousseau
Estepa Línea Tierras
3 Varietals: Malbec, Merlot and Trousseau.
Estepa Línea Mística
2 Varietals matured in barrels:
Malbec and Merlot.
Exports to: United States, United Kingdom, France, Holland, Greece and Brazil.

STAFF
Public Relations: Michael Lean Cole
Domestic Commerce: Juan Álvarez
Foreign Commerce:
María Teresa Prieto
Consultant Oenologist:
Juan Carlos Rodríguez Villa
Resident Oenologist:
Alfredo Nieto

ESTEPA MÍSTICA MERLOT 2002

Color is fairly consistent with notes of evolution. Fruit shows wood. Good texture and structure, with tannins of good quality.

ESTEPA MÍSTICA MALBEC 2002

Fairly floral, with good fruit, very fresh. Density is correct, tannins need to mature. Quite characteristic of its variety. A very good Malbec.

ETCHART

Víctor Marcantoni.

WINERY HISTORY

The first Torrontés vines were planted in 1850 at La Florida estate in Cafayate, Salta. These vineyards, located at the foot of the Cafayate Valley, are one of the highest in the world. When Arnaldo B. Etchart bought the estate in 1938, he lent the strength and stimulus of his character to the operations and started the development of wine growing in the area. In just a few years, he added other varieties like Cabernet Sauvignon, Chardonnay, Malbec and Merlot. Today the establishment has 300 hectares.

In 1975, the winery also settled in the main wine growing area of the country: Mendoza. After five years of working together, Etchart handed its great legacy over to the French group Pernod Ricard in 1996.

The combination of technology and tradition produced an innovative company that invests in vineyards, trains technicians, receives advice from world famous specialists and endeavors for excellence in the quality of its wines, with the intention of conquering new markets.

WINERY LOCATION

National Route 40 s/n, km 1047, (4427) Cafayate, Salta.
Tel: 54 3868 421 310
Business Address: Ave. Fondo de la Legua 936, 2nd fl., B1640EDO, Martínez, Buenos Aires province.
Tel: 54 11 5169 8000
Web Page: www.vinosetchart.com
e-mail: sacbuenosaires@pernod-ricard-argentina.com

VINEYARDS

300 hectares, Cafayate (Salta)
6 hectares, Luján de Cuyo (Mendoza)
65 hectares, La Consulta (Mendoza).
Varieties: Malbec, Cabernet Sauvignon, Merlot, Tannat, Syrah, Bonarda, Caladoc, Petit Verdot, Tempranillo, Torrontés, Chardonnay, Sauvignon Blanc, Chenin and Viognier

VAT CAPACITY

Cafayate: 11 million liters
Mendoza: 4.5 million liters
Storage Capacity:
Cafayate: 150,000 bottles
Mendoza: 600, 000 bottles
Quality Norms: GMP and HACCP

BRANDS

Domestic Market: Etchart Privado, Etchart Cafayate, C. Rosa, Etchart International Line, Arnaldo B. and Etchart Torrontés Tardío.
Foreign Market: Rio de Plata, Etchart Privado, Arnaldo B.and C. Rosa
Exports to: Over 35 countries: Latin America, Holland, Canada, United States, United Kingdom and Germany.

STAFF

Winery Director and Chief Winemaker: Victor Marcantoni
Second Oenologists: Juan Carlos Mosca and Daniel Goméz
Agronomist: Ing. Mariano Bustos
Agronomist (Salta):
Ing. Ramiro Barbosa

Visits: In Cafayate: Mondays to Fridays, 9 a.m. to 5 p.m. Saturdays, 9 a.m. to 1 p.m. Consult in vacation periods.
Gift Shop: Yes.

ETCHART PRIVADO TORRONTÉS 2004

Moscatel notes and very aromatic herbs. Refreshing, good acidity. A true Torrontés.

ETCHART PRIVADO CABERNET SAUVIGNON 2004

Frank color, not very intense. Nose of flowers and spices, smoked notes. Medium structure. Wine with character that will gain charm with time.

ARNALDO B. 1999

Lots of red fruit, not very complex with good grape maturity. An elegant wine. Silky tannins, rather good quality. Medium persistence. A pleasurable wine.

FABRE ⚜ MONTMAYOU

Hervé and Diane Joyaux.

WINERY HISTORY

Located in Vistalba, Luján de Cuyo, Fabre Montmayou welcomes visitors with the special charm of their gardens and cool galleries anticipating an artisan winery, producer of quality wines.

The permanent presence of its owners, Hervé and Diane, can be seen in every detail of this establishment.

Together with their professional teams, they attain that each wine shows a well defined personality. This style is undoubtedly the fruit of their passion for the art and craft of top quality wines, and their respect for the singular expression of the terroir.

WINERY LOCATION
Roque Saenz Peña s/n, CP (5507)
Vistalba, Luján de Cuyo, Mendoza.
Tel: 54 261 4982330
Fax 54 261 4982511
Business Address:
Roque Saenz Peña s/n, CP (5507)
Vistalba, Luján de Cuyo, Mendoza.
Tel: 54 261 4982330
Fax: 54 261 4982511
Web Page:
e-mail:
export@bodegasdomvistalba.com.ar

VINEYARDS
Vistalba and Las Compuertas (Luján de Cuyo): 30 ha for Malbec; 5 ha for Merlot; 20 ha for Cabernet Sauvignon and 25 ha for Chardonnay.

VAT CAPACITY
1,000,000 liters
Storage capacity:
250,000 bottles.

BRANDS
Domestic and Foreign Market:
Fabre Montmayou, Phebus, Trilogie.
Exports to: 25 countries.

STAFF
President: Hervé Joyaux Fabre
Exportation Manager:
Diane Joyaux
Oenologist: Matías Riccitelli
Public Relations:
Verónica Riccitelli

Visits: Monday to Friday from 3 p.m. to 6 p.m. Saturday from 10 a.m. to 1p.m. By previous appointment. Tel. 54 261 4982330.
Gift Shop: Yes.

FABRE MONTMAYOU GRAN RESERVA MALBEC 2003

An impressively dense Malbec, purple reflections reveal a sumptuous bouquet of smoke, graphite, blackberries, cassis, licorice and lavender. Great body, a touch of toasted sweet wood exceptional concentration, purity and definition. A wine at its best for a decade

FABRE MONTMAYOU GRAND VIN 2002

Intense black. Black fruit nose with strong notes of smoked wood that do not overpower the wine. Well balanced, dense and firm tannins. Powerful wine with very good concentration and long finish. Should age very well.

FAMILIA ALTO VERDE

Rodolfo and Carla Nale.

WINERY HISTORY

Familia Alto Verde is headed by Dr. Rodolfo Nale. The winery started in 1988 with the aim of producing San Juan regional products, with high extra value and international quality.

In 1993 the Nale family decided to use organic norms in their vineyard and wine elaboration processes. This initiative was in response to the requirements of developed countries to consume pollution free healthy products.

Since then, the winery philosophy has been to produce within a system sustainable over time and by rational management of natural resources, with the latest technology and efficiency of all those involved in the project.

This vision allows us to achieve excellent wines recognized in all the countries where they are sold.

WINERY LOCATION
Ruta 40, between 13 and 14 streets, Pocito - San Juan. CP (5427).
Tel./Fax: 54 264 421 2683
Business Address: Catamarca 202 Norte, Ciudad, San Juan (5400).
Tel./Fax: 54 264 421 2683
Web Page:
www.familiaaltoverde.com
e-mail: altoverde@amet.com.ar

VINEYARDS
Finca La Urpila (Caucete): Malbec, Chardonnay, Finca Cepas (Sarmiento-Media Agua): Syrah, Chardonnay, Cabernet Sauvignon and Pedro Ximénez. Finca Buenas Ondas (Rawson): Chardonnay and Malbec.

VAT CAPACITY
2,200,000 liters
Storage capacity: 100,000 bottles
Quality Norms: Argentine organic quality norms (Law N° 25.127), equivalent to European norms and U.S.A. Organic National Program. Argencert.

BRANDS
Domestic Market: Nuestra Esencia, Montgaillard and Cheval de Marly (Sparkling).
Foreign Market: Buenas Ondas, Nuestra Esencia, Touchstone and Ecológica.
Exports to: Sweden, England, United States, Canada, Ireland and Germany.

STAFF
President: Dr. Rodolfo Nale
Vice President: Susana Fiorello
General Manager: Carla Nale
First Oenologist: Lic. Rafael Pérez
External Consultants: Cellar · World International by Angela Muir.
Oenology Director:
Lic. Duncan Killer

Visits: Monday to Friday from 9 a.m. to 8 p.m. Saturday from 9 a.m. to 1 p.m. By previous appointment.
Gift Shop: Yes. Wine bar and tasting room.

BUENAS ONDAS
SYRAH ROSÉ
2004

Fairly oily. Kind in the mouth. Fresh and easy to drink.

BUENAS ONDAS
SYRAH 2004

Medium intense color. Nose not too intense with hints of spice and a touch of vegetable. Straightforward wine, balanced and pleasant.

FAMILIA BARBERIS

Humberto Arnaldo, Walter Fabián, Humberto Adrián, and Mauricio Javier Barberis.

WINERY HISTORY

With the purchase of the first vineyards in 1965, Don Humberto Barberis accomplished an old family dream: building a winery capable of making top quality wines.

The experience acquired through long years devoted to the growth and care of its grapevines led him in 1989 to buy Vistalba winery, a very important step toward the elaboration of quality wines.

During the following years, the wine produced was sold to other establishments, which recognized its virtues. This gave birth to the idea of participating in various international competitions, where they received several important prizes.

Nowadays, with the active participation of Don Humberto's children, Adrián, Walter, Liliana and Mauricio, the family tradition is gaining new impulse, shown in the winery modernization and the national and international marketing of wines bearing their trademark.

WINERY LOCATION
Roque Sáenz Peña 5516, Vistalba, Luján de Cuyo, Mendoza
Telephones: 54 261
4983311/4981951
Business Address:
Roque Sáenz Peña 5516, Vistalba, Luján de Cuyo, Mendoza, Argentina
Telephones: 54 261
4983311/4981951
Web Page:
www.familiabarberis.com
e-mail:
mendoza@familiabarberis.com

VINEYARDS
At Vistalba (Luján de Cuyo), Maipú and San Martín, Mendoza.
Varieties: Malbec, Cabernet Sauvignon, Chardonnay, Tempranillo, Syrah.
Third party vineyards:
At Tupungato, Agrelo and Vistalba (Luján de Cuyo) and San Martín., Mendoza.
Varieties: Merlot, Malbec, Cabernet Sauvignon, Tempranillo and Sauvignon Blanc.

VAT CAPACITY
5,000,000 liters.
Storage capacity:
300,000 bottles.

BRANDS
Domestic Market: Familia Barberis, Talento, Humberto Barberis, Blasón del Valle, Cava Negra and Primera Cava.
Foreign Market: Familia Barberis, Talento, Humberto Barberis, Blasón del Valle, Finca La Daniela, Cava Negra and Antigua Cava.
Exports to: U.S.A., Japan, England, Russia, Spain, Canada, Germany, Belgium, Panama and Brazil.

STAFF
President: Humberto Barberis
Vicepresident: Adrán Barberis
Directors: Liliana Barberis, Walter Barberis and Mauricio Barberis
Oenologists: Rolando Lazzarotti and Mónica Calderón.

Visits: By appointment. The winery has a restaurant, "Cuba 131", reservations necessary.
Gift shop: Yes.

BLASON DEL VALLE CHARDONNAY 2004

Pale yellow. Green fruit nose. Great deal of acidity, somewhat lineal, balanced and very refreshing.

TALENTO MALBEC 1999

Ruby red with cigar and dried flower scents. Mild, not very heavy, easy to drink. Intense finish.

FAMILIA BARBERIS MALBEC 1999

Red with hints of violet. It is an elegant wine, very fine and medium concentration. Good expression of Malbec; the wine is correct.

FAMILIA CASSONE

Cassone family.

WINERY HISTORY

The Cassone Family settled in Argentina in the 19th Century, when Celestino Cassone, born in the Italian Piedmont, arrived. Today they own vineyards that have grown here for more than 90 years. In 1998, the family decided to restart viticulture activities building a small winery that preserved the simplicity of the production and development of quality wine with fruit grown in their own vineyards, according to traditional methods.

Familia Cassone keeps its original spirit unaltered, and applies all their resources to the production of wines, mainly Malbec, with a personality and character of its own. Their basic aim is the international market and they seek to satisfy wine lovers' senses with the stamp of Argentine wines.

Working with special care aided by the necessary technology, they produce -with grapes from their own vineyards- naturally balanced wines. This allows them to maintain the desired quality and ensure the continuity of the product. The winery permanently seeks to establish fluid communication, dynamic and personalized with its customers.

WINERY LOCATION
Terrada y Anchorena, Mayor Drummond, Luján de Cuyo, Mendoza.
Business Address: Mitre 1367, Ciudad, Mendoza, (5500).
Tel./Fax: 54 261 4233203.
Web Page:
www.familiacassone.com.ar
e-mail: bodegacassone@familiacassone.com.ar

VINEYARDS
14 ha in Mayor Drummond, Luján de Cuyo. 15 ha in Lunlunta, Maipú and 45 ha In Agrelo, Luján de Cuyo, Mendoza
Varieties: Malbec, Cabernet Sauvignon, Chardonnay, Merlot and Chenin Blanc.

VAT CAPACITY
350,000 liters in stainless steel tanks, French and American oak casks.
Storage Capacity:
200,000 bottles
Quality Norms:
HACCP and ISO9001 (certifying).

BRANDS
Domestic and Foreign Markets:
Obra Prima, Finca La Florencia and Madrigal
Foreign Market: Familia Cassone (for United States)
Exports to: United States, England, Belgium, Holland, Denmark, Ireland, Mexico and Brazil.

STAFF
President:
Eduardo Cassone
Production Management:
Martín Cassone
Foreign Commerce and Domestic Market Management:
Florencia Morales de Cassone and Martín Cassone
Oenologist: Fabián Giardino.

Visits:
By previous appointment.
Gift Shop: No.

OBRA PRIMA ROSADO DE CABERNET SAUVIGNON 2004

Fairly good, fruity, excellent texture with a good finish. A Rosé with persistence and very pleasant aromas.

FINCA LA FLORENCIA CABERNET SAUVIGNON 2002

Nice color, not too intense but with good brilliance. Fruit notes with a few vegetables. An elegant wine. Pleasant; will gain more charm with a little bit more of roundness and strength.

OBRA PRIMA MALBEC 2002

Color not very intense; somewhat developed, but fairly interesting Memories of ripe fruit and floral notes on the nose. Middle of the mouth is medium. Tannins are present and at finish are still a little firm.

FAMILIA GIMENEZ RIILI

Pablo, Juan Manuel and Federico Gimenez Riili.

WINERY HISTORY

Don Pedro Gimenez started this endeavor in Mendoza around 1940 and transmitted his love of wine to his heirs.

About a decade ago, Eduardo Gimenez and Susana Riili, together with their children, decided to change the winery's production profile from large volumes to a limited number of high quality varietals. The phillosophy supporting the family business is producing excellent wines in a modern style, keeping the freshness of the fruit.

The grapes that give origin to Gimenez Riili wines come mostly from the family grapevines in Maipú, Mendoza. This estate is 800 meters. above sea level and the average rainfall 200 mm a year with a wide range of temperatures. Grapes ripen slowly and uniformly, yielding intense and well defined fruity aromas. The harvest is done by hand in small 12 kg. boxes. Then the clusters are selected so the raw material is top quality. Then they are sent into vats by gravity, without using pumps, beginning a lengthy fermentation and maceration (20 to 40 days), which gives complexity and color to the excellent finished products.

WINERY LOCATION
Avda. de Acceso Este, Km 1.027, Maipú, Mendoza.
Business Address: Serú 270, Barrio Bombal, Mendoza City (5500).
Tel / Fax: 54 261 4245973 / 4242147
Web Page:
www.gimenezriili.com.ar
e-mail: info@gimenezriili.com.ar

VINEYARDS
Acceso Este km. 1027, Maipú, Mendoza. 10 ha.
Varieties: Malbec and Merlot.
Third party vineyards:
At Maipú, Mendoza: 15 ha.
Varieties: Cabernet Sauvignon.

VAT CAPACITY
160,000 liters.
Storage capacity:
100,000 bottles.

BRANDS
Domestic Market: Perpetuum and Terramedia.
Foreign Market: Gimenez Riili, Perpetuum and Terramedia.
Exports to: United States, Mexico, Paraguay, Brazil, African countries and United Kingdom.

STAFF
General Management:
Eduardo Gimenez
Foreign Commerce Management:
Federico Gimenez Riili
Marketing Management:
Juan Manuel Gimenez Riili
Oenologist: Lic. Norberto Moreno

Visits: Serú 270, Ciudad, Mendoza. Monday to Friday, from 9 a.m. to 1 p.m. and from 5 p.m. to 8 p.m. Saturday from 10a.m. to 1 p.m.
Gift Shop: Yes. Serú 270, Mendoza City.

PERPETUUM
TORRONTÉS
2004

Fairly discreet on the aromatic level, but with great finesse and good freshness in the mouth.

PERPETUUM
MERLOT
2003

Evolved color, not very strong, orangey notes. The wine is fairly smooth, with spice aromas, and also hay and dry herbs. Easy to drink.

FAMILIA MARGUERY

Guillermo Donnerstag.

WINERY HISTORY

As direct descendants of Arturo and Eduardo Marguery, we founded Familia Marguery Casa Vinícola in 2000. Under the inspiration of the fruitfulness of their lives, we began in the project, and with the support of our talented oenology advisors, we started making our wines. Familia Marguery produces its wines at Cruz de Piedra, Maipú, Mendoza. We are committed to top quality wine production, in limited quantities by using the latest technology. Our grapes come from selected aged vineyards at Vistalba, Tupungato, La Consulta and Tunuyán. This geographic diversity gives us the chance to use the particular characteristics from each area. We want wines with good concentration, complex, elegant and lively, and we work towards this at the vineyard. We believe in the loyalty our ancestors instilled in us and understand this project as a combination of loyalties to them, to the land, to those who till it and all those who share a bottle with us, our friends.

WINERY LOCATION
Callejón Zapata s/n, Cruz de Piedra, Maipú, Mendoza
Business Address:
Olascoaga 1219 1 Piso Of. 4., Mendoza. Tel. 54 261 425-4837
Web Page:
www.marguerywines.com
e-mail:
info@marguerywines.com

VINEYARDS
4 hectares at Villa Seca, Tunuyán, Mendoza.
Varieties: Malbec
Outside Suppliers:
At Vistalba, La Consulta and Tupungato.
Varieties: Malbec and Cabernet Sauvignon.

VAT CAPACITY
40,000 liters.

BRANDS
Domestic Market: Familia Marguery and Casa Marguery
Foreign Market: Familia Marguery and Casa Marguery
Exports to: England, Germany, Brazil, Colombia and USA.

STAFF
Partners: Alejandro Margery, María Enriqueta Marquez and Guillermo Donnerstag.
Oenologists: Ing. Pedro F. Rosell and Ing. Cristián Allamand.

Visits: We do not receive visitors for the moment.

FAMILIA MARGUERY MALBEC 2000

Medium intense color with somewhat orangey notes, but bright and fairly pleasant. Nose is a little floral, also with fruit and faint hints of wood. Texture is medium. A classic good level wine.

FAMILIA MAYOL

A view of the winery.

WINERY HISTORY

The owners are in charge of everything from managing the vineyard, making the wine, to dealing with customers, everything is part of a father and son management team.

Regular quality grape suppliers to large firms (they own more than 80 hectares vineyards in the main producing areas in Mendoza: Tupungato, Luján de Cuyo and Vistalba), three years ago they decided to begin a winery of their own. The winery has positioned itself abroad with a diverse and exclusive varietal offer.

The endeavor bears the personal seal of Pedro Mayol, a professional architect profoundly passionate about viticulture, has given new impetus to the family's legacy, a life long connection with grapes.

The facilities have 25 stainless steel tanks and a room for 400 barrels. Pedro and his son, Matías, keep their objective clearly in mind: a winery that can produce a maximum of 144,000 bottles a year with 80% of the production for exportation.

WINERY LOCATION
Ruta Provincial 89, Tupungato, Mendoza.
Business Address: Necochea 183, piso 1, Tel. 54 261 4499920
Fax: 54 261 4499917
Web Page: www.familiamayol.com
e-mail: info@familiamayol.com

VINEYARDS
80 ha at Luján de Cuyo, Tupungato and Vista Flores.
Varieties: Chardonnay, Bonarda, Pinot Noir, Malbec, Tempranillo, Syrah and Cabernet Sauvignon.

VAT CAPACITY
150,000 liters.
Storage capacity:
100,000 bottles.

BRANDS
Domestic Market: Familia Mayol and Mayol IV.
Foreign Market: Familia Mayol, Kaleido and Mayol IV.
Exports to: United States, Germany, Brazil and Norway.

STAFF
Project Director and Winemaker: Matías Mayol
Winemaker Consultant:
Steve Clifton

Visits: only by previous appointment by phone 54 261 4499920 / 154 189 911.

MAYOL SYRAH 2002

Interesting color, fairly intense. Good ripe fruit, not very concentrated. Balanced wine, not very dense, but with finesse and a long finish.

MAYOL MALBEC 2003

Medium intense color, frank. Good nose of fruit with a hint of flowers. Elegant wine, not very dense, harmonious with smooth tannins.

MAYOL IV 2002

Pleasant color, fairly intense. Nose of ripe fruit, ample volume. Good texture, good density with mature tannins.

FAMILIA SCHROEDER

Dr. Herman Heinz Schroeder and Graciela Demo de Schroeder.

WINERY HISTORY

Of European origin and with deep Patagonian roots, the Schroeder family decided in 2001 to devote themselves to viticulture. Their activity began in San Patricio del Chañar with 120 hectares of meticulously cared for vineyards. In Neuquén, this soil is ideal for producing top quality wines: stony soil, deep and of medium thick texture, relatively low humidity, a wide range of temperatures and irrigated by melt water. Here Malbec, Pinot Noir, Merlot and Cabernet Sauvignon, Chardonnay and Sauvignon Blanc grow.

In 2002, while building the winery, some fossils of a millennial dinosaur were found. This inspired the name "Saurus", which identifies two of the wine lines. The winery is recognized for its functionality and architectural beauty: it was built on five levels, each assigned to a stage of wine production, utilizing gravity as a quality principle.

The Schroeder Family applies their vast experience in successful endeavors known for excellence and innovation to their ambitious project.

WINERY LOCATION

Calle N° 7 Norte, (8305) San Patricio del Chañar, Neuquén.
Tel.: 54 9 299 5086767
Fax: 54 9 299 5880359
Business Address:
Calle N° 7 Norte - (8305) San Patricio del Chañar, Neuquén, Argentina.
Tel.: 54 9 299 5086767
Fax: 54 9 299 5880359
Web Page:
www.familiaschroeder.com
e-mail: info@familiaschroeder.com

VINEYARDS

120 ha at San Patricio del Chañar, Neuquén.
Varieties: Malbec, Pinot Noir, Merlot, Cabernet Sauvignon, Chardonnay and Sauvignon Blanc.

VAT CAPACITY

2 million liters in stainless steel tanks and 180,000 in oak barrels.
Storage capacity: 350,000 bottles
Quality Norms: In certification process of BPA, HACCP, ISO 9001:2000 at the estate and in BPM, HACCP and ISO 9001:2000 in the winery.

BRANDS

Domestic Market: Saurus, Familia Schroeder, Saurus Patagonia Select.
Foreign Market: Saurus, Familia Schroeder, Saurus Patagonia Select.
Exports to: United Kingdom, Germany, Hungary, United States, Canada, Mexico and Brazil.

STAFF

Director: Roberto Schroeder
Oenologist: Leonardo Puppato
Oenological adviser: Juan Carlos Rodríguez Villa
Agronomist: Rodolfo Perinetti
Commercial Department: Sebastián Pizarro

Visits: Everyday, by previous reservation by phone or e-mail to: info@familiaschroeder.com
Restaurant at the winery
Gift Shop: Yes.

SAURUS PATAGONIA SELECT MERLOT 2003

Fruity and vegetable at the same time, fresh. Good fruit. Is fairly elegant, has a long finish and ends with powerful tannins. It is a good wine that will improve its expression with time.

SAURUS PATAGONIA SELECT MALBEC 2003

Intense color, fairly deep. Good fruit. The wood dominates a little with very noticeable vanilla notes that give firm tannins at the finish. The middle of the mouth is correct. A fairly balanced wine.

SAURUS PATAGONIA SELECT PINOT NOIR 2003

Attractive color. On the nose, one can appreciate pleasant fruit and good maturity of the grape. Elegant and powerful wine. Rather harmonious. this Pinot Noir has lots of charm. A very well made wine.

FAMILIA ZUCCARDI

Sebastián and José Alberto Zuccardi.

WINERY HISTORY

Familia Zuccardi had its origin as a result of the interest its founder, Engineer Alberto Zuccardi, had in creating an irrigation system that would adapt to the area's characteristics.

In 1963, Zuccardi bought a plot of land in Maipú, Mendoza province, to test the system. His love of viticulture led him to enlarge wineyards and begin building the winery in 1968. At the time the activity focused on the domestic market. Soon they started analyzing the conditions of the world market. As a result, the Zuccardi family decided to make quality wines to be sent abroad, which implied a deep change in the winery's vision and the training of its human resources.

After participating in the principal countries, they began to develop the local market, but only with top quality products. Innovation is valuable and is the way to conceive the search for quality. The development of varietals like Tempranillo or Bonarda, the careful study of over 30 wine varieties and new types like Santa Julia Tardío or the Malamado are examples of this tradition in the search of new ways to enjoy the pleasure of wine.

WINERY LOCATION

Ruta Provincial 33, km 7,5. Maipú, Mendoza. Tel.: 54 261 4410000
Fax: 54 261 4410010
Business Address: at winery.
Web: www.familiazuccardi.com
e-mail: info@familiazuccardi.com

VINEYARDS

Fray Luis Beltrán (Maipú): 170 ha. Santa Rosa: 440 ha.
Varieties: Syrah, Malbec, Cabernet Sauvignon, Merlot, Tempranillo, Bonarda, Chenin Blanc, Sangiovese, Chardonnay, Viognier, Sauvignon Blanc and Torrontés. 53 ha with 35 experimental varieties.

VAT CAPACITY

4,500 barrels and 8 million liters in stainless steel.
Storage capacity: 700,000 bottles
Quality Norms: HACCP. ISO 9001:2000. Certified organic farming: 285 ha. Organic farming in transition 200 ha. Certification Jas Norms (Japan) first Argentine enterprise certified to import organic products to Japan.

BRANDS

Domestic Markets: Zuccardi Zeta, Zuccardi Q, Santa Julia, Vida Orgánica, Finca Beltrán Dúo and Malamado.
Foreigh Market: Zuccardi Zeta, Zucardi Q. Santa Julia, Vida Orgánica and Malamado.
Exports to: England, United States, Holland, Belgium, Brazil, Japan, Switzerland, Scotland, Mexico, Ireland, Finland, Canada, Germany, Norway, Sweden, Taiwan, Denmark, France, the Philippines, Spain, Italy, Singapur, Peru, India, Australia, Panama, Ecuador, Colombia, and others.

STAFF

Director: José Alberto Zuccardi
Domestic Market: Ana Amitrano
Foreign Market: José Asensio
Oenology: Rodolfo Montenegro
Production: Rubén Ruffo
Agriculture Manager: Edgardo Cónsoli
Visits: Monday to Saturday: 9 a.m. to 5.30 p.m. Sunday and holidays: 10 a.m. to 4.30 p.m.
Gift Shop: Yes.

ZUCCARDI Q MALBEC 2002

Intense black color, good concentration. A suggestive wine with good density, freshness and good varietal definition.

ZUCCARDI Q TEMPRANILLO 2002

Black color is intense. Good aromas, toasted, a little coffee and wood are somewhat noticeable. Very good material, elegant with good density and good tannins. the wine is characteristic of its variety with a finish that brings to mind wine from la Rioja, Spain. Very interesting wine, well made.

SANTA JULIA RESERVA CABERNET SAUVIGNON 2002

Attractive color, bright intense ruby. Fruity, fresh with good harmony, smooth. Could have more persistence. A very pleasant wine to drink.

FILIPPO FIGARI

Roberto Losada, Cesar Mengoni and Manuel Gallardo.

WINERY HISTORY

The winery's name has a special meaning for its founder: Filippo Figari was his grandfather who immigrated from Genoa, Italy at the beginning of the last century. The winery was founded in 1937 by Carlos Bertona, who ran it until his death in 1982. The property was abandoned for 15 years until the current owners began renovating the winery and vineyards. Fourteen hectares have been planted with Malbec, Cabernet Sauvignon, Merlot, Pinot Noir, Syrah and Sauvignon Blanc, creating distinct unique wines year after year.

The land is located near the mountains in Mendoza at 980 meters above sea level. It is one of the best and most privileged areas for growing Malbec and Cabernet Sauvignon. It is rocky terrain that has limited yields, but produces top quality grapes.

Located in Luján de Cuyo and Maipu, this area is part of the northern oasis in Mendoza province and receives water from the Mendoza River, whose flow comes from the meltwaters of the Andes mountain range.

WINERY LOCATION

Brandsen 505, Perdriel, Luján de Cuyo, Mendoza. Tel. 54 237 4830761

Business Address: Av. La Plata 249, 7th fl. Off. A, Buenos Aires City

Fax: 54 11 4904 0436

Web Page:
www.filippofigari.com.ar

e-mail: info@filippofigari.com.ar
sales@fillipofigari.com.ar

VINEYARDS

Perdriel, Luján de Cuyo, Mendoza: 17 ha.

Varieties: Malbec, Cabernet Sauvignon, Syrah, Merlot, Sauvignon Blanc and Pinot Noir.

Third party vineyards: Perdriel, Luján de Cuyo, Mendoza (depending on our needs)

VAT CAPACITY

1,400,000 liters

BRANDS

Domestic Market: Anastasia, Filippo Figari (still wines), Filippo & Co. (sparkling).

Foreign Market: Anastasia, Filippo Figari, MJ Galliard, Green Frog, Bullrich, Four Bucks, Forever Tango (still wines), Filippo & Co., Da Rosa (sparkling).

Exports to: United States, Canada, Brazil, Colombia and Hong Kong.

STAFF

President and Oenologist: Cesar Mengoni

Executive Vice President and Commercial Director: Roberto Losada

Visits: From 9 a.m. to 12 noon, and 3 p.m. to 6 p.m.

Gift Shop: Yes.

FILIPPO FIGARI MALBEC 2003

Fairly attractive color and sustained. Nose has aromatic notes that display the character of this variety. Lacks a bit of density. Middle of the mouth is pleasant and tannins are somewhat firm at the finish. Elegance can be found in this wine.

FINCA ALMA

María Alejandra Lozano.

WINERY HISTORY

Finca Alma is the fulfillment of an ecological and commercial view shared by María Alejandra Lozano and Marcelo Manghi early in 1998.

The objective of this enterprise is to offer consumers limited consignments of fine wines, in accord with advanced concepts.

Through their proprietors' international oenology and commercial experience, Finca Alma is committed to producing and selling varietal wines with an excellent price-quality ratio.

WINERY LOCATION

Finca Alma produces in several establishments. The most representative of them is Cavas del Conde, Dorrego s/n, Coquimbito, Maipú, Mendoza. Tel.: 54 261 497 2624.

Business Address:
Coronel Trole 1057, Ituzaingó, (B1714FPU) Buenos Aires.
Tel./Fax: 54 11 4661 2574
Web Page: www.fincaalma.com.ar
e-mail: info@fincaalma.com.ar

THIRD PARTY VINEYARDS:

30 hecatares at Cruz de Piedra (Maipú).
40 hectares at Tunuyán.
Varieties: Chenin Blanc, Malbec, Merlot, Bonarda, Chardonnay and Sauvignon Blanc.

BRANDS
Domestic Market:
Finca Alma, Alhue.
Foreign Market:
Finca Alma, Alhue, Mirlo Heights, Casanovas Vidal.
Exports to: United States, Canada, Korea, Japan, United Kingdom, Czech Republic, Germany, Spain and Peru.

STAFF
Owner and Technical Director:
María Alejandra Lozano
Owner and Commercial Director: Marcelo Manghi

FINCA ALMA ALHUÈ SAUVIGNON BLANC CHARDONNAY 2002

Yellow with green reflections. Aromas of smoke and touches of cassis. Citric fruit. Good character, interesting, balanced, very fresh finish. A pleasurable wine.

FINCA DON DIEGO

Main door of the winery.

WINERY HISTORY

Located on Route 60 in the Fiambalá Valley of Catamarca, Finca Don Diego, belongs to the Centurion family, and produces top quality wines at 1,505 meters above sea level. In the middle of the Andes mountain range, the winery covers 80 hectares planted with the best Syrah, Cabernet Sauvignon, Malbec and Chardonnay grape stock.

Blending in with pre-existing buildings, it is the first Argentine winery to be built completely from the adobe on its own land. These walls, whose foundation has stone from the mountain range, cane roof and wood, house the latest technology to meet current vinification requirements.

With international awards, such as Vinitaly 2003 and 2004, Las Vegas 2003, Prodexpo 2002 (Russia) and at numerous competitions in Argentina and Central America, Don Diego is the winery that has won the most prizes in the region. The company exports to the United States, Brazil, Holland, Colmbia, Costa Rica and in the near future to Paraguay and France. In February 2005, Don Diego obtained the organic certification for all its vineyards from the International Agriculture Organization.

WINERY LOCATION

Avenida de las Americas s/n, Route 60, San Pedro, Fiambala, Catamarca (5345).

Business Address: Sarmiento 1988, 1st fl., (1044) Buenos Aires
Tel.: 54 11 4954 6835
Fax: 54 11 4953 8001
Web Page:
www.fincadondiego.com
e-mail: info@fincadondiego.com

VINEYARDS

Fiambalá, Catamarca, 40 ha.
Varieties: Syrah, Cabernet Sauvignon, Malbec and Chardonnay.

VAT CAPACITY

125,000 liters
Storage capacity: 100,000 in bottles, 100 oak barrels.
Quality Norms: OIA (International Agriculture Organization): Organic Winery, as from February 2005

BRANDS
Domestic and Foreign Markets: Don Diego
Exports to: the United States, Brazil, Holland, Colombia, Costa Rica and in the near future, Paraguay and France.

STAFF

Fifteen people
President: Lic. Elvio E. Centurion
Oenologist: Lic. Edgardo Ibarra
Agronomist: Engineer Marcelo Casazza

Visits: Monday to Friday, 9 a.m. to 11 a.m. Saturday, 5 p.m. to 7 p.m.
Contact: Ruth Reynoso, turismo@fincadondiego.com
Tel. 54 3837 15691512
Gift Shop: Yes

DON DIEGO
SYRAH 2004

Pretty bright, bordeaux red color. Aromas of ripe fruit well integrated with the wood. Good first taste in the mouth with volume and persistence. A good syrah wine.

FINCA FLICHMAN

Ricardo Rebelo.

WINERY HISTORY

This winery dates back to 1873, when the first vineyards and the winery were established in Barrancas, Maipú. In 1910 the winery was reinaugurated by its founders and registered under the family surname. One of the family members, Sami Flichman, was responsible for developing the first grapevines in a hollow produced by the flow of the Mendoza river. In 1926, Sami was succeeded by his son Isaac, whose deep interest in viticulture led him some years later, to study oenology in France. Thus the trademark "Caballero de la Cepa" started in France in 1947.

In 1998, the winery was purchased by the Sogrape group from Portugal, one of the major family wine companies worldwide, internationally recognized for its Mateus wines and its Ferreira, Offley and Sandeman ports.

This was the starting point of a new stage of important investments in vineyards as well as in the winery.

Nowadays, Finca Flichman makes and sells well-known quality wines with an Argentine character and international style capable satisfying consumers the world over.

WINERY LOCATION
Munives 800 (M5517AOA), Barrancas, Maipú, Mendoza.
Tel./Fax: 54 11 4326 7300
Web Page: www.flichman.com.ar
e-mail: marketing@flichman.com.ar

VINEYARDS
276 ha planted, out of a total of 949, at Barrancas and Tupungato.
Varieties: Cabernet Sauvignon, Malbec, Syrah, Merlot and Chardonnay

VAT CAPACITY
1,500 oak barrels.
Storage capacity:
1,500,000 bottles
Quality Norms: GMP, BPA, ISO 9001, HACCP, BRC, IFS, ISO 14000, OSHAS, SGC.

BRANDS
Domestic Market: Dedicado, Pasaje de Barrancas, Paisaje de Tupungato, Caballero de la Cepa, Finca Flichman Varietales, Claire, Jubilé and Aberdeen Angus.
Foreign Market: Delicado, Paisaje de Barrancas, Paisaje de Tupungato, Caballero de la Cepa, Finca Flichman Varietales, Finca Flichman Reserva, Tanguero, Viña de Barrancas, Argenta.
Exports to: United Kingdom, Brazil, Denmark, United States, Germany, Ireland, Canada, Japan, Austria, Belgium, China, Colombia, Spain, Estonia, Finland, France, Netherlands, Peru, Norway, Panama, Portugal, Sweden.

STAFF
General Manager: Ricardo Rebelo
Production Manager:
Juan Evangelista
Marketing and Corporate Communication:
María Inés González
Oenology Manager:
Luis Cabral de Almeida

Visits: From Wednesday to Sunday from 10 a.m. to 1 p.m. and from 2 p.m. to 5 p.m.
Gift Shop: Yes

PAISAJE DE TUPUNGATO 2002

Intense frank color. Lots of fruit, wood and notes of vanilla. Red and black fruit, ripe grape. Good texture, good medium taste, fairly dense, firm tannins typical of a good quality young wine. A very interesting wine.

PAISAJE DE BARRANCAS 2002

Attractive and fairly frank color. Light red fruit aromas. Medium volume and complexity. Tannis show their presence at the end in the mouth. Pleasant, agreeable wine that should show even more presence and charm with time.

DEDICADO 2001

Very strong intense color. Nose is fairly complex with a mixture of red fruit, cedar and well-ripened grape. Density in the mouth is good with volume. Tannins are fairly firm, noticeable and good quality. It is a powerful wine with very good global quality.

FINCA LA ANITA

Antonio and Manuel Mas.

WINERY HISTORY

Only a decade after their initiation in the field, Finca La Anita is already a legend in Argentine vitiiculture.

This small winery is on a 7 hectare estate in Agrelo heights, Luján de Cuyo Department, in the province of Mendoza.

La Anita is a committed undertaking by brothers Manuel and Antonio Mas -both professionals- who installed the spirit of the best European wineries in their winery. They are loyally devoted to grape growing and to producing wines in limited number but in a highly professional manner.

The orthodox production of their wines is still unique. Its fundamental guidelines show in the quality of all their products that are unique, inimitable.

WINERY LOCATION
Calle Cobos s/n, Alto Agrelo, Luján de Cuyo, Mendoza
Tel/Fax: 54 261 490 0255
Business Address:
Av. Del Libertador 260, piso 16, Of. B, (1001) Buenos Aires
Tel.: 54 11 4325 4498
Fax: 54 11 4328 6402
Web Page:
www.fincalaanita.com
e-mail:
info@fincalaanita.com

VINEYARDS
Alto Agrelo, Luján de Cuyo: 70 ha.
Varieties: Syrah, Malbec, Cabernet Sauvignon, Merlot, Tocai Friulano, Semillón, Chardonnay, Petit Verdot and Sauvignon Blanc.

VAT CAPACITY
260,000 liters.

BRANDS
Domestic Market: Finca, Finca La Anita, Luna, Cuarto de Milla.
Foreign Market: Finca, Finca La Anita, Luna, Cuarto de Milla.
Exports to: Spain, United Kingdom, Denmark, Germany, Italy, United States, Uruguay, Brazil, Colombia, Paraguay, Peru.

STAFF
President: Eng. Manuel Mas
Vicepresident, Responsible for Poduction and Oenology:
Ing Antonio Mas
Commercial Manager:
Ing. Fernando Telo

FINCA LA ANITA MALBEC 2002

Pretty color, lots of ripe fruit, pleasant with good intensity. The wood is well integrated, fine and elegant, with good tannins. A wine that is complete finesse, very agreeable, well balanced.

FINCA LA ANITA SYRAH 2002

Pretty color, lots of ripe fruit with notes of somewhat overripe grapes. Oily, very silky in the mouth. Good tannins, somewhat dry at the finish, but with good power and harmony. A wine from the sun with a bit of alcoholic notes. Nice wine.

FINCA LA ANITA TOCAI FRIULANO 2003

Fruity, charming, balanced, fairly delicate and fresh at the same time.

FINCA LA CELIA

Main façade of the winery.

WINERY HISTORY

Finca La Celia is both historic and modern at the same time; a winery that produces top quality elegant wines, with the personality and distinctive character of the Valle de Uco, a terroir traditionally recognized for its climatic qualities. On the basis of the selected genetic material, and careful management of vineyards, we produce wines like the intense Malbec and an alluring Cabernet Franc.

Founded in 1890 by Eugenio Bustos, Finca La Celia was later inherited by his only daughter, Celia Bustos. With a powerful personality and leadership, she worked her land and turned it into renowned vineyards.

Purchased in 2000 by Viña San Pedro SA, the winery was enlarged and remodelled, although keeping its original structure of the 20's and the architectural taste of its first owners. It was also equipped with French and Italian machinery that incorporated the latest technology.

Its excellent facilities, with stainless steel vats and French and American ilex barrels, allow the production of wines today recognized, enjoyed and prized, in Argentina and internationally.

WINERY LOCATION
Av. Circunvalación s/n., CP (5569). Eugenio Bustos, San Carlos, Mendoza.
Tel.: 54 2622 45112
Business Address: Av. España 1340, Ciudad. CP (5500), Mendoza, Argentina.
Tel.: 54 261 4134400
Fax: 54 261 4134422
Web Page: www.fincalacelia.com.ar
e-mail: info@fincalacelia.com.ar

VINEYARDS
611 hectares
Location of vineyards: San Carlos, Valle de Uco, Mendoza.
Varieties: Sauvignon Blanc, Chardonnay, Pinot Grigio, Merlot, Malbec, Syrah, Cabernet Franc, Pinot Noir and Cabernet Sauvignon.

VAT CAPACITY
Total 6,600,000 tons.
French and American oak barrels: 2,600.
Storage capacity: 500,000 bottles.
Quality Norms: BMP, HACCP, ISO 14.001, certified by BVQI.

BRANDS
Domestic Market: La Celia Reserva, La Consulta.
Foreign Market: La Celia Reserva, La Consulta, Furia and Angaro.
Exports to: Brazil, Canada, Denmark, United States, Finland, Holland, Ireland, Mexico, Norway, Poland, United Kingdom and Sweden.

STAFF
Oenologist: Cristian García
Foreign Commerce Manager: Diego Mohammad
Finance Manager: Mauricio Boullaude

LA CELIA RESERVA CABERNET FRANC 2002

Very good color. Nose is a mixture of hints of wood and red fruit. Touches of leather, some subtle can be found. The wine is elegant in the mouth with good tannins. Balanced, harmonious, very easy to drink with agreeable finesse.

LA CELIA RESERVA MALBEC 2002

High intense color. Good fruit aromas, black fruit, fairly ripe and intense. The wine is balanced, harmonious and elegant. Being a Malbec, it could be a bit more concentrated, but it really is a very pleasant wine.

LA CELIA RESERVA SYRAH 2002

Intense black. Nose is very smoky with slight hints of smoked pork, intense fruit and delicate floral notes. Correct density. A balanced wine. A little bit more volume and middle taste would be advisable to round it out.

FINCA LAS MORAS

Entrance to winery receptor.

WINERY HISTORY

Finca Las Moras is a winery dedicated to producing top quality wines in the province of San Juan. This region, under the spectacular protection of the ring of the Andes mountain range in the Tulum Valley, is located between the Andes and Sierra Pie de Palo, at an altitude of 630 meters. Our vital source of irrigation comes from the meltwaters that forms the San Juan River. Top quality irrigation systems, hydric stress, canopy management, green pruning and harvesting by hand are some of the techniques we use to guarantee the products we harvest and receive at the winery have a clear varietal definition. And also that they maintain the quality of the fruit, an essential characteristic of all our wines. Our leadership in technology includes 1,400 oak barrels and new stainless steel tanks.

Finca Las Moras offers wine lovers a wide range of varieties: Chardonnay, Sauvignon Blanc, Viognier, Rose Shiraz, Cabernet Sauvignon, Bonarda, Malbec and Shiraz. Its line has bi-varietals, 100% varietals, Reserve and Premium.

WINERY LOCATION
Rawson s/n (5439), San Martin, San Juan
Export Business Address:
Nueva Mayorga s/n, Maipú, Mendoza
Tel.: 54 261 520 7218
Fax: 54 261 520 7221
Domestic Business Address:
Arenales 480 (B1638BRD), Vicente Lopez, Buenos Aires.
Web Page: www.fincaslasmoras.com
e-mail: info@fincaslasmoras.com.ar
pabloghiorzi@fincaslasmoras.com.ar

VINEYARDS
120 ha in San Juan
Varieties: Sauvignon Blanc, Viognier, Malbec, Chardonnay, Bonarda, Cabernet Sauvignon, Shiraz and Tannat.
Third party vineyards:
In Pedernal, San Juan
Varieties: Malbec, Cabernet Sauvignon and Chardonnay.

VAT CAPACITY
4,000,000 liters in stainless steel tanks and 315,000 in oak barrels
Quality Norms: BPM, HACCP and BRC.

BRANDS
Domestic Market: Mora Negra, Finca Las Moras Reserva, Finca Las Moras Varietals and Finca Tulum.
Foreign Market: Mora Negra, Las Moras Reserva, Las Moras Varietals and Intis.
Exports to: United States, Puerto Rico, Ecuador, Colombia, Brazil, Venezuela, Mexico, Lativia, Trinidad and Tobago, Paraguay, United Kingdom, Denmark, Ireland, Finalnd, Poland, Italy, Norway, Japan, Austria, Holland, Belgium, Estonia, Bahamas, Lithuania, Ghana and Peru.

STAFF
Winemaker: Daniel Ekkert
Agronomist:
Engineer Claudio Rodriguez
Export Manager: Pablo Ghiorzi
Marketing Manager:
Pablo Moraca
Brand Manager: Andrea Gonzalez
Trade Marketing: Sebastian Nunez
Visits: Only importers for now

LAS MORAS RESERVA CABERNET SAUVIGNON-SHIRAZ 2003

Interesting color with good intensity. Light notes of red fruit. Good material with a somewhat dry finish. Agreeable wine with a delicate elegance.

MORA NEGRA 2002

Good color. Agreeable intensity of ripe red fruit. Wood is rahter noticeable with notes of vanilla and good aromatic freshness. Fairly dense in the mouth, powerful with lots of tannins. Intense, very good for drinking with meals.

LAS MORAS VIOGNIER 2004

Attractive golden yellow color. Character of white fruit with floral notes. Oily, with volume and a slightly bitter touch at the finish.An interesting wine.

FINCA SOPHENIA

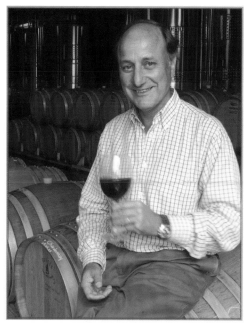

Roberto Luka.

WINERY HISTORY

Finca Sophenia is a winery with top quality wines and recognized Argentine character destined to international markets. Its director is Roberto Luka, who is at the head of a small group of friends, who arpartners.

Roberto Luka, the main shareholder has been President of the Argentine Wine Growers Association and Wines of Argentina.

The winery aims to be the benchmark of the high quality Argentine wine in the world. Since its foundation, the international press has had favorable comments about their wines.

After some a few years' research, the group chose the area of Tupungato, Mendoza, where it found and purchased some land never been tilled before at an altitude of 1,200 m, at the foot of the Andean Range. There they found the ideal ecosystem.

Luka partnered with Gustavo Benvenuto to begin the winery and named it Finca Sophenia in honor of their daughters, Sophia and Eugenia. In 2002, the building was finished and the winery was ready to start producing top quality wines.

WINERY LOCATION

Ruta 89, kilómetro 12.5, Tupungato, Mendoza.
Business Address: Juramento 2089, piso 10°, oficina 1009. CP (1428), Buenos Aires
Tel/Fax: 00 54 11 47819840
Web Page: www.sophenia.com.ar
e-mail: consultas@sophenia.com.ar

VINEYARDS

124 ha for Cabernet Sauvignon, Malbec, Merlot and Chardonnay.

VAT CAPACITY

Stainless steel tanks: 500,000 liters. 200 French and American oak barrels.
Storage capacity: 300,000 bottles.

BRANDS

Domestic Market: Finca Sophenia and Altosur
Foreign Market: Finca Sophenia and Altosur.
Exports to: United Kingdom, Germany, Austria, Norway, Brazil, United States, Mexico and Japan.

STAFF

President: Roberto Luka
Oenologic Consultant: Michel Rolland
Oenologist: Matías Michelini

ALTOSUR SAUVIGNON BLANC 2004

Pale yellow. Aromas fairly intense, reveal touches of cassis. Good freshness, agreeable acidity, slightly bitter at the finish. Its characteristics make it a very refreshing summer wine.

FINCA SOPHENIA MALBEC 2003

Frank color, very vivid. Good aromas of ripe fruit. Lots of finesse and elegance in this wine with silky tannins, fairly smooth. Not very powerful in the mouth, but agreeable with good harmony.

SOPHENIA SYNTHESIS 2002

Interesting color although with a bit of evolution. The bouquet shows a lot of spice and fruit. The wood is well integrated. Dense wine, powerful, with a lot of finesse, elegance and ripe tannins. It is still young, but with great power that deserves to be cellared. Very good quality.

FINCA URQUIZA

Eduardo Gómez Vargas.

WINERY HISTORY

Finca Urquiza is a family company based on the premise of producing top quality wines.

Finca Urquiza products are the result of the meticulous care given the vineyards growing in the Valle de Uco at the foot of the Andes.

Production is carried out with the latest technology and the appropriate infrastructure to sell the products all over the world.

Eduardo Gómez Vargas, for 20 years CEO of Bodegas Santa Ana, one of the major wineries in Argentina, combines his experience and performance in the management of this endeavor and its quest for excellence.

WINERY LOCATION
Bodega San Carlos Sud: San Martín 295, Chilecito, San Carlos, Mendoza.
Business Address:
San Juan de Dios 1747, Dorrego, CP 5519, Mendoza.
Tel/Fax: 54 261 4323293 / 4314582
Web Page: www.fincaurquiza.com
e-mail: bodega@fincaurquiza.com

VINEYARDS
100 ha at Tunuyán, Mendoza.
Varieties: Malbec, Cabernet Sauvignon and Merlot.
Third party suppliers: San Carlos (La Consulta, Chilecito, El Cepillo and Pareditas) Valle de Uco, Mendoza, 400 ha.
Varieties: Malbec, Cabernet Sauvignon, Merlot, Tempranillo, Syrah, Semillón and Chardonnay.

VAT CAPACITY
4,472,000 liters
Storage capacity:
500,000 bottles.

BRANDS
Domestic Market: Finca Urquiza, Finca Los Abedules.
Foreign Market: Finca Urquiza, Southern Willows, Relincho.
Exports to: United States, European countries and Brazil.

STAFF
Executive Director:
Eduardo Gómez Vargas.
Oenologists: Daniel Ramonda and Norberto Richardi.

FINCA URQUIZA MERLOT 2002

Medium intense color. Good aromatic expression, elegant and refined wine with good quality tannins, fairly silky. Should improve in character and expression.

FINCA URQUIZA CABERNET SAUVIGNON 2001

Color a little developed. Nose shows a lot of fruit and sweets, tannins are powerful. A wine for easy drinking.

GOYENECHEA

Alberto Goyenechea.

WINERY HISTORY

The firm was founded in 1868 by brothers Santiago and Narciso Goyenechea, Basque immigrants from Bermejo, Biscay, who arrived in Argentina in 1852.

Goyenechea opened a "pulpería" (a type of pub) in a building on a side street of Plaza de Mayo, which after some time became a general store. Santiago died in 1872 and was succeeded by his son in-law, Pedro Bilbao, until the beginning of the 20th century. Then the company changed its name and bought vineyards and a winery in Villa Atuel in southern Mendoza. The third generation managed the company during the first half of the century under Agustín Goyenechea's leadership, and by 1965 the fourth generation took over with production changing to fine wines.

In 1993, Goyenechea founded the first Board of Origin Control Guarantee (San Rafael), in Argentina. It was the first South American winery to export wine with that guarantee (D.O.C.). Finally in 1998 the fifth family generation joined, the only example in Argentina of such continuity.

WINERY LOCATION
Sotero Arizu s/n (5622) Villa Atuel, San Rafael, Mendoza.
Tel.: 54 2625 470 005
Fax: 54 2625 470 181
Business Address: Adolfo Alsina 1974 (1090) Buenos Aires, Argentina.
Tel. 011 - 4952 0269
Web Page: www.goyenechea.com
e-mail: bodega@goyenechea.com
administración@goyenechea.com

VINEYARDS
Finca "La Vasconia" at Villa Atuel, San Rafael, Mendoza, 130 ha planted with Cabernet Sauvignon, Malbec, Merlot, Syrah, Sauvignon Blanc, Chardonnay, Tocai Friulano and Chenin Blanc.
Third party Vineyards:
Located at San Rafael: Cabernet Sauvignon, Malbec, Syrah, Sauvignon Blanc, Tocai, Bonarda and Sangiovese.

VAT CAPACITY
14,000,000 liters.
350 French oak barrels
Storage capacity:
2,000,000 bottles
Quality Norms: DOC San Rafael, Traceability of products.

BRANDS
Goyenechea, Marqués del Nevado, Vasconia and Tero Real.
Exports to: England, Germany, Netherlands, United States, Mexico, Brazil, Canada, Colombia, Paraguay, Czech Republic, Spain, Norway, Ireland and Belgium.

STAFF
Javier Goyenechea, Luis Goyenechea, Alberto Goyenechea, Rafael Goyenechea, José Luis Goyenechea.
Penologist: Raúl Arroyo

Visits: Monday to Friday from 8 a.m. to 12 noon and from 3 p.m. to 6 p.m.
For visits on Saturdays and for groups, a two week in advance reservation is required.
Further information:
visitas@goyenechea.com

GOYENECHEA QUINTA GENERACIÓN MALBEC 2001

Pleasant color. Wood dominates the fruit in the bouquet. The middle of the mouth is smooth, fairly easy. Finish is correct with rather good quality tannins. A simple and pleasant wine to drink.

GRAFFIGNA

Central yard of the winery and museum entrance.

WINERY HISTORY

As one of the oldest wineries in Argentina, Bodegas y Viñedos Santiago Graffigna, has become a symbol in San Juan province.

Don Santiago Graffigna, an Italian immigrant, arrived in Argentina in 1870. His commitment to the art of wine making, steadfastly continued by his heirs, were the pillars that supported what is now the agro industrial complex. The vineyards that grow in the west of the Tulum Valley, at the foot of majestic Andean Range, benefit from the dry climate, the wide range in temperatures and the San Juan clear sky.

Santiago Graffigna has the honor of being a pioneer in wine exports in Argentina. The vineyards and the wineries have been totally updated in recent years; and have now obtained the consistency required in quality and service demanded today by consumers all over the world.

WINERY LOCATION
Colòn Norte 1342, Desamparados, San Juan. Tel.: 54 264 4210669 / Fax: 54 264 4210669
Business Address: Jujuy 1197 Bella Vista, B1661KTA, Buenos Aires. Tel.: 54 11 4469 8000
Fax: tr 11 4469 8023
e-mail: graffigna@adsw.com

VINEYARDS
Own: 500 ha. At Sarmiento (Cañada Honda), Pocitos, San Juan.
Third party suppliers: 1,500 ha.
Varieties: Cabernet Sauvignon, Malbec, Merlot, Syrah, Viognier, Pinot Grigio, Chardonnay, Sauvignon Bland, Torrontés, Bonarda and Tannat.

VAT CAPACITY
Total: 16,300,000 liters.
Stainless steel: 8,340,000 liters
Concrete: 7,960,000 liters
1,800 American and French oak barrels of 225 liters.
Storage capacity: 12,000,000 liters.
Quality Norms:
ISO 9001. ISO 14000 in process.

BRANDS
Domestic Market: Graffigna, Santa Silvia and Colòn.
Foreign Market: Graffigna, Santa Silvia, Finca de la Montaña and Colón.
Exports: to 30 countries on five continents.

STAFF
Wine Division Director:
César Azevedo
Chief Oenologist: Gerardo Danitz

Visits: Graffigna Museum
Tuesday to Friday 9 a.m. to 1 p.m.
Saturday: 9 a.m.to 8 p.m.
Sunday: 10 a.m. to 2 p.m.

GRAFFIGNA SYRAH 2002

Lots of fruit and aromatic freshness. Syrah's character is noticeable with strong nuances of sun and almost honey-like features.
The middle of the mouth is rather pleasant, with volume. Tannins at the end are slightly dry. It is a wine with great persistence and complexity. Quite correct.

GRAFFIGNA PINOT GRIGIO 2004

Normal color. Aromas typical of the variety. Fairly balanced, fresh, a little bitter at the finish. Rather pleasant wine and fresh.

INFINITUS

Main façade of the winery.

WINERY HISTORY

The vast Rio Negro Valley is located 39 degrees south latitude. There in the Patagonia, near the end of the earth, these wines were born as man's homage to the infinite.

The grapes from this oasis at the far end of the world obtain a special identity in this soil. They have substances from a far.

These winds from the far end of the world acquire a special identity from this desert soil where sunny days and cold nights give them a harmonious balance.

The magic of the soil gives them unique aromas, textures and flavors. Where the winery ends, the desert, wine and mystery begin.

A wild area, almost unexplored gives wine lovers Semillon's citric aromas, Chardonnay's elegance, Malbec's typical Argentine flavor, Cabernet Sauvignon's quality and Merlot's smooth roundness.

WINERY LOCATION
Ruta 22, J.J. Gomez, General Roca, Rio Negro
Business Address: Domaine Vistalba S.A. Roque Saenz Pena s/n (5507), Vistalba, Luján de Cuyo, Mendoza
Tel.: 54 261 4982330
Fax: 54 261 4982511
Web Page:
www.bodegasinfinitus.com
e-mail:
export@bodegasdomvistalba.com.ar

VINEYARDS
70 ha in Rio Negro
Varieties: Cabernet Sauvignon, Malbec, Merlot, Syrah, Chardonnay and Semillon.

VAT CAPACITY
1,300,000 liters
Storage capacity: 200,000 bottles

BRANDS
Domestic and Foreign Markets: Infinitus
Exports to: 25 countries

STAFF
President: Herve Joyaux Fabre
Technical Director and Oenologist: Daniel Renna
Export Manager: Diane Joyaux

Visits: By previous appointment, contact the Commercial Office

INFINITUS
MERLOT
GRAN RESERVA
2002

Good color with interesting intensity. Fruit, fresh, elegant, a great deal of finesse in the aromas; good persistence, finishing with silky tannins. Not a powerful nor extroverted wine. Easy to drink and very charming.

JESÚS CARLOS FANTELLI E HIJOS

Jesús Carlos Fantelli.

WINERY HISTORY

A family company that started in 1977 with grapevine plantation and the winery construction. Since 1995 their wines have participated in international competitions, winning over 150 prizes in France, Belgium, England, United States, Brazil, Argentina, Turkey, Italy, countries where we send our products.

Among our quality wines are Chardonnay, Chenin Blanc, Torrontés, Sauvignon Blanc, Malbec, Syrah, Bonarda, Cabernet Sauvignon, Tempranillo, Merlot. The winery also produces organic wines and has more than 150 certified hectares. Consumers now appreciate liquor wines, especially mistela. In March 2004, our company was honored to win with the Europe Arch Prize for quality and technology in Frankfurt, Germany.

At present, the winery has storage capacity for 10 million liters and a storage room with capacity for 1,000,000 bottles.

WINERY LOCATION
Retamo S/N, Santa Rosa, Mendoza.
Tel.: 54 2623 497089 / 90
Postal Address: Rivadavia 278, San Marín, Mendoza CP. 5570
e-mail:
fantelli@sanmartinmza.com.ar
Web Page:
www.bodagafantelli.com.ar

VINEYARDS
240 ha at Santa Rosa, Mendoza. Implanted with Chardonay, Chenin, Torrontès, Sauvignon Blanc, Malbec, Merlot, Syrah, Bonarda, Cabernet Sauvignon and Tempranillo.
Third party vineyards:
280 hectares at Rivadavia, Junín San Martín and Maipu planted with Chenin Blanc, Tocai, Chardonnay, Malbec, Syrah, Cabernet Sauvignon and Bonarda.

VAT CAPACITY
10,000,000 liters
Storage capacity:
1,000,000 bottles.
Quality Norms: BPA, BPM, HACCP and Traceability implemented.

BRANDS:
Domestic Market: Fantelli, Casa Latina 2x4 Tango and Raíces
Foreign Market: Fantelli, Casa Latina, 2x4 Tango, Vinos del Sol.
Exports to: United States, Canada, Mexico, Brazil, Peru, England, Luxemburg, France, Germany, Japan, Croatia, Ireland, China, Scotland and Belgiium.

STAFF
Manager Partner:
Jesús Carlos Fantelli
Partner: Carlos Pedro José Fantelli
Oenologist: Hugo Zamora

Visits: Not at present.

FANTELLI
COSECHA PRIVADA
MERLOT SYRAH
2001

Good color, fairly intense and bright. Good fruit with Syrah's character dominating. The wine is elegant and fairly pleasant. Finishes on a tannic note, but good quality. A wine with fruity character, a little black fruit and very agreeable.

GRAN RESERVA
1999

Color is fairly strong with a hint of somewhat orangey evolution. Nose has aromas of flowers, dry fruit and a little tobacco. The middle mouth is rather elegant, not very dense but harmonious. Tannins end a bit dry. A classic wine of good level. Well made.

JOSÉ LUIS MOUNIER

José Luis Mounier and his wife Mercedes.

WINERY HISTORY

The family enterprise began 10 years ago and is focused on wine-tourism. The tour consists in a walk around the place, an ancient Indian settlement, the vineyards, the winery, ending with a wine tasting session. Regional cheese may also be tried there, in a gallery with an excellent view.

Finca Las Nubes is 5 km from Cafayate square, at the foot of the El Cajón mountains range, in Salta.

The management of the vineyards is natural, without herbicides or inorganic fertilizers. Vinification is artisan, respecting health and oenology norms, in order to obtain healthy wine. We begin with healthy ripe grapes so wines are characteristic of the stock and the area's denomination. The family's passion is an additional contribution to be taken into account: Mercedes, at the head of tourism, Ana Lucía, in charge of public relations and José and Pablo, in production.

Nearly 3 hectares of the vineyard have Malbec, Cabernet Sauvignon and Tannat. Wines made are a blend to cellar (Malbec, Cabernet Sauvignon and Tannat), a rosé, a varietal Torrontés and a young wine, a blend of Cabernet Sauvignon and Malbec. Yearly production is 45,000 bottles.

WINERY LOCATION
El Divisadero, Alto Valle de Cafayate, Salta: Tel.: 54 3868 422129.
Business Address: El Divisadero 4427, Cafayate, Salta.
e-mail: japmounier@yahoo.com.ar

VINEYARDS
Located at El Divisadero, Alto Valle de Cafayate, Salta.
Varieties: Malbec, Cabernet Sauvignon and Tannat.
Oher suppliers' vineyards: 3 ha vineyards with 40 year old Torrontés.

VAT CAPACITY
25,000 liters, 50 barrels.
Storage capacity: 15,000 bottles.
Quality Norms: Industrial security.

BRANDS
Domestic Market: Finca Las Nubes and José L. Mounier.
Foreign Market: José L. Mounier.
Exports to: San Pablo, Brazil

STAFF
Proprietors: Family enterprise owned by José Luis and Mercedes Mounier, and their children Ana Lucía, José Omar and Pablo Luis.

Visits: Everyday from 9 a.m. to 5 p.m. On Sunday, by previous appointment Mercedes de Mounier and her children Ana, José and Pablo will receive you personally.

FINCA LAS NUBES 2004

Fairly strong color. Aromas not very complex, with notes of spice, toasted and fruit. Medium structure, still a little hard with young tannins that need to evolve a bit to give greater roundness.

JOSÉ L. MOUNIER 2002

Interesting color, good aromas of ripe fruit and small red fruit with vanilla and well integrated wood together with a smoked touch. Good persistence with pleasant tannins. Dense and powerful, good quality, well balanced, can still age some. Still has a little warm side at the finish, but is a good quality wine.

JOSÉ L. MOUNIER TORRONTÉS 2004

Elegant, good aromas, freshness. Still needs a bit of balance in the middle of the mouth, but has a refreshing finish.

LA AZUL

Shirley Hinojosa.

WINERY HISTORY

La Azul is a viticulture endeavor with a precise technological profile devoted to producing top quality wines for demanding consumers. The process is followed thoroughly from the vineyard to marketing.

At the foot of the Andean Range, in Tupungato, Mendoza, stands Finca La Azul, led by Shirley Hinojosa, who with passionate enthusiasm heads a team that shows solid professional and technical skill. In the 90's Finca La Azul set its course to produce high quality wines. Altitude, rocky soil, wide range of temperatures are elements that contribute to the quality of its products.

Equipped with the latest technology, the winery utilizes as much skill and care as the vineyard. After the harvest, Finca La Azul grapes are put in small machines and then sent to steel tanks with temperature control.

New French and American oak barrels receive part of the wine for maturation.

In 2003, La Azul winery began producing three lines of wine. The best grapes from the vineyard were used but they are only a small portion of its total production.

WINERY LOCATION
Ruta Provincial N° 89 s/n, Tupungato, Rivadavia 120, Tunuyán 5560 Mendoza.
Tel. Fax: 54 2622 423593
Business Address:
Av. del Libertador 15.937, (1642CKG) San Isidro, Buenos Aires.
Tel/Fax: 54 11 47323770
Web Page: www.bodegalaazul.com
e-mail: ventas@bodegalazul.com

VINEYARDS
Finca La Azul: 116 ha at Agua Amarga, Tupungato, Mendoza.
Varieties: Bonarda, Semillón, Chardonnay, Cabernet Sauvignon, Malbec, Syrah and Merlot.
Third Party Vineyards: Bodega La Azul wines come exclusively from its vineyards.

VAT CAPACITY
Stainless steel: 60,000 liters.
Oak casks: 10,125 liters.
Quality Norms:
In process: EURET-GAP and Good Agriculture Practices.

BRANDS
Domestic Market:
Azul, Bodega La Azul
Foreign Market:
Azul, Bodega La Azul
Exports to: United States

STAFF
Director: Shirley Hinojosa
Oenologist: Lic. Flavia Manterola
Corporate Image: Estudio Zemma & Ruiz Moreno
Commercial Representative and Press: UMAMI Gourmet
Consultant: Lic. Alfredo Sáenz, Bernard Claus.

Visits: Contact Mendoza office to arrange a visit.

AZUL CABERNET SAUVIGNON 2003

Good steady color. Nose shows notes of pepper and flowers with good intensity. The middle of the mouth is correct. It is full, with good density. Tannins typical of Cabernet Sauvignon, barely hard. A good wine.

AZUL MALBEC 2003

Good color with fairly strong shades of red. A lot of fresh fruit, although not very complex. Smooth with a good finish and pleasant tannins. It has a great deal of elegance.

AZUL MERLOT 2003

The nose is a mixture between floral and fruity with medium intensity. There is good material at the beginning, although the wine does not last very long. Finishes with somewhat harsh tannins.

LAGARDE

Sofía Pescarmona.

WINERY HISTORY

It was founded in 1897 and it still maintains the élan of artisan production and elaborating. Since 1976 its proprietors, the Pescarmona family, continue the Mendoza tradition of this time bonded historic winery.

Walking in the patios and the family house, we breathe the atmosphere of old times, long gone. Lagarde was one of the earliest Argentine wineries devoted to the highest quality wines. It is a founding member of the first D.O.C. in Mendoza (Controlled Origen Nomenclature- Denominación de Origen Controlada de Mendoza), at Luján de Cuyo.

Our project and ambition focus on the unceasing search for quality and the definition of our own style, elegant and identifiable as coming from Mendoza, not following the latest trends, just for the pleasure of those who enjoy our wines year after year.

That is why Lagarde is determined to make wines only with grapes from their own vineyards, and thus reproduce the qualities of each plot of land. We also seek to incorporate the wisdom and inspiration of our oenologists and owners to make wine with personality.

WINERY LOCATION
San Martín 1745. Luján de Cuyo (5507), Mendoza
Tel/Fax: 54 261 4980011
Business Address:
Av. Eduardo Madero 942, Piso 19
Buenos Aires. C1106ACW
Tel.: 54 11 50770807
Web Page: www.lagarde.com.ar
e-mail: info@lagarde.com.ar

VINEYARDS
240 ha in four Perdriel estates and two estates in Mayor Drummond (Luján de Cuyo); Los Árboles (Tupungato).
Varieties: Cabernet Sauvignon, Malbec, Merlot, Syrah, Cabernet Franc, Petit Verdot, Tempranillo, Chardonnay, Viognier, Sauvignon Blanc, Semillón and Moscato Amarillo.

VAT CAPACITY
1,800,000 liters
Storage capacity:
360.000 bottles
Quality Norms: certifying BPM and HACCP.

BRANDS
Domestic Market:
Henry, Lagarde and Altas Cumbres.
Foreign Market: Henry, Lagarde and Altas Cumbres.
Exports to: Denmark, United Kingdom, France, Spain, Switzerland, Hungary, Czech Republic, Brazil, Mexico, Colombia, Ecuador, Puerto Rico, Peru, Uruguay, Costa Rica, Nicaragua, U.S.A. and Japan.

STAFF
General Manager:
Sofía Pescarmona
Oenologist: Juan Roby Stordeur

Visits: Monday to Friday from 9.30 a.m. to 1 p.m. and from 2 p.m. to 6 p.m. Saturday and holidays from 10 a.m. to 1 p.m.
Gift Shop: Yes

LAGARDE SYRAH 2003

Interesting color, not very deep, but fairly bright and high. Fruity with medium intensity. Syrah's character is noticeable. The wine is rather elegant with powerful tannins.

HENRY CABERNET FRANC 2003

Very good, intense and frank color. Aroma displays wood, smoked touches that predominate with a good fruit finish. Good texture stands out and then finishes with firm tannins.

LAGARDE SEMILLÓN 2004

An original wine with hints of honey. slightly sparkling. Fairly oily with good persistence. A novel and different wine.

LA RIOJANA COOP.

Roberto Mantovani, manager (left) and Mario Gonzalez, president.

WINERY HISTORY

In the framework of the Famatina high peaks and the deep blue of the Velazco hills in the Famatina Valley, Chilecito, La Riojana has been active since 1940. Sixty-five years after its foundation, it has 496 shareholders that are about 80% of the small and medium producers in the province. The winery uses a mixture of traditional techniques and advanced technology.

In 1998, they started a process of continuous quality improvement and ISO 9001/2000 certification norms, in addition to other international parameter: Organic Production, FLOI, JAS, HACCP and BCR.

In 2003 it added a winery in El Peral, a privileged area in Mendoza, enlarging and diversifying production. In January 2005, they began producing organic extra virgin olive oil.

The spirit of growth based on sustainable development, genuine investment of national capital, professional advice, experience and solidarity associative work for over half a century prevail in La Riojana.

WINERY LOCATION
La Plata 646, (5360) Chilecito, La Rioja. Tel. 54 3825 423150
Business Address: Fragueiro 1334. CP (5000), Córdoba.
Tel.: 54 351 4716611
Web Page: www.lariojana.com.ar
e-mail: lariojana@lariojana.com.ar

VINEYARDS
Valles de Famatina: 3.987 ha.
Varieties: Cabernet Sauvignon, Tempranillo, Bonarda, Merlot, Syrah, Barbera, Malbec, Torrontés Riojano, Chardonnay, Pinot Grigio, French Colombard and Sauvignon Blanc.
Third Party Vineyards: 801 ha at Famatina Valleys.

VAT CAPACITY
74,152,700 liters
Quality Norms: ISO 9001/2000, HACCP, Organic Production Norms, FLOI Norms, JAS and BRC

BRANDS
Domestic Market: Viñas Riojanas, Pircas Negras, Santa Florentina, NEO, Valdeviña, Raza Argentina and Nacari.
Foreign Market: Additional to those of the domestic market, we must add Inti.
Exports to: England, Germany, Belgium, Sweden, Lithuania, Norway, Denmark, Brazil, Peru, Ecuador, Colombia, Paraguay, Canada, United States, Netherlands, Mexico, Costa Rica, among others.

STAFF
Manager: Roberto Mantovani
Assistant Manager: Jorge Macqueen
Domestic Market Commercial Manager: Leonardo Monguzzi
Foreign Market Commercial **Manager:** Walter Carol
Production Technical Staff: Mauricio Fogliatti, Rodolfo Griguol, René Vicentini, Juan Navarro, Jorge Ruitti, Julio Ocampo, Alberto Neyra, Viviana Michel and Pablo Nasif.
Visits: Monday to Friday, from 9 a.m. to 3 p.m. Saturdays, from 9:30 a.m. to 12 noon.
Gift Shop: Yes.

SANTA FLORENTINA PINOT GRIS 2004

Yellow with lively green reflections. White fruit aromas and good acidity. Fresh wine, easy to drink.

SANTA FLORENTINA TORRONTÉS 2004

The Wine is whole without any flaws. Lots of complex aromas. Good mouth, with interesting acidity and persistence. Clean and very pleasant to drink.

LA RURAL

Lic. Mariano Di Paola, winery's oenologist.

WINERY HISTORY

Recognized since its foundation in 1885 for the quality of their wines, Bodegas La Rural also stands because of its Wine Museum, the most important of its kind in America.

The Museum houses 5,000 pieces, machinery and tools of the vinegrowing process, and old carriages that reflect the history of this activity as well as the daily life of each era.

A tour through the museum allows visitors to return to the early rudimentary days of wine making and then see present day winery where modern technology and French oak barrels can be appreciated.

The innovation and capability of the professional team reflect the special style of their wines.

WINERY LOCATION
Montecaseros 2625, Coquimbito, Maipú, Mendoza.
Tel.: 54 261 4972013
Business Address: Av. Rivadavia 413, Piso 8, Buenos Aires.
Tel.: 54 11 4343 5224
Web page:
www.bodegalarural.com.ar
e-mail:
administracion@bodegalarural.com.ar

VINEYARDS
263 ha Chenin Blanc, Sauvignon Blanc, Chardonnay, Pinot Noir, Syrah, Merlot, Cabernet Sauvignon, Malbec, Gewurstraminer and Cabernet Franc.
Third Party Vineyards: 500 ha at Maipú, Vista Flores, Agrelo, La Consulta and Tupungato.
Varieties: Chenin Blanc, Sauvignon Blanc, Chardonnay, Tempranillo, Merlot, Syrah, Bonarda, Malbec and Cabernet Sauvignon.

VAT CAPACITY
11,000 liters. Storage Capacity: 3,000 barrels and 1.7 million liters in casks.
Quality Norms: in process.

BRANDS
Domestic Market: Pequeña Vasija, San Felipe, Cepa Tradicional, Felipe Rutini, Trumpeter, Colección Rutini.
Foreign Market: The same as above plus Felipe Rutini Reserva, Felipe Rutini Encuentro and Felipe Rutini Apartado.
Exports to: United States, Canada, Latin American countries, France, Holland, Denmark, Netherlands, China, United Kingdom, Indonesia, Singapore and others.

STAFF
Administrative and Financial Manager:
Accountant Carlos Fernández
Production Manager:
Lic. Mariano Di Paola
Commercial Manager:
Lic Enrique Coscia
Export Manager: Lic Alfredo Matilla
Visits: Monday to Saturday from 9 a.m. to 5 p.m. Sundays from 10 a.m. to 2 p.m.
Gift Shop: Yes.

RUTINI MERLOT 2002

Interesting color, fairly intense with good density. Fruit and smoked notes in its aromas, with a little of pleasant vanilla. The wine is round and smooth. Good Persistence with pleasant young tannins. Time will give it great harmony.

RUTINI MALBEC 2002

Fairly intense and bright red. Nose is an interesting combination between fruit and smoked notes: hint of meat. Mouth is rather intense with good texture. Finishes with mature tannins. Wine with good longevity.

FELIPE RUTINI 1999

Pretty color, intense with light notes of evolution. Nose combines wood, fruit, tobacco, grass and dried fruit. The middle of the mouth is good and well balanced and ends with mature tannins. Good level of acidity that adds freshness. A Great wine.

LÓPEZ

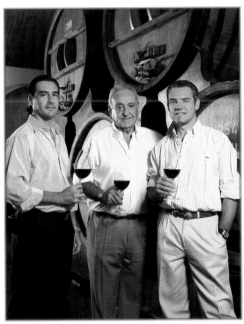

Eduardo López Laurenz, Carlos López and Carlos López Laurenz.

WINERY HISTORY

Bodegas López, that began over a hundred years ago, still remains in the hands of the founding family and is managed by the third and fourth generation. The wise combination of ancestral traditions and permanent technological updating give their wines a special characteristic: classic and modern at the same time.

It began elaborating its own wines in the best areas, with its own grapes and on a principle that has been followed ever since: to control every step in the elaboration process, to take care of every single detail.

Nowadays the Winery has an important reserve volume, red wines aged in French oak casks of over 5,000 liter capacity; and whites placed at low temperatures in epoxy pools and stainless steel tanks.

Throughout the process, from the vineyard to the finished product, technology is at the service of the family's knowledge and expertise gained from over 100 years of wine making experience.

The excellence of their wines, the result of a style carefully maintained for several generations, has created their own unique characteristic: the López style.

WINERY LOCATION
Ozamis 375 (5511) Maipú, Mendoza.
Tel.: 54 261 4811091
Fax: 54 261 973610
e-mail:
lopezmza@bodegaslopez.com.ar
Web Page:
www.bodegaslopez.com.ar
Business Address: Godoy Cruz 2000 (C1414CYP) Buenos Aires.
Tel.: 54 11 47747071
e-mail:
lopezbue@bodegaslopez.com.ar

VINEYARDS
1,081 ha at Maipú (Cruz de Piedra and Lunlunta), Luján de Cuyo (Agrelo) and Tupungato, Mendoza.
Varieties: Cabernet Sauvignon, Malbec, Merlot, Sangiovesse, Petit Verdot, Pinot Noir, Syrah, Chardonnay, Semillon, Chenin Blanc and Sauvignon Blanc.

VAT CAPACITY
40 million liters.
Storage capacity: 500,000 bottles
Quality Norms: ISO 9001/2000, renewed in 2005.

BRANDS
Domestic and Foreign Market:
Montchenot, Château Vieux, Rincón Famoso, López, Traful, Vasco Viejo, Varietals Casona López Cabernet Sauvignon, Malbec, Merlot, Syrah, Chardonnay, Semillon, Xero Malbec, Cabernet Sauvignon and Chardonnay. Jerez Federico López. Champagnes: Montchenot, López and Mont Reims. Olive oil extra virgin López.
Exports to: USA, Peru, Germany, Mexico, Guatemala, Uruguay, Venezuela, Spain, Canada, Czech Republic, Netherlands, Italy, Lithuania, Latvia, Bolivia, Brazil, Costa Rica, Panama, Paraguay, Puerto Rico, Ecuador and Colombia.

STAFF
350 employees

Visits: Monday to Friday from 9 a.m. to 5 p.m. Saturday and Holidays: 9.30 a.m. to 12.30 p.m.
Gift Shop: Yes

CASONA LÓPEZ SYRAH 2003

Fruity with some vegetable notes, typical of the grape. Intense ruby red; elegant, refined, firm tannins. It is a wine to drink quickly.

CASONA LÓPEZ MALBEC 2002

Enriched color corresponding to the vintage. The wine always has the same style with notes of tobacco, cigar and wood. It is a typical traditional Argentine wine.

MONTCHENOT 1995

The color is enriched as is the nose with hints of dried flowers and hay in keeping with its age. The nose is well balanced and has medium length. It is long lasting.

LUCA WINERY

Laura Catena.

WINERY HISTORY

Laura Catena is creating a new category of Argentine wines: with limited production and handcrafted quality, these products reflect their respective "terroirs" with total loyalty. Advanced elaboration and careful maturing in (preferably French) oak casks raise these wines to the quality level demanded by real connoisseurs.

Final blends give strength as well as complexity and elegance. They are the maximum expression of meticulous treatment of the wine, agricultural experimenting, irrigation controls, skilled enological management, and a permanent quest of quality. Present day production includes Chardonnay, Pinot Noir, Malbec and Beso de Dante.

The project is dubbed Luca, the name of Laura Catena's eldest son. The family McDermott's coat of arms shown on the label belongs to Dan, Laura's husband. Laura feels permanent inspiration in the synthesis of cultures existing in her own family and this international inspiration pervades the style and quality of her wines.

Luis Reginato, a young, but experienced enologist and respected grapevine consultant in Mendoza, is the Luca Winery enologist.

WINERY LOCATION

Luca Winery uses third party wineries to produce its wine. Contact Cecilia Rázquin, Commercial Director, telephone 54 261 5198644
Commercial contact:
Tel: 54 261 5198644,
Fax: 54 261 4900217
e-mail: ceciliar@lucatikal.com.ar

OWN VINEYARDS

45 ha. at Vista Flores, Tunuyán, Mendoza. 40 ha at Altamira, La Consulta, San Carlos, Mendoza. Varieties: Malbec, Syhrah, Cabernet Franc and Cabernet Sauvignon.
Third party vineyards: Altamira 5 ha, La Consulta 3 ha, Vista Flores 6 ha and Tupungato 3 ha.
Varieties: Chardonnay, Pinot Noir, Malbec, Syrah and Cabernet Sauvignon.

VAT CAPACITY

varies according to the year.
Storage capacity:
varies according to the year.
Quality Norms: The winery where Luca wines are produced has ISO 9000 certificate.

BRANDS
Domestic and Foreign Markets: Luca
Exports to: United States, Brazil, Denmark and Canada.

STAFF
Proprietor: Laura Catena
Oenologist and Agronomist: Luis Reginato
Commercial Director: Cecilia Rázquin

Visits: Our production is limited and no one is specifically in charge of looking after visitors at present. Please contact Cecilia Rázquin if you need further information about our wines.

LUCA
CHARDONNAY
2002

Dark gold color. Good ripe fruit, peach, pear and floral notes. Silky, oily, opulent. Powerful wine, long finish.

LUCA
BESO DE DANTE
2000

Attractive color. Fruity with hints of red fruit that will improve with maturity and complexity. Elegant refined long lasting wine. Finish is a little tannic. A wine that will grow with cellaring.

LUIGI BOSCA

Alberto Arizu.

WINERY HISTORY

Luigi Bosca winery in Mendoza produces wines with highly refined characteristics and great personality, resulting from the meticulous work done at their own wineries in Luján de Cuyo and Maipú, Mendoza, and the permanent experimentation with a number of varieties developed in different climates, soils and altitudes.

With an extensive background, Luigi Bosca is presently one of the few wineries that have remained in the hands of their founders, in this case the Arizu family. Already in their fourth generation, they have expanded notably on the local market and become a benchmark for Argentine wine.

Their introduction to the European market and subsequent expansion at the international level succeeded in consolidating prestige gained through experience and the search for excellence through innovation, dynamism and technology. Now Luigi Bosca offers three product lines with clear features of their own, that are exported to 40 countries: Finca La Linda, young and fresh, Luigi Bosca Reserva, wines with elegance and distinction, and Línea Alta Gama, which includes the exclusive collection Finca Los Nobles, Bohème, a sparkling wine and the new Gala 1 & 2.

WINERY LOCATION
San Martín 2044, Mayor Drummond (5507) Luján de Cuyo, Mendoza.
Tel.: 54 261 4981947
Fax: 54 261 4982086
Business Address:
Alicia Moreau de Justo 740 PB Of. 7 & 8 (1101) Buenos Aires.
Tel.: 54 11 43312206
Fax: 54 11 43318863
Web Page: www.luigibosca.com.ar
e-mail: luigibosca@luigibosca.com.ar

VINEYARDS
600 ha at Luján de Cuyo and Maipú
Varieties: Syrah, Malbec, Cabernet Sauvignon, Merlot, Pinot Noir, Pinot Meunier, Viognier, Tempranillo, Chardonnay, Sauvignon Blanc, Riesling and Gewürztraminer.

VAT CAPACITY
7,000,000 liters: 3 million in stainless steel; 3 million in concrete; 1 million in American and French oak casks..
Storage capacity:
700,000 bottles.
Quality Norms: HACCP granted by PhF Specialists Inc., U.S.A.

BRANDS
Domestic Market: Finca Los Nobles, Gala, Bohème, Luigi Bosca, Finca La Linda and Viña Paraíso.
Exports to: Germany, Brazil, Belgium, Canada, Chile, China, Colombia, Costa Rica, Denmark, Ecuador, Spain, Israel, Finland, France, Hong Kong, Russia, Malaysia, United Kingdom, Ireland, Japan, Mexico, Norway, Paraguay, Puerto Rico, Singapore, Sweden, Switzerland, Trinidad & Tobago, Uruguay, U.S.A.

STAFF
Board of Directors: Alberto Arizu, Raúl Arizu, Roberto Arizu, Estela Arizu and Roberto Brugaletta.
Commercial Director: Alberto Arizu (Jr.)
Oenologists: Lic. José Hernández Toso and Lic. José Irrera.

Visits: By previous appointment.
Gift Shop: Yes.

FINCA LOS NOBLES CABERNET BOUCHET 1997

Intense color, good depth. Ripe red and black fruit, great aromatic intensity. Good texture and persistence. With good tannins. Fairly powerful, dense and deserves to age, but with lots of character. Taking into account its age, it has remarkable intensity.

LUIGI BOSCA GALA 1 2002

Interesting color, not very intense but fairly bright. The nose has ripe fruit, light simultaneous notes of grass and tobacco. Excellent after taste with density and ripe tannis. A very agreeable and correct wine.

LUIGI BOSCA GALA 2 2002

Intense and shiny color. Nose combines fruit and floral notes. Medium concentration, but round in the middle of the mouth, ending with fairly typical Cabernet Sauvignon tannins, and a lasting finish.

LUIS SEGUNDO CORREAS

Agronomist Julián Correas, winery's president.

WINERY HISTORY

In the las Acequias Valley, Mendoza, on estates the family has owned for over two centuries, Luis Segundo Correas' winery is a symbol of elegance in the production of top quality wines. The company is in the hands of the fourth generation winery owners, who inherited the sensibility and art of combining and highlighting aromas and flavors.

With the knowledge of the various soils, stocks, climates and vineyards age, they produce elegant wines, with unique features and personality, the distinctive family seal.

In the winery only top quality wines are made, all from grapes raised on their own estates, which guarantees precise handling of the harvest and production.

In addition to respect for their ancestors traditional handcraft philosophy, new technological advance, new knowledge and modern facilities have been incorporated. The company is growing constantly and maintains an interesting presence in the international market.

WINERY LOCATION
Carril 3 Acequias s/n, Medrano, Mendoza, CP: 5585
Tel/Fax: 54 261 4230604
Business Address:
Granaderos 888, CP 5500, Mendoza.
Figueroa Alcorta 3033, piso 1, Buenos Aires, CP. 1425.
Tel/Fax: 54 11 48016569
Web Page:
www.bodegacorreas.com.ar
e-mail:
exports@bodegacorreas.com.ar

VINEYARDS
Medrano: 270 ha.
Barrancas: 15 ha.
Luján de Cuyo: 7 ha.
Rivadavia: 112 ha.
Varieties: Malbec, Cabernet Sauvignon, Syrah, Sangiovese, Merlot, Chardonnay, Tocai Friulano, Torrontés and Semillón.

VAT CAPACITY
3,700,000 liters
Storage capacity:
100,000 bottles.
Quality Norms:
In process: Traceability, Good Manufacturing Practices and Good Agricultural Practices

BRANDS
Domestic Market:
Luis Segundo; Valle Las Acequias; El Ciprés, Cuatro Ríos.
Foreign Market:
Luis Correas, Valle Las Acequias, El Ciprés, Don Luis, Cuatro Ríos.
Exports to:
United States, United Kingdom, Belgium, Spain, Brazil, Germany, Canada, Paraguay and Caribbean Islands.

STAFF
President: Ing. Agr. Julián Correas
Commercial Director:
Cdor. Francisco Correas
Exportation: Nicolás Albino
Administration: Adriana Ponce
Oenologist: Daniel Mayorga

Visits: By previous appointment only.

VALLE LAS ACEQUIAS MALBEC 2003

Intense color, fairly dense, rather bright. Lots of fruit, material, and density. A nice wine with lots of character and material.

VALLE LAS ACEQUIAS CHARDONNAY 2003

Pale gold. Floral and fruity. Fairly balanced, good freshness.

LURTON

Jacques and François Lurton.

WINERY HISTORY

In 1988, Jacques and François Lurton, André Lurton's sons, created the winery that bears their last name, in Burdeos, France, in order to produce wines in different parts of the world.

They believed that good wine can be made in every region where the grapevine grows under normal conditions. So they created a large range of wines, each with a style of its own, with excellent price-quality relationship to meet current demand. For this purpose, they selected the best "terroirs", where, with their oenologist team, they process the wines they sell.

In 1992, Jacques and François Lurton arrived in Argentina. They bought 300 hectares in Mendoza: in Vista Flores (Tunuyán) and Barrancas (Maipú). Tunuyán, in Valle de Uco, was selected because of its altitude and special microclimate.

Argentine wines are exported to USA, Canada, Mexico, England, Switzerland, Sweden, Finland, Germany and Holland. Important shipments have been made to such countries as Japan and China.

Jacques and François produce wines in six countries: France, Argentina, Spain, Uruguay, Chile and Australia.

WINERY LOCATION
Ruta Provincial 94, Km 21, Vista Flores, Tunuyán.
Tel./Fax: 54 2622 492067-78
Business Address: Echeverría 1744, Godoy Cruz, Mendoza. Tel.: 54 261 4248 400 Fax: 54 261 4248 404
Web Page: www.jflurton.com
e-mail: bodega@bodegalurton.com

VINEYARDS
Vista Flores, Tunuyán: 225 ha.
Barrancas, Maipú: 90 ha.
Varieties: Cot, Malbec, Cabernet Sauvignon, Syrah, Bonarda, Chardonnay, Torrontés, Pinot Gris, Viognier and Tokai Fermunt.
Third party Vineyards:
La Consulta, San Carlos: 5 ha.
Varieties: Malbec

VAT CAPACITY
3,100,000 liters.
Storage capacity: 125,000 bottles
Quality Norms: HSCP: Norms for the prevention of risk in food handling required by the EU.

BRANDS
Domestic and Foreign markets: Tierra del Fuego, Varietal, Reserva, Gran Lurton, Piedra Negra and Chacayes.
Exports to: United Kingdom, Germany, France, Netherlands, United States, Canada, Finland, Brazil, Russia, Spain and Japan.

STAFF
General Manager:
Andrés Heiremans
Administration Manager:
Alejandro López Grossi
Commercial Director:
François Lurton
Technical Director:
Jacques Lurton
Oenologist: Guillaume Martineau

Visits: Monday to Friday, from 10 a.m. to 5 p.m. by previous appointment.
Gift Shop: Yes.

GRAN LURTON CABERNET SAUVIGNON 2001

Interesting color, slightly evolved, but very intense. Good nose with fruit leaning towards dried fruit, to apricot. Good density in the mouth, round and persistent. Good quality tannins that are not dry. A powerful wine that deserves to be cellared, but can be enjoyed now.

CHACAYES 2002

Good color, lively and bright. With a mixture of ripe red and black fruit, hints of hazelnuts; good density in the mouth, elegant and refined. Finishes with tannins still a little firm although good quality and ripe. A wine with potential. Excellent and well made.

J&F LURTON PINOT GRIS 2004

Good attractive color. Fruit bouquet, good complexity. Pleasant wine, balanced, harmonious and delicate.

MAURICIO LORCA

Mauricio Lorca.

WINERY HISTORY

Little over 100 km from Mendoza Capital, in the Valle de Uco, Bodegas y Viñedos began under Mauricio Lorca's guidance, Lorca is the winemaker and in charge of the project to produce top quality wines.

With an innovative concept, a vineyard was designed with 6,850 plants per hectare to ensure the best supply of raw material and produce highly concentrated and complex wines.

Mauricio's vision, enriched by his experience of over 12 years, includes the idea of producing typical varietal wines with a sensitive personality honoring nature's generosity that combines a wide range of temperatures, the Andean melt water, the virtues of the soil and a kind climate.

With great optimism, Bodegas y Viñedos Mauricio Lorca seeks to set a trend of intense wines that display the potential of the Argentine soil.

WINERY LOCATION
Callejón Troilo s/n, Vista Flores, Tunuyán, Mendoza.
Business Address:
San Martín 5039, Luján de Cuyo, Mendoza
Tel.: 54 261 4961579
Fax: 54 261 4961240
Web Page:
www.mauriciolorca.com
e-mail:
info@opalowines.com

VINEYARDS
29 ha At Vista Flores, Tunuyán, Mendoza.
Varieties: Cabernet Sauvignon, Cabernet Franc, Malbec, Syrah, Petit Verdot, Sauvignon Blanc and Viognier.

VAT CAPACITY
150,000 liters.
Storage capacity:
50,000 bottles.

BRANDS
Domestic Market: Ópalo, Lorca Poético and Lorca Fantasía.
Foreign Market: Ópalo, Lorca Poético and Lorca Fantasía.
Exports to: Brazil, Peru, Colombia, Mexico, United States, Switzerland, Germany, England and Austria.

STAFF
Proprietor and Oenologist:
Mauricio Lorca

Visits:
By previous appointment.

MAURICIO LORCA
ÓPALO MALBEC
2003

Black in color, fairly intense. A nose with very ripe fruit. In the mouth, it has good density, ends with good tannins. It is a very interesting wine that can still improve in quality.

MONTEVIEJO

Catherine Péré Vergé.

WINERY HISTORY

Catherine Péré-Vergé the owner of Monteviejo who participated in the Argentine adventure Clos de los Siete began her viticulture history 19 years ago in Pomerol, Bordeaux region, when she bought Château Montviel, later on Château La Gravière in 2000, and in 2002, having decided to revive some of the first Pomerol vineyards, chose Château Le Gay.

Monteviejo is 120 km from Mendoza City, in the district of Vista Flores, Tunuyán, at the foot of the Andean Range, at an altitude of 1,100 meters. Monteviejo has 121 planted hectares on a total area of 850 hectares. The winery's construction began in 2001 and the first harvest in 2002. The clones selected came from France, high quality and low production. As concerns Malbec, local grape stock was chosen from old vineyards, with excellent adaptability to the soil.

Monteviejo is a team of young people committed to achieving top quality products backed by prestigious winemaker Michel Rolland's sensitivity and experience.

WINERY LOCATION
Clodomiro Silva s/n Vista Flores, Mendoza.
Tel.: 54 2622 422054
Fax: 54 2622 422209
Business Address:
Clodomiro Silva s/n Vista Flores, Mendoza
Tel.: 54 2622 422054
Fax: 54 2622 422209
Web Page: www.monteviejo.com
e-mail: mapeller@ciudad.com.ar

VINEYARDS
Total 121 ha.
Varieties: Malbec, Merlot, Syrah, Cabernet Sauvignon and Chardonnay.

VAT CAPACITY
Total: 1,700,000 liters.
Stainless steel: 1,250,000 liters
Oak barrels: 1,000
Storage capacity:
1,500,000 bottles.
Quality Norms: ISO 9002 in process.

BRANDS
Domestic and Foreign Markets: Lindaflor Malbec, Lindaflor Chardonnay, Monteviejo, Petite Fleur and Festivo.
Exports to: United States, France, England, Belgium, Japan, Switzerland, Russia, Brazil, Spain, Canada, South Korea, China, Denmark, Ireland, Peru and Colombia.

STAFF
Owner: Catherine Péré Vergé, Helene Parent, Henri Parent.
French Oenologist: Michel Rolland
Argentine Oenologist:
Marcelo Pelleriti
Public Relations:
Gustavo Paolucci

Visits: Monday to Friday from 9 a.m. to 3 p.m.

LINDAFLOR
2003

Bright intense red color with purple tones and reflections. Complex aromas of ripe plum and licorice, black pepper and subtle notes of nutmeg. Round body, well structured and harmonious. Outstanding finesse in a sustained finish. A complex and elegant wine.

PETITE FLEUR
2003

Intense red. Aromas of cassis and ripe cherries and hints of mint and eucalyptus. Smooth tannins, ripe and integrated with aromas of ripe fruit and hints of spice. Round and well concentrated, balanced and ample. Finesse in its sustained finish.

LINDAFLOR
CHARDONNAY
2004

Beautiful yellow color with green tones. Buttery with aromas of tropical fruit, without neglecting citric notes. Oily mouth and ripe with a sustained finish in harmony with delicate wood that reflects the terroir's potential.

NAVARRO CORREAS

Main façade of winery.

WINERY HISTORY

Tradition, prestige and elegance are the concepts that mark Navarro Correas among Argentine wineries.

Navarro Correas family descends from "los Correas", a family with an old winegrowing tradition. Its origin dates back to 1798, when Don Juan de Dios Correas planted the first vines in Mendoza. Since the mid 1800's and through a century, the family sold their grapes and wines to other producers. But in 1974, Don Edmundo Navarro Correas decided to present their wines under the family name.

Navarro Correas inaugurated their winery in Godoy Cruz, Mendoza, to increase production and storage capacity, and meet the challenge of exporting and integrating the tourism wine routes. With a total investment of 3 million dollars, the new facilities on the 3.5 hectare premises include a Visitor Center, Wine Bar, Wine Tasting room, an exhibition room, a reception with items for sale, two underground cellars and a fermentation, conservation and harvest area.

WINERY LOCATION
San Francisco del Monte 1555. Godoy Cruz, Mendoza.
Tel/Fax: 54 261 4315 987/8/9
Business Address:
Bouchard 680, Piso 7, C1106ABJ, Buenos Aires
Tel: 54 11 57762800
Fax: 54 11 57762900
Web Page: www.ncorreas.com

VINEYARDS
500 hectares, located at Tupungato, Tunuyán, San Carlos (La Consulta), Maipú and Luján de Cuyo, (Perdriel and Agrelo)
Varieties: Malbec, Cabernet Sauvignon, Merlot, Syrah, Pinot Noir, Chardonnay and Sauvignon Blanc.

VAT CAPACITY
2,000,000 liters in stainless steel tanks, 5,500 liters in French and American oak barrels.
Storage capacity: 3,500,000 liters.
Quality Norms: ISO 9001:2000

BRANDS
Domestic Market: Ultra, Gran Reserva, Colección Privada, Los Árboles, Finca Dolores and Sparkling Wines.
Foreign Market: Ultra, Gran Reserva, Colección Privada, Los Árboles, Finca Dolores and Sparkling Wines.
Exports to: United States, Peru, England, Sweden, the Caribbean, Germany and the Dominican Republic.

STAFF
General Manager:
Ana María Urrutia
Senior Brand Manager:
María Virgina López
Plant Manager: Flavio Alexeef
Oenologist: Juan Marco.

Visits: Visit Center: San Francisco del Monte 1555, Godoy Cruz, tel. 54 2614315 987/8/9
mail: centrodevisitas@ncorreas.com
Monday, Wednesday and Friday at 10 a.m., 12 noon and 3 p.m. by previous appointment.

COLECCION PRIVADA MALBEC 2003

Good color, fairly intense with some orangey hues. Fruity nose is rather fresh and medium intensity. Well balanced in the mouth with a finish of ripe tannins. Correct, elegant wine.

GRAN RESERVA CABERNET SAUVIGNON 2002

Attractive color with good intensity. Fruit and wood aromas, a little floral. Tannins need to round out, but it has good structure and texture.

NIETO SENETINER

Winery's façade.

WINERY HISTORY

The history of Bodegas Nieto Senetiner dates back to 1888. Founded and built by Italian immigrants in the small town of Carrodilla, Luján de Cuyo, it developed in the hands of several families in the early 1900's. This special feature gave rise to the winery's architecture, a reminder of the style seen in the Italian countryside.

In 1969, the vineyards and vinery were bought by the Nieto Senetiner family, who enlarged the facilities and began a new stage of growth. In 1998, the winery was bought by the Perez Companc family, the founder of the Perez Companc Family Group.

At present, the winery has the latest technology for producing top quality wines, but it has not changed the original spirit of their products.

Nieto Senetiner exports to over 30 countries and has won important prizes at prestigious international competitions.

WINERY LOCATION

Guardia Vieja s/n, Vistalba, Luján de Cuyo, Mendoza.
Tel.: 54 261 4984027 / 0315
Business Address: Uruguay 4075, Victoria, Pcia. de Buenos Aires.
Tel.: 54 11 4340 1900 /1921
Web Page:
www.nietosenetiner.com.ar
e-mail:
amantesdelvino@nietosenetiner.com.ar

VINEYARDS

300 ha at Luján de Cuyo (Agrelo, Vistalba) and Tupungato, Mendoza.
Varieties: Pinot Noir, Chardonnay, Merlot, Cabernet Sauvignon, Syrah, Malbeck, Bonarda, Cabernet Franc and Tannat.

VAT CAPACITY

1,703,900 liters
Storage capacity: 500,000 bottles.
Quality Norms: ISO 9001
Version 2000.

BRANDS

Domestic Market: Cadus, Bonarda, Don Nicanor, Nieto Senetiner and Benjamín Nieto Senetiner.
Foreign Market: Cadus, Bonarda Partida Limitada, Don Nicanor, Nieto Senetiner and Benjamín Nieto Senetiner.
Exports to: United States, Brazil, Europe and Japan. In smaller amounts, to the rest of Asia and Latin America.

STAFF

General Manager: Juan Molina
Operation Manager: Milton Kuret
Oenology Manager:
Roberto González
Agricultural Manager:
Tommy Hughes
Visits: Summer: Monday to Sunday from 10 a.m. to 4 p.m.
Rest of the year: Monday to Sunday from 10 a.m. to 3 p.m.
Tours in Spanish and English.
turismo@nietosenetiner,com,ar

Gift Shop: Yes. Vistalba Gift Shop and also Enophil School Gift Shop, Scalabrini Ortiz 2439, Cap. Fed.

CADUS MALBEC 2002

Important color with good intensity. Fairly deep, always fresh. Lots of fruit, notes of vanilla, black fruit and good maturity. Elegant with good middle of the mouth and very good tannic finish. Has lots of potential.

PARTIDA LIMITADA BONARDA 2002

Suggestive color with lots of depth. Nose is typical of the variety with hints of red fruit, very little vegetable and intense. The middle of the mouth expresses good acidity and freshness. Ends with slightly rustic tannins, but is faithful to the Bonarda style. Strong and powerful. A top quality wine with lots of expression and character.

CADUS SYRAH 2002

Good intense color. Fairly fresh and pleasant fruit. Not very dense in the mouth but it is balanced and harmonious. Finishes with very good quality tannins.

NOFAL

Ferina Alonso and her daughters Ercilia, Tere, Nora and Beatriz Nofal.

WINERY HISTORY

Bodega Nofal, belonging to the Nofal Alonso family, dates three generations devoted to the production of wine made from their own grapes in Mendoza.

In 1950 Gabriel Nofal founded "Bodega y Viñedos Nofal" and its prestigious brands of top quality Santa Ercilia, Viejo Tonel and Tunquelén were sold in Argentina and abroad. As an enterprising business-man Gabriel Nofal gave new impetus to Mendoza vitiviniculture, and by 1965 he founded the Argentine Wines exporter consortium.

Long before that, in 1917 don Ceferino Alonso, another pioneer, had started producing Malbec wines from grapes coming from his own vineyards in Maipú. The Nofal Alonso family, managed by Gabriel Nofal and Ferina Alonso's daughters (Ercilia, Beatriz, Nora and Teresa) continue the family tradition of pro-ducing top quality wines.

Bodega Nofal's philosophy is to create limited series of modern wines with personality and intense aro-mas, combining new technologies with the care and passion of their ancestors.

WINERY LOCATION
Calle Gutiérrez s/n Alto Verde,
San Martín, Mendoza.
Web Page:
www.bodeganofal.com.ar
e-mail:
buenosaires@bodeganofal.com.ar
mendoza@bodeganofal.com.ar

VINEYARDS
Finca Ferina 76 ha, at Los Sauces,
Tunuyán, Mendoza.
Varieties: Malbec, Cabernet Sauvignon, Tempranillo, Bonarda, Sangiovese, Barbera d'Asti and Syrah. At Finca Gabriel, 45 hectares, Alto Verde San Martín, Mendoza: Pinot Blanc, Ugni Blanc, Pedro Ximénez and Syrah.

VAT CAPACITY
1,700,000 liters
Storage capacity:
300,000 bottles.

BRANDS
Tunquelén, Santa Ercilia and Nofal Alonso
Exports to: United States, Brazil, Italy, Spain, Holland and France.

STAFF
Board of Directors: Ercilia, Beatriz, Nora and Teresa Nofal Alonso.
Oenologist: Carlos González Ramponi.
Agronomist: Ing. Antonio Rizzato
In charge of Estate Production: Rafael Alonso

TUNQUELÉN
TEMPRANILLO 2003

Agreeable and intense color. Very fruity on the nose, fresh fruit. Aromas that coincide with the varietal characteristics. An elegant wine that is easy to drink.

SANTA ERCILIA
MALBEC 2003

Intense typical Malbec color. Lots of spice on the nose. Balanced, agreeable with a long finish. An elegant wine.

NÓMADE WINES

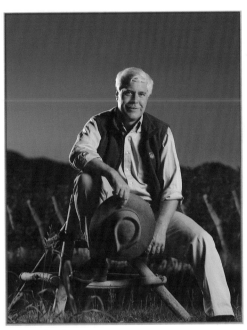

Tomás Achával.

WINERY HISTORY

Nómade's dream began in 1994, when Tomás Achával was president of Bodegas Chandon, fell under the spell of the Andes and its vineyards. Then he discovered what was going to become the axis of his life: wine and its culture.

As a true traveler, he knew how to learn from people with experience, who taught him the valuable knowledge that helped him lead Bodegas Chandon to the highest international level

After 2002, with the experience he had gained and the passion and energy that identify him, Tomás decided to make wines that surprise and inspire consumers. For this purpose, he personally traveled the whole length of the Andean region, and found the places and climates most favorable to the development of various stocks. He discovered vineyards with a great enologic riches and unique in their history and people.

Gabriela Celeste, executive director of Eno-Rolland, and other distinguished professionals experienced in the elaboration of top wines and vineyard management accompany Tomás in this project.

WINERY LOCATION
Vinos y Viñedos Nómade, España 1094, La Consulta, Mendoza.
Business Contact:
Tel.: 54 9 11 4 993 7752
Fax: 54 2320 4 99053
Web Page:
www.nomadewines.com
e-mail:
tomasachaval@nomadewines.com

CONTROLLED VINEYARDS
Mendoza: Las Mulas, Campo Los Andes 5 hectares, Sauvignon Blanc, Cabernet Sauvignon and Merlot at 1,150 meters.
Don José, La Consulta: 3 hectares for 1932 Malbec.
Altamira, La Consulta: 2 hectares, Parral Syrah and 2 hectares for Malbec.
El Pini, Vista Flores: 3 hectares, of 1913 Malbec.
Patagonia Cinco Saltos: Merlot and Pinot Noir.

BRANDS
Domestic and Foreign
Markets: Nómade and 7 Lunas
Exports to: Brazil, United States and Northern Europe countries.

STAFF
President: Tomás Achával
Oenology and laboratory:
Ing. Gabriela Celeste from Eno-Rolland.
Vineyards:
Gabriela and Tomás.
Marketing: Tomás Achával
Administration:
Estudio García Ojeda

Visitor Center:
Under construction.
Visits: reservations required. Call 54 911 4993 7752.

NÓMADE RESERVA MALBEC 2004

Black, almost violet. Nose of plums, intense candy, notes reminiscent of nuts and wood. Good material, dense, intense, complex; a wine to copy. Should age for a good number of years.

NÓMADE RESERVA SYRAH 2003

Good deep color, very high Good aromas of fruit, wood, a little of candy, somewhat overripe. Interesting density with good persistence. There is much that stands out in this wine, with a fairly potent tannic finish. Without a doubt, it has good potential.

NORTON

Miguel Halstrick.

WINERY HISTORY

Bodega Norton was founded in 1895 by Edmund J. P. Norton, an Englishman who arrived in Mendoza as an engineer working on the railway that connected Mendoza and Chile. Amazed by this land and with good foresight, he planted the first grapevines brought over from France. Norton was the first vineyard south of the Mendoza River, a viticulture area renowned as one of the best in the country. Also the Norton brand became a wine benchmark in Argentina.

In 1988, Austrian entrepreneur Gernot Langes-Swarovski traveled to Mendoza and was impressed by the beauty of the region, the warmth of its people and conditions that favored wine growing. He foresaw Argentina's great potential in the world and in 1989 bought the winery for a clear purpose: producing wines known for their quality the world over. His son Michael is responsible for managing the winery, heading an excellent team of professionals. A new stage of substantial investment, modernization and growth began.

Today Norton is the leading brand in Argentine wine exportation and one of the most important wineries in the country.

WINERY LOCATION
Ruta Prov. N° 15 Km. 23,5 Perdriel, Luján de Cuyo, Mendoza.
Tel.: 54 261 4909700
Fax: 54 261 4909799
Business Address:
Tronador 4890, 9° piso (Sur) Edif. Panamericana Plaza (Av. Gral. Paz and Panamericana) Buenos Aires.
Tel.: 54 11 57778400
Fax: 54 11 57778499
Web Page: www.norton.com.ar
e-mail: norton@norton.com.ar

VINEYARDS
Medrano, Mendoza: 71 ha.
Lunlunta, Mendoza: 19 ha.
La Colonia, Agrelo; Mendoza: 1,082 ha.
Perdriel, Luján de Cuyo, Mendoza: 105 ha.

VAT CAPACITY
Vats and tanks: 10,000,000 liters.
In barrels: 800,000 liters.
Storage capacity: 500,000 bottles:
Quality Norms: ISO 9001/00, HACCP.

BRANDS
Domestic Market:
Norton and Perdriel.
Foreign Market:
Norton and Perdriel.
Exports to: Asian, European, American and African countries.

STAFF
General Manager:
Michael Halstrick
Operation Manager: Luis Steindl
Oenologist: Jorge Riccitelli

Visits: Monday to Saturday
Gift Shop: Yes. Wine Bar.

NORTON RESERVE MALBEC 2002

Pleasant color, very frank and bright. Good nose of ripe fruit. Smooth, elegant wine, persistent with kind tannins. Lots of harmony and balance. A pleasurable wine.

PERDRIEL SINGLE VINEYARD 2001

Fairly interesting color, sustained and deep. Good aromatic quality with ripe fruit. The wood is integrated with an evolution towards notes of tobacco and older wine. Interesting density, good tannins that respect the wine's elegance and finesse. It is long and still has a great deal of potential.

PERDRIEL DEL CENTENARIO 2002

Fairly deep and bright color. Nose of ripe fruit, with good quality grapes. Smooth, elegant. It lacks nothing. A pleasurable wine.

NQN

Lucas Nemesio and Luis Maria Focaccia.

WINERY HISTORY

We were born a short time ago. We have the impulse of what is new. Our project is clear: to produce wines in Patagonia, wines that will be recognized and singled out all over the world. We know that top quality needs excellent land, the latest technology, demanding professionals, love of the craft, perseverance and patience. And we have it all. We grow the best grapes so our winery has excellent raw material in order to produce top quality international wines. We have invested in the latest equipment to create the conditions in these southern lands that best guarantee the success of our wines. We have 162 ha planted with fine varieties and their growth can be seen: in the 2004 harvest we produced 500,000 bottles of the different varietals, a volume that justified the construction of our winery, whose total production capacity will be 2,600,000 liters a year.

WINERY LOCATION
Ruta Prov. N° 7, Calle 15, San Patricio del Chañar, Neuquén.
Tel/Fax: 54 299 155810000 /155886000 / 0800-9992NQN (676)
Business Address:
Ruta Prov. N° 7, Calle 15, San Patricio del Chañar, Neuquén.
Web Page:
www.bodeganqn.com.ar
e-mail:
bodeganqn@bodeganqn.com.ar

VINEYARDS
San Patricio del Chañar: 127 hectares planted
Varieties: Malbec 48 ha; Merlot 38 ha.; Cabernet Sauvignon 27 ha; Pinot Noir 8 ha; Sauvignon Blanc 3.5 ha and Chardonnay 5 ha.

VAT CAPACITY
1,350,000 liters in stainless steel.
51,300 liters in barrels.
Storge capacity:
100,000 bottles.
Quality Norms: In process. ISO 9000, ISO 14000, Good Manufacturing Practices.

BRANDS
Domestic Market:
Picada 15; Malma Clásico 2004; Malma Reserva 2003, Colección NQN and Sparkling Malma.
Foreign Market:
Picada 15; Malma Clásico 2004; Malma Reserva 2003, Colección NQN and Sparkling
Exports to: United States.

STAFF
General Direction: Luis María Focaccia and Lucas Nemesio
Oenologist: Gustavo Agostini

Visits: Monday to Friday 9.30 a.m. to 5 p.m. Weekend and holidays: 10 a.m. to 5 p.m.
Gift Shop: Yes.
Restaurant: Malma Restó bar, open everyday.
Resevations: 54 299 155574154 reservas@bodeganqn.com.ar 0299-155810000 int. 224 (restó bar)

COLECCIÓN NQN 2003

Intense color, almost black. An explosion of fruit, very pleasant, red and black fruit, very good really smooth tannins. A delicate, balanced, very pleasing wine with good over all consistency.

MALMA RESERVA MERLOT 2003

Red, intense Bordeaux color. Not very complex, but with good harmony. Medium density and good persistence. Tannins are still a little firm, but have a nice texture. A wine to drink now when it is young, for immediate pleasure.

MALMA RESERVA MALBEC 2003

Very good color, fruity with lots of very good quality red fruit. Balanced wine, the firm tannins are a bit noticeable at the finish, but it is a young wine. A pleasurable wine with good quality fruit and harmonious finish.

O. FOURNIER

José Manuel Ortega.

WINERY HISTORY

Coinciding with the new millennium, the Ortega Gil-Fournier Spanish family founded a modern winery, at the foot of the Andes in La Consulta, Mendoza.

Bodegas and Viñedos O. Fourier proposes become one of the most distinguished wine making wineries producing top quality Argentine wines, taking advantage of the competitive features of the soil and the climatic conditions of the terroirs, and combining technology and oenological expertise, both national and international.

La Consulta region, where the estates are located at an altitude of 1,200 m. This height has a wide range of temperatures that enables the production of wines with of excellent color and apt for a lengthy aging.

The varieties grown are Tempranillo, Cabernet Sauvignon, Merlot, Malbec, Syrah and Cabernet Franc.

Except for Malbec, plants come from France and Italy and have been root-grafted in American varieties. The harvest is carried out by hand. Two selecting tables are used, at the first, the best clusters are chosen, and the damages ones are eliminated at the second.

WINERY LOCATION
Calle Los Indios s/n (5567), La Consulta, San Carlos, Mendoza.
Tel./Fax: 54 2622 451579 / 088 / 598
Business Address:
Calle Los Indios s/n (5567), La Consulta, San Carlos, Mendoza.
Tel./Fax: 54 2622 451579
Web Page: www.ofournier.com
e-mail: info@ofournier.com

OWN VINEYARDS
100 ha cultivated, from a total of 286, located in San Carlos (La Consulta, Pareditas, Chilecito and El Cepillo), Mendoza.
Varieties: Tempranillo, Merlot, Malbec, Syrah, Cabernet and Sauvignon Blanc.
Third Party Vineyards: 50 ha.
Varieties: Tempranillo, Merlot, Malbec, Syrah and Sauvignon Blanc.

VAT CAPACITY
Total: 1,085,000 liters.
Stainless steel: 868,000 liters.
Concrete: 90,000 liters.
Oak barrels: 290,000 liters.
Storage capacity:
750,000 bottles.
Quality Norms:
IRAM/ISO in implementation process.

BRANDS
O.Fournier, Acrux, Bcrux, Urban Uco
Exports to: Brazil, Peru, Uruguay, United States, Canada, Switzerland, Spain, England, Holland, Germany, Russia, Belgium, Finland and Sweden

STAFF
Owner: José Manuel Ortega Gil-Fournier
President: Federico Cassone
O.Fournier Group Oenologist: José Mario Spisso
Commercial Manager: Celina Brenta
Administration and Finance Manager: Diego M Stortini

Visits: By previous appointment.
Gift Shop: Yes.

ACRUX MALBEC 2002

Good intense color. Lots of fruit integrated with the wood. The wine is soft, well balanced. It offers a tannin finish that is quite strong. It has excellent potential, above all, its finesse, and elegance as well as the complexity it is beginning to show.

BCRUX 2002

A nice color, good intensity, very attractive fruit, cool and fresh. A friendly wine, with round tannin finish. It is a pleasurable wine, extremely enjoyable.

O. FOURNIER SYRAH 2002

Suggestive color, with red fruit aromas and good wood. Elegant and complex with a good middle of the mouth that ends on firm tannins. Young and delicate, an interesting example of the virtues of its area southern Mendoza.

PALO ALTO

Santiago Antognolli and Luis Martínez López.

WINERY HISTORY

We worked in an ancient family winery located in Cruz de Piedra, Maipú. When it was restored the original construction lines were respected while Italian technology was incorporated and a space was created where history and the future co-exist.

We have the capacity to produce 1,800,000 liters, but focus on elaborating reduced volumes of carefully controlled high quality wines.

The grapes come from our Medrano and Tupungato estates, 35 and 15 years old respectively and only high quality varieties are used. Harvesting is done by hand. In the winery, clusters are submitted to strict controls. Fermentation develops at very low temperatures thus favoring the preservation of the fruits characteristics.

Finally wines have two destinations: they are bottled and sent to the cellars to be stowed or go into barrels made from American or French oak to age. Our concept of wine aging aims at achieving a structure permitting the maximum expression of the fruit, with balanced complexity and concentration in order to present the integrity of bottled flavors and aromas without filtering or clarification.

WINERY LOCATION
Videla Aranda 502, Cruz de Piedra, Maipú, Mendoza.
Tel.:54 2614990407
Business Address:
Carlos Pellegrini 1141, 7° Piso, Buenos Aires.
Tel./Fax: 54 11 43270262
Web Page:
www.bodegapaloalto. com.ar
e-mail:
paloalto@vinarium.com.ar

VINEYARDS
Medrano: 24 ha.
Tupungato: 22 ha.
Varieties: Malbec, Merlot, Cabernet Sauvignon, Chardonnay, Sauvignon Blanc and Pinot Noir.

VAT CAPACITY
600,000 (400,000 in steel tanks and 200,000 in epoxy lined pools).
Storage Capacity:
40,000 bottles

BRANDS
Domestic Market:
Coiron, Satomi, Palo Alto.
Foreign Market: Coiron, Satomi, Amadores, Umai.
Exports to: USA, Brazil and Holland.

STAFF
President: Santiago Antognolli
Oenologist: Luis Martínez López
Marketing and Foreign Commerce Management:
Flavia Fernández Fabio

Visits:
Mondays through Fridays: 8.30 a.m. to 5 p.m. Saturdays and Sundays: previous appointment by telephone

PALO ALTO MALBEC 2003

Attractive color, good intensity. Not very complex, a bit lineal but pleasant, well made. Medium intensity in the middle of the mouth. It is a kind wine, easy to drink, with a certain harmony.

PALO ALTO CABERNET SAUVIGNON 2003

Intense color, quite attractive. Fruity aromas, medium density finishing on potent tannins. It is a pleasant wine with decent balance, but needs only a little more harmony.

PALO ALTO SAUVIGNON BLANC 2004

Good color. Its aromas are discrete, with floral notes. Very fluid, consistent finish.

PASCUAL TOSO

Mario Toso.

WINERY HISTORY

In the mid 80's, when Don Pascual Toso left Canale D'Alba Piemonte, Italy, for Argentina, perhaps he never thought he would be founding one of the most prestigious wineries in the country for the consistent and indisputable excellence of its products and the irreproachable course of its commercial activities for over 100 years.

He chose Mendoza as a place to live and initially started out in business, but his wine culture heritage led him to appreciate the exceptional character of the wines produced in Mendoza. He consequently installed his first winery there in 1890.

With exceptional foresight, he extended his vineyards to Maipú, convinced that it was an area of high quality production. He bought "Las Barrancas", an estate where he built a winery for elaboration and storage.

Continuing with its profile of constant improvement, the winery hired Paul Hobbs, with whom they have since carried out a project to renew and improve the style of the wines. The first results are beginning to be seen, with prizes and recognition awarded to their 2002 and 2003 vintages.

WINERY LOCATION
J. B. Alberdi 808, Guaymallén, Mendoza.
Tel.: 54 261 4058000
Fax: 54 261 4058001
Business Address:
Exclusive Distributor Domestic Market:
J. Llorente & Co. SA: Catamarca 70, 1213, Buenos Aires.
Tel.: 54 11 4866 2250
Fax: 54 11 4865 3901
Foreign Market: J. B. Alberdi 808 5519, Guaymallén, Mendoza.
Tel.: 54 261 4058000
Fax: 54 261 4058001
Web page: www.toso.com.ar
e-mail:
Tosowines@bodegastoso.com.ar

VINEYARDS
Barrancas, Maipú, 300 hectares.
Varieties: Cabernet Sauvignon, Malbec, Merlot, Chardonnay, Syrah, Sauvignon Blanc and other varieties as basis for sparkling wines.
Third party suppliers:
Varieties: Cabernet Sauvignon, Malbec, Syrah, Merlot, Chardonnay, Sauvignon Blanc.

VAT CAPACITY
6,000,000 liters in stainless steel tanks, epoxy pools and casks
Storage capacity:
1,500,000 bottles
Quality Norms:
ISO9001:2000 being implemented.

BRANDS
Domestic and Foreign Market:
Pascual Toso, Toso
Exports to: United States, Canada, Brazil, Uruguay, France, Chile, United Kingdom, Sweden, Netherlands, Belgium, Finland, Denmark, Ireland, Japan, Norway, Iceland, Estonia, Korea, Russia, Latvia, Spain, Thailand

STAFF
General Manager: Ing. Mario Toso
Management: Enrique Toso
Export Manager:
Francisco Cortes Lepis
Exportation: Lic. Cecilia Flores
Technical Manager:
Rolando Luppino
Consultant: Paul Hobbs

Visits: by previous appointment.

MAGDALENA TOSO 2002

Fairly intense and shiny color. Interesting aromas of vanilla, red fruit and spice. Good concentration and structure, powerful tannins; also a long and pleasant finish.

PASCUAL TOSO 2003 MALBEC RESERVE

Intense color. Nose expresses wood that is not yet fully integrated, but in the back you can perceive fairly ripe and intense fruit. Medium density in the mouth with still firm tannins. A nice wine.

RUCA MALÉN

Jean Pierre Thibaud and Jacques Louis de Montalembert.

WINERY HISTORY

At the foot of the Andes, Agrelo, Luján de Cuyo, Mendoza. The owners are Jean Pierre Thibaud (Argentine, son of a French couple) with vast experience having been president of Bodegas Chandon in Argentina for 10 years and Jacques Louis de Montalembert, with a viticulture tradition in the Burgundy region of France. Besides their own vineyards, they appreciate the production of other vinegrowers in the area. They preserve the natural conditions of grape culture and privilege the origin as well as man's efforts as valuable resources in the production of great wines. The land offers the quality sought for each varietal, thanks to the relationship among climate, soil and variety.

"Ruca Malén" refers to a Mapuche legend. It says that the native women walked without looking up because of awe before the dazzling sight of a young enthralling god. One day one of them looked up at him and was bewitched by a flash. The god took her up the Aconcagua with him, close to the sun, a rich land of pure waters. There he presented her with a dwelling, Ruca Malen, "the maiden's house". He also gave her some nectar she could drink to revive the joy, the happiness of the man she loved.

WINERY LOCATION

Ruta N° 7, km 1059, Agrelo, Luján de Cuyo, Mendoza
Tel.: 54 261 4106214
Business Address:
Manuel Obarrio 2986, 1° piso, C1425 CQB, Buenos Aires.
Tel.: 54 11 4807 1671
Fax: 54 11 4801 6690
Web Page:
www.bodegarucamalen.com
e-mail:
agarciaestrada@bodegarucamalen.com

VINEYARDS

21 hectares at Agrelo
Varieties: Malbec and Chardonnay
Third Party Suppliers and Varieties: Malbec at Perdriel and Agrelo (Luján de Cuyo, Lunlunta (Maipú) and La Consulta (San Carlos). Merlot at Tupungato and Tunuyán. Cabernet Sauvignon at Agrelo and Ugarteche (Luján de Cuyo), Lunlunta (Maipú) and at La Consulta (San Carlos).

VAT CAPACITY

376,000 liters in stainless steel tanks, and 600 barrels (13,500 l): 80% French and 20% American oak.
Storage capacity: 1,000 m2.

BRANDS

Domestic and Foreign Markets:
Yauquén, Ruca Malén and Kinien
Exports to: United States, England, Holand, France, Sweden, Brazil, Uruguay, Panama, Peru and Paraguay.

STAFF

President:
Jacques Louis de Montalembert
Vice President: Jean Pierre Thibaud
Consultants: Silvia Avagnina,, Carlos Catania and Raúl del Monte.
Oenologist: Juan Manuel Mallea

Visits: Tastings and lunches, Monday to Friday from 10 a.m. to 5 p.m. Saturday from 10 a.m. to 1 p.m. By appointment: tel: 54 261 4106214 Cel.: 154 541 236 Nextel 145*1963 mespinola@bodegarucamalen.com
Gift Shop: Yes.

KINIEN MALBEC 2001

Attractive color, good intense expression of fruit. Elegant in the mouth with medium concentration, but good balance. Finish with ripe tannins. Good aftertaste of spice, characteristic of Malbec. On the whole, a very pleasant wine.

RUCA MALÉN CABERNET SAUVIGNON 1999

Color is fairly bright with some orange hues. Hints of very ripe fruit. A powerful wine with good concentration and a true personality.

RUCA MALÉN CHARDONNAY 2004

Pleasant pale gold color. Floral nose and white fruit. Elegant, fairly smooth, consistent, good persistence. Not very complex, but very agreeable.

SALENTEIN

Inside the winery.

WINERY HISTORY

With a new perception of quality - plantations of classic varietals, preservation of very old varieties, reapplication of European and the latest technology - Salentein produces international quality wines that have been sold in several countries around the world since 2000. The 550 hectares they own have plots with different bearing, soil and altitudes ranging from 1,050 m to 1,700 m, which allows excellent adaptation of the various stocks. Irrigation is done with pure melt water.

The winery, the only construction of its type in the region, is shaped like a cross. Each wing is a small winery with two sections: one at ground level, houses stainless steel French tanks and oak casks for fermentation and storage, while the other, underground, is used for maturing the wine in oak barrels. The two levels allow the wine to descend from the tanks to the barrels by a gravity system. The four wings converge in a center circular space, inspired in the typical amphitheatres of classic times.

WINERY LOCATION
Ruta 89 s/n, Los Árboles, Tunuyán, Mendoza.
Business Address:
In Mendoza: Emilio Civit 778, (M5502GVU), Mendoza.
Tel/Fax: 54 261 4411000
In Buenos Aires: Av. L. N. Alem 855, 6° piso, (C1100AAD).
Tel.: 54 11 4131 1100
Fax: 54 11 4131 1199
Web Page:
www.bodegasalentein.com
e-mail:
info@bodegasalentein.com

VINEYARDS
550 ha in Valle de Uco, Mendoza.
Varieties: Malbec, Cabernet Sauvignon, Merlot, Pinot Noir, Syrah, Tempranillo, Chardonnay and Sauvignon Blanc.

VAT CAPACITY
Total: 3,012,725 liters.
Stainless steel: 1,842,200 liters.
Oak casks: 91,200 liters.
Oak barrels: 1,079,825 liters.
Storage capacity:
1,000,000 bottles.
Quality Norms: ISO 9000 and HACCP.

BRANDS
Domestic and Foreign Markets:
Salentein Primus, Salentein.
Exports to: Europe, United States, Canada, Brazil, Japan, China and Hong Kong.

STAFF
Commercial Manager:
Alejandro Panighini
Oenologist: Laureano Gómez
Agronomist: Ing. Gustavo Soto

Visits: Monday to Sunday: 10 a.m. to 4 p.m.
Gift Shop: Yes.

SALENTEIN MERLOT ROBLE 2002

Strong color, good brightness. Aromas of ripe fruit, black fruit, together with vanilla and smoked notes of wood. Elegant. Good density, volume, tannins are tender, but noticeable. A wine with medium power that can be cellared for a time or enjoyed now.

SALENTEIN PRIMUS PINOT NOIR 2002

Fairly strong and interesting color. Very pleasant typical aromas, intense and fresh. In the mouth, the wine is rather dense and powerful, maintaining the grape's finesse. It has good persistence. The finish is long with no harshness or bitterness. Well balanced.

SANTA ANA

Rodolfo Sadler.

WINERY HISTORY

Santa Ana was founded in 1891 by Luis Tirasso, a pioneer in Argentine viticulture. The quality of their processes, guaranteed by their professionals dedicated work, place the winery among the main fine wine producers in South America.

As a result of its growth and consolidation in the Argentine market, Santa Ana decided to enter the demanding international markets and has done so successfully. The sustained growth of their exports proves this.

With a top wine growing and enological team, Santa Ana has shown its strength, uniting tradition and technology to produce wines whose quality has been recognized internationally with over 100 awards.

Santa Ana, leader in the Argentine wine growing industry, stands out for its knowledgeable combination of experience and innovation. It has lasted over time as a close and beloved winery, positioned among the most successful on an international level.

WINERY LOCATION
General Roca and Urquiza, Guaymallén, Mendoza.
Tel: 54 261 5207219
Fax: 54 261 5207221
Business Address: Arenales 460, Vicente López, Buenos Aires.
Tel: 54 11 5198 8000/8600/9000
Web Page:
www.bodegas--santa ana.com.ar
e-mail:
avivas@bodegas-santa-ana.com.ar

VINEYARDS
400 hectares in Luján de Cuyo and Maipú (Mendoza); in Tulum Valley (San Juan).
Varieties: Malbec, Cabernet Sauvignon, Bonarda, Chardonnay, Chenin Blanc, Sauvignon Blanc, Cabernet Franc, Tocai Friulano, Riesling, Tannat and Viognier.
Third party vineyards:
750 hectares in Luján de Cuyo, Tunuyán, Tupungato, Maipú, San Carlos, Santa Rosa, San Martín and Rivadavia, Mendoza.
Varieties: Malbec, Cabernet Sauvignon, Merlot, Syrah, Bonarda, Chardonnay, Pinot Noir, Sauvignon Blanc, Chenin Blanc and Tempranillo.

VAT CAPACITY
12 million liters
Storage Capacity:
200,000 bottles.
QUALITY NORMS:
BPM, HACCP and BRC

BRANDS
Santa Ana, Carácter, Casa de Campo and La Mascota
Exports to: More than 40 countries, the most important of which are Switzerland, Denmark, Brazil and Japan.

STAFF
Export Manager: Adriano Vivas
Oenologist: Rodolfo Sadler
Agronomist: Ing. Guillermo Yaciófano

Visits: Consult via email.

SANTA ANA CEPAS PRIVADAS CABERNET SAUVIGNON 2003

Pleasant color. Fruity aromas, fresh and intense. Middle of the mouth is correct with a tannic finish. A wine that is somewhat concentrated and elegant. Easy, not very complex, but good.

SANTA ANA CEPAS PRIVADAS MALBEC 2003

Good color, fairly vivid. Fresh and fruity. With volume and density in the mouth that ends with strong tannins. A pleasant wine, somewhat fresh, fairly noticeable acidity and pretty liveliness.

FUSSION 2001

Color is fairly vivid and attractive. Good fresh fruit, pleasant in the mouth with some density. Pleasing wine with character and personality. Fresh, agreeable, for drinking now and full enjoyment.

SAN HUBERTO

Leonardo Spadone.

WINERY HISTORY

Bodegas San Huberto was founded in 1905 in Valle de Aminga, La Rioja province, 1,450 m above sea level, a privileged area thanks to its geographical location, especially its climate conditions: deep sandy soil, a dry climate, scarce yearly rainfall, hot summers and very cold winters, moderate winds, good sunshine, with 95% sunny days and a wide range of temperatures the entire year: A land with excellent conditions for producing fine wine.

In 1998, the Spadone Group bought the winery and undertook an expansion plan with a clear objective: increasing their penetration in domestic and foreign markets, based on an essential premise, the quality of their products. In order to carry out this plan, improvements were made, both in the vineyards and the facilities: drip irrigation was incorporated, new oak barrels and stainless steel tanks and other important investments.

WINERY LOCATION

Ruta Nacional 75, kilómetro 82,5 (5301) Aminga, Castro Barros, La Rioja.
Tel.: 54 3827 494040
Business Address:
Rìo Cuarto 1242 (C1168AFF), Buenos Aires.
Tel.: 54 11 43035404 / 08
Web Page:
www.bodegassanhuberto.com.ar
e-mail:
info@bodegassanhuberto.com.ar

VINEYARDS

200 ha at Aminga, La Rioja.
Varieties: Cabernet Sauvignon, Malbec, Merlot, Syrah, Bonarda, Cabernet Franc, Petit Verdot, Moscato Giallo, Sauvignon Blanc, Viognier, Chardonnay, Semillón, Chenin Blanc and Torrontès.

VAT CAPACITY

2,200,000 liters.
Storage capacity:
50,000 bottles.
Quality Norms: BPM, BPA and HACCP (in process).

BRANDS
Domestic and Foreign Markets: Nina, San Huberto and Velazco.
Exports to: United States, Mexico, Puerto Rico, Ecuador, Brazil, South Africa, Lithuania, Czech Republic, United Kingdom, Italy, Denmark, Korea and China.

STAFF
President: Leonardo Spadone
Foreign Market Commercial Manager: Marcelo Manghi and Ariana Spadone.
Domestic Market Commercial Manager: Carlos García Castro
Oenologist: Juan Banno

Visits: Monday to Friday from 10 a.m. to 3 p.m. By previous appointment. Call 54 3827 494040 or by info@bodegassanhuberto.com.ar.
Gift Shop: Yes and winery products are for sale.

NINA
PETIT VERDOT
2002

Concentrated with interesting color, dense. Lots of fruit, complex. Sweet tannins. Persistent. Great quality wine.

NINA
CABERNET
MALBEC 2002

Intense dark color. Great concentrarion of ripe fruit and presence of good wood. Elegant wine with firm tannins that can be easily enjoyed over time.

SAN POLO

Maria Marta Giol (president), Carlos Alfonso Giol (vicepresident).

WINERY HISTORY

In 1880, three pioneers of Argentine viticulture: became partners Juan Giol, Bautista Gargantini and Pascual Toso. Fate had it that the owners of Bodegas and Viñedos San Polo would be the fourth generation, direct descendants of these predecessors.

The great grandfather of today's proprietors, Juan Giol, bought the winery in 1915 and the present day estate La Esperanza from Ricardo Bustos, son of Eugenio Bustos, a pioneer in the conquest of the desert. These lands were inherited by Humberto Giol, who, together with his wife Eleonora Gargantini, founded the San Polo Winery and Vineyards around 1930.

Then, with the same spirit that had inspired their parents, they added new hectares to their vineyards and winery capacity in the best vine producing area of Mendoza at the foot of the Andes.

The task is now being continued by Carlos Giol and Clotilde Toso, who inherited the firm purpose of working hard to expand Argentine viticulture.

WINERY LOCATION
San Martín s/n, La Consulta, San Carlos, Mendoza.
Tel/Fax: 54 2622 471200.
Business Address: Granaderos 1.753, Mendoza.
Tel/Fax: 54 261 4236009.
Web Page: www.sanpolo.com.ar
e-mail:
administració@sanpolo.com.ar
laconsulta@sanpolo.com.ar

VINEYARDS
At San Carlos: Finca La Esperanza: 45 ha; Finca La Humbertita: 33 ha; Finca El Cepillo: 65 ha and San Polo: 29 ha.
Varieties: Malbec, Merlot, Chardonnay, Tempranillo, Cabernet Sauvignon, Pinot Noir, Syrah, Semillón and Chenin Blanc.

VAT CAPACITY
4,000,000 liters
Storage capacity: 300,000 liters.
Quality Norms: In process, ISO 9000.

BRANDS
Domestic Market: Auka
Foreign Market: Piuquenes, Auka and La Remonta
Exports to: United States, United Kingdom, Canada and Italy.

STAFF
President: María Marta Giol
General Manager: Rodolfo Masera
Commercial Director: Ángel Morchio
Oenologist: Lic. Pablo Calderón
Oenology Adviser: Alberto Antonini
Agronomist: Christian Ciaglo

Visits: Monday to Friday, from 10 a.m. to 4.30 p.m.

AUKA
MERLOT 2003

Good color, rather dark. Ripe fruit aromas. Good concentration in the mouth with firm tannins. A correct wine that is very good to drink.

SANTA FAUSTINA

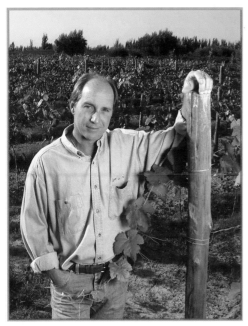

Peter Weinert.

WINERY HISTORY

Santa Faustina is the result of the knowledge and passion for good wines that inspire its producers, Peter Weinert and Graciela Reta, a renowned Argentine winemaker.

The winery makes top quality red wines, among them Malbec and Syrah, in a small winery in Medrano, Mendoza.

Grapevines generally thrive there thanks to the excellence of the land, which has been cultivated organically for over 50 years.

The Syrah comes from a vineyard in Medrano which is about 58 years old. The harvest is done by hand with grapes at their peak ripeness and careful protection gives the wine strong character. Thirty percent of the production is stored in new French oak barrels for 9 months.

The wines from their winery are deep red, expressing the intensity of the fruit in each varietal and preserving their full potential.

WINERY LOCATION
Medrano, Mendoza, Argentina
Business Address:
Primavera 2658 Rivadavia 5577, Mendoza
Tel/Fax: 54 5623 492600
Web Page: in construction
e-mail:
wrwines@infovia.com.ar

VINEYARDS
At Rivadavia: 2 ha Syrah at an altitude of 700 meters.
At Alto Medrano: 5 ha Syrah at an altitude of 750 meters.
Varieties: Syrah
Third Party Vineyards:
16 ha Syrah at Alto Medrano, 750 m altitude, 45 year old vineyard.
10 ha Malbec at Lunlunta, at a 950 m altitude, 35 year old vineyard.
10 ha Tempranillo at Tupungato, at 1,250 m altitude, 80 year old vineyard.
4 ha Tocay at Junín, at 700 m altitude, 20 year old vineyard.

VAT CAPACITY
1,000,000 liters
Storage capacity:
500,000 bottles
Quality Norms: BPM

BRANDS
Santa Faustina and D'Autor.
Domestic Market:
Direct Contact
Exports to:
United Kingdom, Brazil and United States.

STAFF
Director: Peter Costa Weinert
Director: Graciela Reta

Visits: By previous appointment:
wrwines@hotmail.com
Gift Shop:
Under construction.

 SANTA FAUSTINA SYRAH

Cherry color, light and fairly bright. Nose of ripe red fruit. Elegant wine, with silky tannins and good aroma.

TRAPICHE

Winery's façade.

WINERY HISTORY

Trapiche, located in Mendoza at the foot of the Andes, is the Argentine brand with the largest market share in the world.

Its innovative pioneer personality, upheld already for over 120 years, has made it the inevitable benchmark in Argentine viticulture.

Trapiche is rich in diversity. With more than 1,000 ha of its own vineyards and taking advantage of the diversity of soils and climates in Argentina, this winery has specialized in obtaining the best fruit of every "terroir". Its wines faithfully reflect the varietals typical characteristics.

Synergy between the work of the agronomist and the oenologist, both under the direction of the Chief Winemaker, results in fruity wines with great concentration of aroma and color. When they go into the oak barrel, the integration of fruit and wood is refined and natural.

Trapiche combines the generous sun, the melt water from the Andes snow-capped peaks and the natural riches of Argentine soils in its wines.

In its various and complete wine lines, Trapiche offers the best options for each occasion.

WINERY LOCATION

Mitre s/n, Coquimbito, Maipú, Mendoza
Tel.: 54 261 520 7210
Fax: 54 261 520 7209
Business Address: Mitre s/n, Coquimbito, Maipú, Mendoza
Tel.: 54 261 520 7210
Web Page: www.trapiche.com.ar
e-mail: ccorica@trapiche.com.ar

VINEYARDS

1,075 ha located at Coquimbito and Cruz de Piedra (Maipú), Ugarteche and Agrelo (Luján de Cuyo), Santa Rosa and San Martín, Mendoza.
Varieties: Malbec, Cabernet Sauvignon, Merlot, Syrah, Tempranillo, Pinot Noir, Cabernet Franc, Viognier, Chardonnay, Torrontés, Semillón and Sauvignon Blanc.
Third Party Vineyards: in Luján de Cuyo, Maipú, San Carlos, Tunuyán, Tupungato and Pedernal (San Juan).
Varieties: Malbec, Cabernet Sauvignon, Syrah, Merlot, Chardonnay and Pinot Noir.

VAT CAPACITY

15,000,000 liters.
Storage capacity:
1,500,000 bottles.
Quality Norms:
BRC, HACCP and BPM.

BRANDS

Domestic Market: Iscay, Trapiche Medalla, Fond de Cave, Trapiche Colección Roble, Trapiche Varietales, Astica, Septiembre, 1883.
Foreign Market: Iscay, Trapiche Medalla, Trapiche Broquel, Trapiche Oak Cask, Trapiche Varietals, Astica, Falling Star.
Exports to: Over 50 countries. Main destinations: Canada, United States, Japan, Norway, Denmark, United Kingdom, Brazil, Sweden, Ireland and Germany.

STAFF

Chief Oenologist: Lic. Daniel Pi
Oenology Team: Sergio Casé, Sergio Giménez and Diego Levada.
Vineyard Manager:
Ing. Marcelo Belmonte.
Visits: By appointment.

ISCAY 2002

Intense color, fairly bright. The fruit and wood are well integrated. There is a true aromatic complexity. A wine with much elegance and finesse, but powerful at the same time; finishes on delicate tannins. Above all, it has elegance and finesse.

TRAPICHE MEDALLA 2002

Lots of color, intensity and depth. Aromas have ripe black fruit, and smoked notes of wood. Very dense in the mouth, persistent with robust tannins. A powerful wine for today that merits some time to round out more. It is a great wine, well designed.

TRAPICHE ROBLE MALBEC 2003

Pleasant color, fruity aromas. Shows good density in the mouth, with ripe tannins. Balanced. A simple wine, very agreeable, well made, also has good concentration.

TRIVENTO

Winery's entrance.

WINERY HISTORY

The word Trivento means "tres vientos" (three winds). The name was chosen because of the importance of winds in the growth and development of vines. The Polar wind, which flows in winter, cuts through and joins the sap hidden in the vines; then the pruning season begins. In spring, the Zonda comes from the Andes, awakens the vines, the first shoots appear. The third is the Sudestada (Southeastern wind), which comes in summer from the east with refreshing humidity. It revitalizes bunches from the burning sunshine and they ripen fully. The grapes here are what Trivento wine is made from.

The company started in 1996. Its goal is to produce wines of exceptional quality. Thanks to a strong commercial strategy, technology and Concha y Toro "know-how", today Trivento is present in the most important countries and is the Argentine brand with the largest global coverage. In an effort to surpass its customers' expectations, it has certified several quality norms, thus showing the possession of an integrated management system that fulfills all the maximum standards demanded internationally in viticulture.

WINERY LOCATION

Pescara 9347, Russell, Maipú (5517), Mendoza.
Tel.: 54 261 4990270
Fax: 54 261 4990269
Business Address: Pescara 9347 Russell, Maipú (5517), Mendoza.
Web Page: www.trivento.com
e-mail: info@trivento.com

VINEYARDS

922.23 hectares located on seven estates in the Maipú, Tupungato, San Carlos, Luján de Cuyo, Rivadavia and San Martín departments of Mendoza.
Varieties: Malbec, Syrah, Cabernet Sauvignon, Merlot, Petit Verdot, Cabernet Franc, Pinot Noir, Viognier, Chardonnay, Sauvignon Blanc and Chenin Blanc.
Third Party Vineyards: at Vistalba, Luján de Cuyo, Mendoza.
Varieties: Malbec.

VAT CAPACITY

27.9 million liters.
Storage capacity: 300,000 liters.
Quality Norms: ISO 9001:2000, Euregap (Finca Los Ponchos). HACCP.

BRANDS

Domestic and Foreign Markets: Trivento
Exports to: Over 80 countries in Europe, Asia, Oceania, Africa and America.

STAFF

General Manager: Tomás Larrain.
Oenology Manager: Federico Galdeano
Marketing Manager: Mónica Caamaño
Production Manager: Leonardo Royo
Export Manager: Pedro Cortés

Visits: By previous appointment.
Gift Shop: Yes.

TRIVENTO GOLDEN RESERVE MALBEC 2002

Beautiful intense color. Lots of black fruit, smoked, vanilla. Good intensity in the mouth, lots of material, many tannins. Powerful harmonious wine, very elegant, with good persistence, finishes on notes of fruit and very pleasant tannins.

TRIVENTO RESERVE CABERNET / MALBEC 2003

Attractive color. Aromas show freshness, good fruit, not very powerful, but elegant with tannins that are rather noticeable although they are not a bother.

TRIVENTO TRIBU TEMPRANILLO 2004

Medium intense color. Fairly fruity and fresh aromas. Texture is medium to light. A fresh wine, pleasant to drink now and enjoy it.

VAL DE FLORES

Michel and Dany Rolland.

WINERY HISTORY

During his trips around Mendoza, Michel Rolland came across a small 14 hectare estate in Vista Flores where the best Malbec was grown. He always considered that terroir with admiration; in 2001 together with his wife Dany, he acquired shares in the Sociedad Val de Flores SA. It is an estate with top quality plants that are over 50 years old, lying at the foot of the Andes. Some improvements were made there and the first harvest was produced at Monteviejo winery.

Only 27,000 bottles were produced, and the wine was very carefully made, with profound respect for the environment. The wine was soon acquired by customers around the world. The only wine made from the very limited production has received favorable comments from all over.

Dany Rolland declared, "May Val de Flores be a celebration of this preserved piece of nature, and so others may share our passion".

For the time being, the wine matures in the Monteviejo winery, which has top technological qualities, while waiting for their own winery.

WINERY LOCATION
Bodega Monteviejo: Clodomiro Silva s/n 5565 Vista Flores, Mendoza
Tel.: 54 261 500 7263
Social Address:
Tte. Gral. J.D. Perón 1509, 9° Piso (C1037ACC) Buenos Aires, Argentina
54 11 4372 8792
Web Page: www.val-de-flores.com
e-mail: contact@val-de-flores.com

VINEYARDS
At the foot of the Andes, at Vista Flores, South of Mendoza
Varieties: 13 ha Malbec.

VAT CAPACITY
100 barrels
Storage capacity:
20,000 bottles.

BRANDS
Domestic Market: Val de Flores
Foreign Market: Val de Flores
Exports to: France, USA, Switzerland, Great Britain, Asia and Russia

STAFF
Management: Luis Hurovich
In Charge: Marcelo Pelleriti and Gabriela Celeste
Vineyard Manager: Marcelo Canatella
Oenologist: Michel Rolland

VAL DE FLORES

A majestic handsome red. Intense, invites you to drink it. Sensual on the nose. Good balance between the tertiary aromas and fruit. Very good initial taste, expands and acquires balanced structure with the tannins, while oily at the same time. A wine with a very good finish and satisfying memories.

VALENTIN BIANCHI

Valentìn Bianchi.

WINERY HISTORY

In 1928, Don Valentín Bianchi realized the immigrant's golden dream of having his own vineyard and winery. After a long pilgrimage, he saw his hope turn into reality with his first winery, in later years to become Bodegas y Viñedos Valentín Bianchi. Today, 77 years later, Bianchi is one of the leading wineries in Argentina and the family's third generation maintain the quality standards established at the beginning.

To accompany this extraordinary growth, the decision was taken to move wine production completely to Finca Las Paredes. The new winery was built according to the very latest technology.

To produce top quality wines, a boutique winery was created where grape selection is made manually and all the machinery is independent from the main winery, thus ensuring separate treatment, guaranteeing optimum quality of all processes to attain top premium products.

WINERY LOCATION
Ruta 143 y calle V. Bianchi, San Rafael, Mendoza.
Business Address: Cte. Torres 500 (M5600BCJ) San Rafael, Mendoza
Tel.: 54 2627 422046
Fax: 54 2627 430131
Web Page: www.vbianchi.com
e-mail: informes@vbianchi.com

VINEYARDS
343 hectares
Varieties: Cabernet Sauvignon, Malbec, Merlot, Barbera, Syrah, Pinot Noir, Riesling, Chenin Blanc, Chardonnay and Sauvignon Blanc.
Location of vineyards: San Rafael.

VAT CAPACITY
18,670,000 liters (founder winery), 10 millions, 8,7 (new winery)
French oak barrels: 2,000.
Storage capacity: 800,000 bottles, one million for sparkling wines.
Quality Norms: ISO 9001.

BRANDS
Domestic Market: Enzo Bianchi, Stradivarius, Bianchi Particular,Famiglia Bianchi, Bianchi 1887, Cinta de Plata, Don Valentin Lacrado, Bianchi DOC, Champaña Bianchi Extra Brut.
Foreign Market: Enzo Bianchi, Bianchi Particular, Famiglia Bianchi, Elsa Bianchi, Finca Los Primos, Don Valentin Lacrado, Arrabal, Gaucho, Bianchi Sparkling Wine.
Exports to: Canada, Mexico, Panama, Puerto Rico, Venezuela, Colombia, Brazil, Paraguay, Uruguay, Denmark, Norway, United Kingdom, Peru, Italy, Holland, Switzerland, France, Spain, Finland, Sweden, Japan, Taiwan and South Korea.

STAFF
President and Winemaker: Valentín Eduardo Bianchi
Director: Ricardo Stradella Bianchi
General Manager: Eduardo Lomanto
Oenologists: Francisco Martínez and Roberto Leleu
Consultants: Robert Pepi (Napa Valley) and Corinne Lateyron (France)
Estate Management: Marcelo Garretón
Exports: Andrés Kemeny
Tourism: Tel/Fax: 54 2627 435600/ 435353, mescoriza@vbianchi.com
Gift Shop: Yes.

ENZO BIANCHI 2002

Delicate fruity nose with some notes of animal aromas. Has good density in the mouth, fairly noticeable acidity and freshness. Tannins are evolving. It is still a young wine, that with time will certainly develop all its power and elegance. As a whole, it is very harmonious.

BIANCHI PARTICULAR MALBEC 2002

The nose, with notes of animal and red fruit, has good intensity. Middle of the mouth is expressive, with volume, grease and persistence. Finishes with powerful tannins. Very good, on the whole.

FAMIGLIA BIANCHI CABERNET SAUVIGNON 2002

Elegant wine. Fruity and fresh in the mouth. Complex aromas of a Cabernet Sauvignon with strength and lasts well in the mouth.

VINITERRA

Adriano Senetiner.

WINERY HISTORY

Viniterra is a winery whose dimensions were based on a human scale, that is to say, one that due to its volume and capacity is entirely controlled by man in all its processes.

Its objective is to keep producing top quality wines with a strong inclination towards exports but preserving an important presence in the domestic market.

The winery's capacity is 3,340,000 liters in concrete pools with an epoxy lining. The facilities also have stainless steel tanks, two for 30,000 liters, four for 10,000 liters and one for 7,500 liters. This one is basically utilized for fractioning.

The plant contains 430 225 liter oak barrels. Also two 5,000 liter French oak fermentation casks.

WINERY LOCATION
Acceso Sur, km. 17,5. Luján de Cuyo, Mendoza.
Tel: 54 261 4985888 / 0073
Web Page: www.viniterra.com.ar
e-mail: turismo@viniterra.com.ar

VINEYARDS
90 ha at Agrelo, Luján de Cuyo, Mendoza.
Varieties: Malbec, Merlot, Carmenere, Pinot Noir, Viognier, Pinot Grigio and Cabernet Sauvignon.
Third Party Vineyards: 35 ha at Maipú and 50 ha at Luján de Cuyo,
Varieties: Chardonnay, Semillón, Torrontés, Malbec, Merlot, Syrah, Tempranillo, Cabernet Sauvignon and Pinot Noir.

BRANDS
Domestic Market: Omnium Terra, Viniterra, Dolcissimo and Iubileus.
Foreign Market: Cielo, Inacayal and Bycos.
Exports to: United States, Canada, Mexico, Puerto Rico, Peru, Brazil, Germany, Switzerland, Denmark, Czech Republic and Sweden.

STAFF
President: Adriano Senetiner
Directors: Cecilia Zunino, Roxana Senetiner, Omar Rodríguez and Martín Aguinaga.
General Manager:
Ing. Miguel Urrutia
Foreign Commerce:
Fernando Rossi
Oenologist: Juan Carlos Chavero

Visits: Monday to Friday from 9 a.m. to 5 p.m.
Saturday with previous appointment.
Gift Shop: Wine sales and merchandising.

VINITERRA PINOT GRIGIO 2004

Bright lively color. Fruity and spice aromas. In the mouth it has great freshness and balance. Agreeable and pleasant to drink.

TERRA MOMENTO II MALBEC - MERLOT 2003

Interesting color, fairly lively. Noticeable aromas of wood, smoked and chocolate. The wine is balanced and rater fine. The finish is smooth and delicate. Good quality wine.

VINITERRA MOMENTO II MALBEC 2001

Good color, fairly strong. Ripe red fruit, black fruit, vanilla notes. It has volume and stands out, ending with somewhat austere tannins, but good quality that should age well. Overall it is correct, with balance and harmony.

VIÑA AMALIA

Marina, Adolfo, Carlos and Hugo Basso.

WINERY HISTORY

In 1922, brothers Adolfo and Tulio Basso, together with their partner Emilio Tonnelier, took their first steps in the viticulture business, buying "La Purísima" winery, in Mendoza. They produced wine and sold it in 220 liter wooden barrels.

In 1935, the Basso & Tonnelier company bought Santa Ana Winery, an establishment created in 1891. Their descendants turned it into one of the leading wineries in Argentina, and then sold it to the Chilean Santa Carolina Group in 1996.

Among other members of the founding families, Hugo and later on, his son Carlos worked in the winery. Carlos was president from 1981 to 1996.

Hugo and his sons Hugo (Jr.), Carlos and Octavio bought a small winery in Carrodilla, close to Mendoza city in 1997. The grapes they produce come from their own vineyard, Finca La Amalia, purchased in 1990.

Also, in partnership with Adolfo Basso, Hugo's brother, and his daughters Federica, Alejandra and Claudia, they planted a 200 ha vineyard, called Los Montes Negros.

WINERY LOCATION
San Martín 7440, Carrodilla, Luján de Cuyo 5505, Mendoza.
Tel. 54 261 4360677 / 4360363
Business Address: San Martín 7440, Carrodilla, Luján de Cuyo, 5505, Mendoza.
Tel 54 261 4360677 / 4360363
Web Page:
www.vinamalia.com.ar
e-mail:
fincamalia@nysnet.com.ar

WINEYARDS
Finca La Amalia located at San Carlos: 214 ha.
52 ha Cabernet Sauvignon (planted in 1970 and 20 ha Malbec (planted in 1968 and 1999).
Finca Los Montes Negros, located at Los Árboles, Tunuyán, Valle de Uco: 200 ha Cabernet Sauvignon, Malbec, Syrah, Pinot Noir, Merlot, Petit Verdot, Chardonnay, Sauvignon Blanc and Viognier.

VAT CAPACITY
750,000 liters.
Storage capacity: 200,000 bottles in outside underground chamber.

BRANDS
Domestic Market: Viña Amalia
Foreign Market: Viña Amalia and Carlos Basso
Exports to: United Kingdom, Sweden, Switzerland, Brazil, United States, Canada, Denmark, Russia, Ecuador, Ireland, Germany, Belgium, Mexico, Italy, France, Austria and Uruguay.

STAFF
President: Carlos M. Basso
Marketing: Octavio Basso
Administration: Nicolás Pérez
Oenologist: Jorge Rodríguez
General Secretary: Marina Basso
Trainee: Adolfo Basso

Visits: Monday to Friday: 10.30 a.m. to 12.30 p.m. and 3 p.m. to 5 p.m. Weekend or holiday: call to confirm.

VIÑA AMALIA SAUVIGNON BLANC 2004

Pale yellow color with green reflections. Aromas that bring cassis, citrus and floral to mind with a slight vegetable note. Good acidity and refreshing. A very pleasant wine to drink.

CARLOS BASSO VINO TINTO 2003

Good color, fairly bright and deep. Good floral and wood notes on the nose. The wine is fairly consistent with a good middle of the mouth and agreeable tannins. Pretty material at the finish. On the whole It has good concentration and elegance.

VIÑA DOÑA PAULA

Stefano Gandolini, winemaker in Viña Doña Paula.

WINERY HISTORY

Viña Doña Paula was founded in 1997 for the express purpose of offering "New World" wines, ultra premium quality products. The areas they chose for their vineyards in Ugarteche, Luján de Cuyo, and Tupungato, were carefully selected to attain maximum potential in the combination of soil, climate and stock.

An infrastructure with state-of-the-art technology allows the oenologists to create a unique style and identity, which makes Doña Paula a quality brand with permanent innovation.

In 2002 the winery began to expand its commercial activities exporting 95% of its production and 3 years later, it proudly participates in over 30 markets, offering the quality and characteristics that only Luján de Cuyo, Ugarteche and Tupungato "terroir" can produce.

Doña Paula offers a new concept. With wines that show a typically Argentine character and a management style based on quality, long term investment and the support of a solid structure at international level, Doña Paula is positioning itself as an important player in the wine world for the coming years.

WINERY LOCATION
Poliducto YPF, Ugarteche, Luján de Cuyo, Mendoza.
Business Address:
Paso de los Andes 467, Luján de Cuyo, Mendoza.
Tel.: 54 261 4884410
Fax: 54 261 4986374
Web Page:
www.donapaula.com.ar
e-mail:
info@donapaula.com.ar

VINEYARDS
Ugarteche, Luján de Cuyo, Mendoza: 760 ha, of which 208 are producing. At Tupungato, Mendoza: 60 ha, 53 of which are producing.
Varieties: Malbec, Merlot, Cabernet Sauvignon, Syrah, Chardonnay, Sauvignon Blanc, Pinot Noir and Cabernet Franc.

VAT CAPACITY
Total 3,433,750 liters.
In stainless steel tanks: 3,400,000 liters.
In oak barrels: 33,750 liters.
Storage capacity:
800,000 bottles.

BRANDS
Domestic and Foreign Markets: Los Cardos, Doña Paula Estate, Selección de Bodega.
Exports to: United States, Denmark, Canada, Brazil, Germany, Cyprus, Hong Kong, Estonia, Philippines, Austria, Belgium, Netherlands, Poland, the Czech Republic, Switzerland, Peru, Mexico, Taiwan, Ireland, Australia, Colombia, Panama, Costa Rica and United Kingdom.

STAFF
Oenologists: Stefano Gandolini and David Bonomi
Operations Manager: Edgardo Del Popolo
Export Manager: Carlos Trad

Visits: By previous appointment, Monday to Friday from 10 a.m. to 5 p.m.

DOÑA PAULA SELECCION DE BODEGA MALBEC 2002

Pleasant color, failry frank, sustained and lively. Ripe black fruit mixed with notes of toasted coffee coming from the wood. Noticeable intensity, mature tannins with good general harmony and long finish. Well balanced and interesting.

DOÑA PAULA ESTATE MALBEC 2003

Very attractive color. Aromas of good ripe black fruit, with a hint of well integrated wood. Wine with texture and structure, good tannins, persistent finish. Elegant wine with an interesting concentration.

DOÑA PAULA SELECCIÓN DE BODEGA CHARDONNAY 2002

Suggestive color, very golden. Floral aromas and subtle toasted notes that give an overall elegance. Fresh, with good acidity, pleasant finish.

VIÑEDOS LOS MAITENES S.A.

Antonio C. Sottano, Raúl Correas (h), Raúl A. Correas.

WINERY HISTORY

The winery is located in the Perdriel district, Luján de Cuyo. The buildings date from 1904 and were constructed for the elaboration of exclusive top quality wines.

The construction keeps its original features, though with important infrastructure and technology enhancements, applied to the production process.

The grapes come from their own vineyards, located in the heart of the best production area in Mendoza. The very old plantations in ancient limy soil irrigated by melt water channels that balance the plants naturally.

The wine making process prioritizes manual treatment of the clusters. The fruit is selected on conveyor belts and then is macerated, prior to being fermented in cold small sinks. The wine is then transferred to French and American oak barrels for aging. Bottles are stowed during 12 months.

As wines reach their optimum point of development, the establishment has begun expanding to new destinations, while maintaining an excellent relationship with the domestic market.

WINERY LOCATION
Cobos 4285, Perdriel, Luján de Cuyo, Mendoza.
Tel.: 54 261 4881236
Fax: 54 261 4292527
Business Address:
Av. España 512, piso 2, of.2 Ciudad, Mendoza.
Tel./Fax: 54 261 4292527
Web Page:
www.losmaitenes.com
e-mail:
info@losmaitenes.com

VINEYARDS
Barrancas, Maipú.
Varieties: Malbec, Cabernet Sauvignon.
Third Party Vineyards:
Rusell, Maipú: 10 ha.
Varieties: Merlot, Malbec and Cabernet Sauvignon.

VAT CAPACITY
300,000 liters
Storage Capacity:
30,000 bottles.

BRANDS
Domestic Market:
Maestre de Campo Merlot, Maestre de Campo Malbec and El Corregidor
Foreign Market:
Maestré de Campo Merlot.
Exports to: USA, Belgium and Puerto Rico.

STAFF
President: Dr. Raúl Alberto Correas
Vicepresident:
Dr. Antonio Carlos Sottano
Oenologist: Walter Bressia
Commercial Manager:
Raúl Correas (h).

Visits:
From 9 a.m. to 5 p.m.

MAESTRE DE CAMPO MERLOT 2002

Good color, slightly orangey. The nose shows stewed fruits and good intensity. The mouth is round, a bit sugary, the finish is tannice. An interesting wine that will gain a little more vivacity with time.

YACOCHUYA

Arnaldo Etchart.

WINERY HISTORY

The Etchart family has been part of the wine business since 1850. Arnaldo Benito Etchart purchased the estate and La Florida winery in the middle of the 20th century and his son Arnaldo developed the "Etchart" brand quite successfully in Argentina and abroad.

In 1998, Arnaldo Etchart summoned Michel Rolland to develop red wines for the winery. This was one of the first instances of Rolland's expert advice outside of France. A work and friendly relationship started with one of the best oenologists in the world.

Etchart winery was sold to the Pernod Ricard group in 1996, and one year before, Arnaldo already had the wines for his new endeavor: San Pedro de Yacochuya. The new winery began activities in 1998 and the first harvest was in February '99. The establishment is located at an altitude of over 2,000 m above sea level: one of the highest vineyards in the world. The estate has 16 hectares, planted with Malbec, Cabernet Sauvignon, Tannat and Torrontés. The cellar is equipped with state-of-the-art technology. In 2001, San Pedro de Yacochuya exported its first premium wine: Yacochuya M. Rolland Vintage 1999, without neglecting the local market.

WINERY LOCATION
Finca Yacochuya, Cafayate, Salta.
Tel.: 54 3868 421233
Fax: 54 3868 421487
Business Address: Suipacha 1087, 8 B (1008), Buenos Aires.
Tel./Fax: 54 11 4312-2810
Web Page: www.yacochuya.com
e-mail: info@sanpedrodeyccochuya.com.ar

VINEYARDS
Located in the estate, in Cafayate, Salta.
Varieties: Malbec, Cabernet Sauvignon, Tannat and Torrontés.

VAT CAPACITY
90,000 liters.
Storage capacity: 100,000 bottles.

BRANDS
Domestic Market: Yacochuya and San Pedro de Yacochuya.
Foreign Market: Yacochuya and San Pedro de Yacochuya.
Exports to: France, England, Spain, Germany, Brazil, Puerto Rico and United States, Uruguay, Peru and Colombia.

STAFF
Owners:
Arnaldo Etchart and Michel Rolland

Visits: Yes, confirm appointment by phone 54 3868 15638240

YACOCHUYA 2002

Intense petroleum black color, elegant. Complex aromas with an initial touch of vanilla and spice. Sweet mouth, persistent, harmonious in its four elements (acidity, bite, alcohol and sweetness). Its firm structure augurs a long cellaring. Excellent.

SAN PEDRO DE YACOCHUYA 2003

Pretty black cherry color, lively and bright. Aromas of fresh fruit with notes of strawberries, cassis, black cherry are rather exuberant. Structured, but harmonious, with lots of roundness. Its elements make it an agreeable wine that can be enjoyed now or kept for some years.

SAN PEDRO DE YACOCHUYA TORRONTÉS 2005

Golden yellow color, almost amber, bright and exciting. Aromas of rose petals and litchi overwhelm the glass with a smoothness that only this grape stock has. Mouth is round with a refreshing finish of minty notes. A wine to be served chilled, but not cold.

BIBLIOGRAPHY

AGUERRE, Javier y Mariana Cerutti. **Las inversiones en el sector vitivinícola a partir de 1990**. Inédito.

ALCALDE, Alberto. **Cultivares vitícolas argentinos**. Instituto Nacional de Tecnología Agropecuaria (INTA). Mendoza, 1989.

ASPIAZU, Daniel y Eduardo Basualdo. **El complejo vitivinícola argentino en los noventa: potencialidades y restricciones**. División de Desarrollo Productivo y Empresarial, de la Comisión Económica para América Latina y el Caribe (CEPAL). Diciembre, 2000.

CATANIA, Carlos y Silvia Avagnina de del Monte. **Los cultivares para vinos en la Argentina**. Centro de Estudios Enológicos, Estación Experimental Agropecuaria Mendoza.

Datos del Centro de Estudios para la Producción. Secretaría de Industria, Comercio y Minería de la Nación. Argentina, 2002.

DRAGHI LUCERO, Juan. **Miguel A. Pouget y su obra**. Revista de la Junta de Estudios Históricos de Mendoza. 1949.

GIRINI, Liliana. Tesis doctoral **Arquitectura, industria y progreso. Las bodegas vitivinícolas de Mendoza**.

Grandes Vinos. 2000. En: Bodegas y Vinos. Número 3. Diario Los Andes, Mendoza.

GUAYCOCHEA de ONOFRI, Rosa. **Arquitectura de Mendoza**. Facultad de Arquitectura y Urbanismo, Universidad de Mendoza. 1978.

Instituto Nacional de Vitivinicultura. *Censos y Registro de actualización de viñedos 2001*.

La vitivinicultura en 1910. Centro Vitivinícola Nacional. Buenos Aires, 1910.

Libro de oro de la Vendimia 1936 – 1986. Medio siglo de historia. Editado por Diario Mendoza.

MARZO, Miguel y Osvaldo Inchauspe. **Geografía de Mendoza** (Tomo II). Editorial Spadoni. Mendoza, 1967.

MEARDI, Luis. **Historia de la vitivinicultura de Argentinba**. Disertación presentada en la reunión de la Academia Italiana de la Vid y el Vino. Centro de prensa. 1987.

Revista Vinífera, Instituto Nacional de Vitivinicultura.

RODRÍGUEZ, José, Susana Matus y María Ocvirk. **Ampelografía práctica**. Cátedra de Viticultura, Facultad de Ciencias Agrarias, Departamento de la Vid y el Vino, Universidad Nacional de Cuyo. Mendoza, 1997.

RODRÍGUEZ, José y Susana Matus. **Torrontés Riojano** y **Bonarda: gran cepaje tinto revalorizado**. Cátedra de Viticultura, Facultad de Ciencias Agrarias, Universidad Nacional de Cuyo. Julio 2002.

VIDAL BUZZI, Fernando y Augusto Foix. **Argentina, viñedos, bodegas y vinos**, Ed. Llamoso, Buenos Aires, 2000.

ACKNOWLEDGMENTS

Robert Parker, journalist and wine critic. Raúl de la Mota, master of winemakers. National Viticulture Institute: Chairman, Eng. Raúl Guiñazú, Eng. Cristina Pandolfi, Press Department and Library's personnel. National Institute of Agricultural Technology, Experimental Station Mendoza: Oenological Research Center, Eng. Carlos Catania and Oenologist Silvia Avagnina de Del Monte. Viticulture Section Research Workers. Engineers José Rodríguez and Susana Mathus, School of Agronomy, Universidad Nacional de Cuyo. Architects Mario Yanzón and Eliana Bórmida. Mendoza Hyatt Hotel. Eng. Laura Bravin and Designer Ana Argerich, in charge of The Wine Route project. Arch. Liliana Girini, specialized in Cultural Heritage. Arch. Leandro Henríquez. Eng. Gabriela Celeste, Eno-Rolland Mendoza. Studio Ehq, Mr. Luis Hurovich, Misses Silvia Tarditi and Genara Vacirca. Ms. Stéphanie Rolland.

Printed in Talleres Gráficos Aprinta S.A.,
Patagones 2772 (1437) Capital Federal,
Argentina, in December 2005.